# Diary of a Rural GP

# About the Author

Dr Michael Sparrow has charted an unconventional course from the immaturity and uncertainty of life as a medical student, through hospital jobs and a six-year spell in the Royal Air Force, to the immaturity and uncertainty of life as a rural GP. Now retired, he lives on the Devon/Cornwall border.

# DIARY OF A RURAL GP

## Hilarious true stories from a country practice

Michael Sparrow

DUCKWORTH

This edition published in 2020 by Duckworth,
an imprint of Duckworth Books Ltd
1 Golden Court, Richmond, TW9 1EU, United Kingdom

www.duckworthbooks.co.uk

Print ISBN: 9781788420747
Ebook ISBN: 9781788422246

3 5 7 9 10 8 6 4 2

# Have you read them all?

For Laura. Once, twice, third time a lady.

# Contents

*Introduction*                                                    9

1   Lost for Words – Part I                                     17
2   Why Does It Have to Happen to Me?                           21
3   Groundhog Day – Part I                                      37
4   Lost for Words – Part II                                    52
5   Everyone Needs a Jason                                      68
6   Home Delivery                                               80
7   The 100 Club                                                91
8   Not on My Watch                                            106
9   The Rule of Evelyn                                         115
10  Lost for Words – Part III                                  127
11  Groundhog Day – Part II                                    138
12  You Can Get Anything in a Volvo                            150
13  Cynthia (and the Ogre and the Vicar)                       161
14  Matters of Life and Death                                  173
15  Bill and Ben, and Some Unusual Bequests                    189
16  Mrs Axleby's Knickers and the Tractor Episode              205
17  Lost for Words – Part IV                                   214

# Introduction

*29 July 2017*
*The Arundell Arms, Lifton*

Dinner was over, and I rose to speak for the final time as a GP. The staff had changed the computer password to "end of an era" to mark the occasion. After twenty-nine years at Lifton, twenty-six of those as the "boss", I was finally retiring. I cleared my throat, and steadied myself. It was an emotional occasion for us all. Off I went.

'So,' I began, 'this is the last ever speech from me, but hopefully not my last ever Lifton gathering. Thank you all for coming, and it's nice to see some old friends here after such a long time. Lorna – if Carlsberg ever started appointing counsellors, you would probably be at the top of their list. Seated next to me you can see Fee and Polson, my two oldest friends from medical school, both of whom I have known for over forty years.

'When I was sitting in my office last night, trying to decide what I was going to say, for some reason I started thinking about musical allegories, a song for every occasion. The best I could come up with for tonight was a cheerful ditty, one of my favourites from university days: "This is the End" by the Doors. It is an uplifting tale about someone who loses their only friend and then probably commits suicide, so you have lost the will to live by the time you get to the end of the song. And then I began to theorise about which musical acts some of you might be associated with – Ali W and Claire, probably Steps and S Club Seven for you; Karen, Fairport Convention or anyone in a kaftan; Marion, I think somebody in a cardigan, Perry Como perhaps, or Val Doonican. And Julie I have down as a closet Bay City Rollers fan.

'The question I have most been asked over the last few months is, I suppose not surprisingly, "What are you going to do when you retire?" and I don't really have a precise answer for that. A bit of gardening, more cooking, a shift or two behind the bar of the pub next door. My friend Derek, who, as you know, is the village policeman, suggested that one.

'After a game or two of chess one evening, and a glass or two of wine, he sat me down and asked me the same question, followed by "What else are you good at, Mike, apart from medicine?" After half an hour of deep and meaningful conversation, we realised I wasn't actually particularly good at anything, and the best I could probably hope for would be to drive Derek's white van for him when he retires and sets up as a self-employed builder, and maybe make him some soup.

'So, if this is the end, how did it all start? My wife and I's favourite word is "serendipity" and, appropriately enough, I had never even heard of Lifton until a chance meeting in the early hours in a pub on the Chillaton road to Tavistock changed my destiny in life. I was drifting towards the end of my time in the RAF, with no very clear idea of what I was going to do next, when I met Em Mounce, an old friend of my father-in-law and the matriarch of Lifton at the time, who over a gin and tonic told me that Lifton needed another doctor. That's how it was done in those days – no CV, nothing approaching a conventional interview, not even a job application. Just the simple word of mouth, via a friend of a friend.

'I arrived in Lifton reckoning I had five, maybe seven, years to grow into the job and learn my trade, but, as most of you know, Dr Margaret retired and then died shortly afterwards, from a tumour behind her eye. Suddenly I found myself alone, thinking "I'm not really sure I know what I am doing here". I realised I wasn't experienced enough, and I was well aware I lacked the depth of knowledge to keep my head above ground for very long before someone found me out. But in those days there was no one out there to help, so I set about figuring out how to do things my own way. A blank sheet of paper, a shiny new pen and a plan to be hatched.

'People have tried to criticise it over the years, but I developed what I would later call the "Lifton Way" based on some very simple principles.

When you walk through our door, or ring our practice, you will be greeted by a member of staff in person. Real people, who know you and your family. Who are flesh and blood and live and breathe as you do. Who care about your problems and sympathise with your difficulties. Who will hold your child and take care of your dog, if necessary. Who will offer you a drink if you feel faint, and a lift home if you are weary.

'No one would ever be turned away. If you walked through our door and I could deal with whatever you brought with you, I would do so, and do it there and then. If I couldn't, or somebody else could do it better, I would pass it on to them as soon as I could. I never cared too much about conventional systems or customs, and wouldn't have recognised a "Standard Operating Procedure" if you hit me over the head with a whole catalogue of them. I was never interested in protecting my personal reputation or ticking all the politically correct boxes at the expense of a patient's well-being. And if that got me into trouble from time to time – as it so often did – well, so be it. There were things I cared about more.

'Even at the end of my tenure, just a couple of months ago, I found myself sitting in front of the deputy director of NHS England in a career-defining moment. I had apparently had the temerity to criticise the findings of a Safeguarding Board, which I now understand is tantamount to offering excuses for serial killers, or upholding child molesters' rights. It hadn't seemed to matter to anyone that my observations were well reasoned and correct in each and every respect.

'"You don't remember me, do you, Dr Sparrow?" said Liz, the lady charged with reviewing and then judging my supposed misdemeanours.

'"I'm afraid I don't," I admitted, feeling on the back foot for once.

'"Oh, but I remember you," she said with a smile. "Now let's have a talk about what everybody tells me you've done, and then confine it to history, where it belongs."'

My throat felt as dry as the Sahara by now but, as everyone seemed to be listening still, I thought I'd better press on.

'I think we all wonder at some point in our lives why we end up doing what we do. I also question what I might be really good at, because it has to be out there somewhere. There must be something Derek didn't quite manage to spot, bless him.

'I tell this story in my first book, if my memory serves me correctly, but I think it bears repetition. It was November 1969. I am twelve, walking home in the dark at 9.30 p.m. – because that is what we used to do in those days – from the local youth club with a cheap but precious piece of metal hanging round my neck. It is the "Open to All Comers" five-a-side football cup winner's medal, and our team, in the Under-12s league, have beaten the previously undefeated champions of the Under-19s by six goals to two. It was unprecedented, and because this is my leaving day, I can finally boast that I scored five of the goals.

'As I turn into my road, just a hundred or so yards to go, there is an ambulance outside our house, and my unconscious father is being loaded into it, my mother at his side. They drive off into the night, blue lights flashing, and I have no idea what is going on. When my mother returns a day and a half later, she tells me my father has had a heart attack and is recuperating in a convalescent home over thirty miles away. But she hasn't driven for nearly twenty years, and in those days public transport was thin on the ground. We had no relatives living nearby, and most neighbours did not have their own vehicles. My father was a poorly paid schoolteacher, and regular taxis for the round trip was not really an option.

'"So how are we going to get to see him?" I asked. My mother didn't know and was too shell-shocked to think about it.

'The next day, I took the car keys off the hook in the kitchen, opened the garage doors and reversed my dad's Hillman Imp out on to the drive.

'"If I can get it that far," I said to her, "you can get it to the first lamppost down the road and back again. Then we go to the second one, the third, and by this afternoon I want you to be driving it round the block. Tomorrow, we go together to see my dad."

'I am not, never have been, and never will be an academic. I have never pretended to be a great clinician, spotting conditions that others have missed or having a series of "light bulb" moments that make my colleagues look pedestrian for their diagnostic failures. I will never have a disease or syndrome named after me, and I will end up rightfully in the very small print of medical history. I couldn't rigidly follow a protocol if you paid me and wouldn't ever wish to. Medical administration is what other people do to allow me to drift around the edges of convention, avowing that the rules have never really applied to me.

'Because what I think I have always been good at is getting people through the difficult times in their lives, being there when nobody else was available or cared enough. I'm not sure if that was a calling, a vocation, or just how it was meant to be, as decreed by a force greater than myself. It is what I am proud of, though, and part of the legacy I hope I have left behind me as I disappear over the horizon. At this point, I worry I am beginning to sound like someone accepting a BAFTA award, when all you really wanted to hear was "Thanks, guys," and get back to your pudding.

'So, I hope you will forgive me for all that self-indulgent navel gazing and I promise that we are now coming to the important part of what I have to say this evening, because tonight is not all about me. I need to talk about what I will miss come Monday morning.

'I will not miss the paperwork; the mind-numbing, endless administrative dictats; the ever increasing numbers of hoops we have to jump through just to show that we are actually doing our jobs correctly. I won't miss the daily frustrations of not being able to follow the vocation I think I have actually been rather good at because of the inordinate number of barriers that have been placed in my way.

'I won't miss the diminishing budgets, or the expanding demands. I won't miss the fresh-faced but well-meaning young doctor twenty or more years my junior asking me at an annual appraisal six months before I retire what my personal development plans are. I won't miss any of that at all.

'So what will I miss?

'Some of the patients, of course. Over the years many of them have become friends, and vice versa. You develop a relationship with them on so many levels, a sort of mutual dependency. They needed me to make them feel better about themselves, and hopefully improve their health, and I needed them to make me believe I was valued, and that there was a real point to my being here.

'I will miss the daily routine of walking through the door approximately one minute before morning surgery is due to start, and preparing for the battle that lay ahead each day. I will miss the glass of wine I had from the secret fridge hidden behind my desk at the end of a Friday afternoon, while I sat out on the back step, reflecting upon the week and watching the Canada geese fly over as regular as clockwork in an uneven V-shape on their journey to who knows where. I will miss sharing slow-motion replays of the cricket during a consultation with a fellow devotee. I will miss seeing children I have delivered grow up into adulthood and prepare to take on the world.

'But, although all of that is important, none of it is the most special thing about my time here.'

I took a deep breath and composed myself. It wouldn't do to get this wrong.

'Because what I will really miss is you.

'You have never been the people who worked <u>for</u> me. You've been the people who worked <u>with</u> me, my extended family, my favourite people to socialise with. And we have done stuff, things I doubt many other surgeries have. Christmas parties in Dublin, Edinburgh and Paris, but we never quite made LA. Maybe a reunion one day when we have all finally retired.

'We've each of us had our wobbles along the way, but whenever life has been tough we have stuck together, helped one another out, and found a way through. It is no doubt terribly un-PC to say it, but you have always been "my girls", and I am proud to acknowledge it. If I was on a reality TV programme right now, I would probably say "I love you all" and go for a group hug and loads of selfies, but we are British to the core, and a stiff upper lip is what is required here.

'I've done some really stupid things in my life, both before I came to Lifton and while I have been here, but when I look back, I like to think I have never <u>not</u> done something I felt I should have done, if that makes sense. I have no regrets. I have tried my hardest to make everyone's world a better place, but obviously I haven't always achieved that.

'So, as I finish, a word for my wife, Laura, she of the inexhaustible compassionate companionship, who tolerates my eccentricities with the patience of a saint. If you don't quite get marriage right at the first attempt, make sure you do at the last. She has been my saviour, and I hope I hers. But then again, over coffee in the lounge, she may very well tell you something totally different.

'I would now like to raise my glass to you all. My final thought is that my time here has been a bit like being inaugurated as the captain of a newly built ship, standing on the bridge and embarking on a voyage of uncertainty across troubled seas, until finally making it back into port – even if it wasn't necessarily the one I was aiming for. Thank you all for accompanying me, as you walk down the gangplank to the safety of the shore and the new world that awaits you.

'And that's it. That's me gone. I now pass on the baton I received so long ago to the next generation, to take it wherever they wish to go. I hope that they, you, and everyone still to come runs with it wisely. To Lifton Surgery, and all who continue to sail in her.'

They raised their glasses with me, a hidden tear in all of our eyes, or at least that's what I like to think. And suddenly, in that very last moment, my life and career as a GP at Lifton was finally over. Roll on the new world, wherever it may take me.

After twenty-five years of living outside the village – just across the border in Launceston, Cornwall – and despite firmly vowing never, ever to do so, my wife has finally persuaded me to move back to where I first began. Six months before my retirement we took occupation of an idyllic thatched cottage at the east end of the main road, with a hidden garden at the back.

The newly reopened pub next door, the splendid Fox and Grapes, is just under a minute's walk away of an evening – and no more than two on the way back. It was like coming home again after all these years. A place to sit and remember my history and welcome old friends as they make their way through our gate to share nostalgic memories on the back patio in the early evening sunlight.

But, mostly, they just come for a drink.

What now follow are a few simple tales about some of the people I encountered along the way, and mostly – but not completely – left behind. My memories of them will always persist.

The nightmares too.

I hope you enjoy meeting them as much as I did.

# 1
# Lost for Words – Part I

It is late summer 1998, and I was soon to travel back to Ethiopia on my own for a few weeks. No one could tell for sure what awaited me there.

I had promised to take my children, Charlie and Cressie, to the beach for my last Sunday with them before leaving. The weather was patchy at best, clouds scudding across an angry and unforgiving sky. After a leisurely pub lunch and a game or two of pool we chased the fading light fruitlessly round the south coast before deciding to give it up as a lost cause, and headed for home.

Half an hour later, after meandering aimlessly along picturesque winding lanes, we were approaching the main roads when the sun suddenly burst through an unexpected band of brilliant blue sky. We were just passing a field of recently harvested wheat, glowing golden in the glorious evening light.

'Oh, daddy,' exclaimed Cressie excitedly. 'Look at that!'

'Yes, isn't it lovely?' I agreed, touched by her juvenile perspicacity.

'No,' she said pityingly, 'sunsets are not to die for. But those stacks of hay… can we go and play on them?'

'Oh, you philistine,' I sighed, and then, grinning, 'Yes, of course you can. But don't tell your mother I let you do it.'

The sun was entering its slow, graceful descent on the rapidly vanishing horizon, casting ever longer shadows. Ahead of us lay the great cylindrical bales of straw, scattered at irregular intervals across the gently inclining field of flattened stubble. Falling away in the distance the sea shimmered, ethereally serene, as I reversed into the field, drawing gently to a halt.

'I'm hungry,' announced Charlie suddenly. 'Have we got anything to eat?'

'But you've only just had lunch,' I protested, 'with two helpings of dessert and extra ice cream.'

'He's a growing boy, daddy,' Cressie reminded me. 'And I'm hungry too. Do you have marmite?'

'And what about you?' I asked wearily. 'What's your excuse?'

'I've got worms,' she replied, poker-faced. 'Have you got any crisps?'

I did have crisps, and apples – I wondered why I had apples, because I hate apples – and some chocolate, a thermos flask, a couple of bottles of beer and a blanket.

'Make the most of it,' I said, opening the boot and tossing them the spoils. 'Both the sun and I will be gone for a while, very shortly.'

I spread the blanket on the ground and stretched out on my back, luxuriating in the sheltered warmth and feeling my eyes beginning to close.

'Hey daddy,' I could hear them call in the distance. 'Look at us. We can move them.'

I propped myself up on my elbows and glanced across a few yards to my left where Charlie and Cressie, grinning hugely, had their shoulders braced against one of the straw bales, inching it slowly forward.

'Careful,' I warned. 'Make sure you stay on the uphill side, won't you? They're a lot bigger than you, and much heavier than they look.'

The end of the day, the warmth of the sun, a bottle of beer… and despite all my best intentions, I drifted off to sleep.

I awoke, probably no more than a few minutes later, to shrieks of delight from the children. Sitting bolt upright, struggling as one does to remember exactly where one is in unfamiliar surroundings, my eyes began slowly to focus.

Charlie and Cressie were astride the nearest bale, riding it like jubilant surfers on the crest of a once-in-a-lifetime wave as it rolled steadily down the slope, gradually gaining momentum. They waved, and I waved back cheerily, admiring their footwork as they began to gather speed on the inexorable downhill descent.

My eye caught an irresolute black square just ahead of their path, an abandoned oil can.

'Oh, my goodness,' I thought briefly, though it wasn't really "goodness" at all. 'Supposing it jolts them off…'

Almost as the thought crossed my mind the ever more rapidly moving giant cylinder swallowed up the can in an instant, spitting it out in its wake a second or two later as flat as the thinnest of uncooked pancakes.

'Oh my God,' I breathed, reality dawning. 'Supposing that was one of the kids…'

My mind flashed back:

When Charlie was just three years old (Cressie was yet to emerge from her pram), I took him with me on a call to some new neighbours, less than half a mile down the road.

'Come on, Charlie,' I said, 'let's go for a walk. We'll leave Cressie asleep with your mum. I doubt either of them will wake up before we get back.'

The new arrivals, the Andertons, had scarcely unpacked their furniture, let alone the baby I had been called to see, who was sleeping restlessly in a cot in the garden. I checked him over carefully and pronounced my verdict.

'Teething,' I announced solemnly. 'Teething, colic, and being three months old. Probably a bit stressed, too. But he seems to have settled down now.'

'Stress!' exclaimed Mrs Anderton, 'What do you mean, stress? He's a baby, not some chief executive of a major global organisation. How can a baby get stressed?'

'New home, new surroundings…' I shrugged. 'It must be really difficult for you at the moment, so why not your baby? He has feelings, too, you know, even if he doesn't understand what they are as yet. And besides…'

'Yes?' she said, a worried look on her face. 'Is there anything else, anything serious?'

'Not any longer,' I explained. 'His nappy had managed to twist itself round and was squashing what little there is at the moment of his left testicle. I loosened it up, rearranged his anatomy and gently encouraged things back round to the front, where they ought to be.'

'Oh, thank you,' she sighed, looking embarrassed. 'I'm so sorry…'

'It's okay,' I shrugged. 'All in a day's work – nappy straightening and testicular realignment are two of my specialities. And besides, the previous owners were registered with the opposition.'

19

'Neighbouring practice,' I explained when she raised an eyebrow, 'or the enemy, as we like to describe them – and I've always wanted to have a look around here. Such a fascinating garden – could I?'

'Of course,' she said, jumping to her feet. 'Be my guest – we haven't had a chance to explore properly ourselves yet, what with so much to do. We're not quite sure what's here – watch the steps, though, with your son. They're a bit uneven.'

Charlie had been playing happily in the sandpit during my brief consultation, acquiring a new taste, and was reluctant to leave.

'Come on, son,' I motioned to him, 'up the steps in front of me so I can keep an eye on you.'

'Oh, daddy!' he said, disgruntled, as we made our way round a leafy corner of the garden. 'I was having such fun...'

At which point he disappeared entirely from view, barely two feet in front of me, totally submerged in an ivy-covered pool...

That feeling, that sudden, desperate, paralysing panic which stays with you long after the event is over, hit me again then. The bale had reached a steeper gradient and was gathering speed alarmingly, Charlie and Cressie running faster and faster on top of it to maintain their balance, fear now replacing the previous exuberance in their voices.

I raced behind in their wake, struggling to catch up.

'Jump,' I screamed at the top of my voice, 'jump, as far as you can. Jump for your lives.'

And they jumped, bless them, landing in a sprawling heap by my side and crying in relief as the bale of hay accelerated relentlessly down the hill before disappearing over a precipice to what lay unexpectedly below.

We lay holding each other for what seemed like an eternity, none of us able to speak.

Lost for words.

# 2

# Why Does It Have to Happen to Me?

You never know what a night on the 'Kernowdoc' out-of-hours service might bring, apart from the absence of a good night's sleep.

Other doctors arrived for their midnight shift, crawled into bed and woke seven hours later fully refreshed and reconstituted for the day ahead, but as for me... just turning up on the doorstep signified the outbreak of half a dozen epidemics.

The nearest I ever got to a decent night's sleep came after crawling into bed at 6 a.m. following an exhausting evening's labours, hoping just to close my eyes for a few moments before leaving at seven to attend to my daily duties. At 9.45 I struggled into consciousness as a cleaner stuck her head round the door and announced: 'Here he is, everybody,' to a general sense of relief.

Having failed to arrive at either home or the surgery, and with everyone wondering where on earth I had vanished to, my other half had finally had a flash of inspiration and rung the hospital to check if I had ever got round to leaving it.

Morning surgery ran a little late that day.

I often used to wonder.

Why does a six-week-old cough become suddenly so important at three o'clock in the morning, and why did some stupid doctor sitting in the nice warm triage centre in Truro with a bacon sandwich and freshly brewed coffee send me twenty-five miles out into the night to take a look at it?

There is a law of inverse proportions at work here – the further you have to travel, and the more dreadful the weather through which you have to traverse, and the more difficult it is to find the address you have been given, the less necessary that visit will turn out to be. The really important ones are dying just round the corner on a beautiful summer's morning.

But, I repeat, you just never know precisely what is going to happen on these nights.

Here follows a true record of a single night on call. Not a cobbled together collection of stories for dramatic effect – this is it, just as it unfolded, hour by hour. At the time I felt certain God had some issues with me, but it could have been worse. I just didn't know how.

11.55 p.m. I arrive at the hospital on a cold, bleak night.

It is just beginning to rain, an ominous sign. The driver, Terry again, and the doctor from whom I am taking over are sitting watching the end of the late-night film on TV, with that horribly smug 'We haven't even been out of the building all shift' look on their faces.

'Evening, gentlemen,' I say. 'Quiet night?'

'As the proverbial grave,' answers Simon, the doctor, standing and stretching before gathering up his belongings. 'Well, I'm off home to bed. Hope the peace and quiet lasts for you.'

I look at Terry, and he looks at me.

'I'll give it fifteen minutes,' I say philosophically. 'Twenty at the outside,' and the bleep goes off before I've even had the chance to sit down.

We have a name, an address, and a time of intended completion, but no details of the problem. This would not usually worry me unless it's an ASAP (as soon as possible), which means the patient is probably seriously ill and I'll have to actually get out of the car when we arrive.

Our drivers, a godsend to GPs who had been used to doing their own navigating and driving as well as dealing with patients, have now been doing their jobs for some three years, developing an encyclopaedic knowledge of the local area along the way.

Terry, who knows roughly where we are going, sighs good-naturedly as yet another decent film has to be left with the final twenty minutes unseen. We head down to the car and drive off.

The vehicles are all leased from a local garage and are specifically chosen for their benevolent characteristics and doctor-friendly suitability, i.e. they are ponderously slow and cripplingly uncomfortable. They have radios that don't work and mobile phones that are frequently out of range.

'Kernowdoc' is emblazoned on the side in consumer-friendly green, and we have a not-always-working flashing light on the roof that we are only allowed to use under certain circumstances. Hurrying back to the hospital to catch the end of a football match is not generally held to be one of them.

And most people ignore it anyway, no doubt thinking that Mr Whippy has downsized and taken to delivering ice creams at unusual times and places. I had argued vociferously for a siren or, failing that, a megaphone through which I could bellow 'Make way, I'm a doctor!'

Deaf ears.

Out in the inky nocturnal darkness the weather is rapidly deteriorating, with worse to come. Half an hour later we arrive at our destination, a small residential home on the outskirts of yet another quasi-idyllic Cornish village called – you've guessed it – Tre-something, where cloth-sandalled Liberal Democrats pretend to holiday in the summer while actually going to "Ibeetha". I stand in the wind and rain banging on the wrong door for five minutes before a member of staff emerges from the right one to see if we had yet arrived.

'And what can we do for Mrs Alder?' I ask brightly, pathetically glad to be indoors and out of the rain for a moment.

'Pronounce her dead,' she says flatly. As she spots the look on my face, she adds 'Oh. Didn't they tell you?'

Terry has reversed the car round and is waiting for me, engine running.

'Got a collapse back in Werrington,' he says tersely. 'No more details as yet, but it's an ASAP.'

'Can we put the green flashing light on?' I plead innocently.

'You are such a child, Mike,' he retorts, throwing me a look of mock disdain.

'Please?' I beg, and he gives in.

'Okay,' he sighs grudgingly. 'But I'm not going to let you make those woo-woo siren noises again.'

We find 5 Broad Street with comparative ease, and an elderly lady in a pink candlewick nightdress meets me at the door.

'He's...' she says hesitantly, looking upwards, 'but I think... I think...'

I run up the narrow stairs and on to the landing, turning to the right and almost falling over the half-clad body of a man in his late seventies lying on the floor, half in and half out of the bathroom. A small pool of vomit lies just beneath his head, and a woman in her mid fifties is gently cleaning his face.

'I've tried to give him the kiss of life,' she says, looking up at me with tears in her eyes, 'and press his chest, but it's so cramped... Do you think I could have done anything else?'

'Is he... are you?' I ask, not wanting to get anything wrong.

'His wife, yes,' she answers, understanding at once, adding as I look down at her husband, 'He was older than me, you see.'

Older, and sadly very dead. I could see at a glance. Probably before we had got the call, probably before she had picked up the telephone, and probably even before she had sped up the stairs having heard his body fall to the floor.

Later we sit downstairs in the cluttered kitchen, hob kettle screeching, waiting for the police to arrive. Mrs Carter and her mother tell me about their day in the matter-of-fact tones you so often hear at moments like these.

'We'd had such a lovely day,' says his wife. 'Friends round, laughing and joking just like old times, and he really enjoyed himself.'

'And he ate well,' puts in her mother. 'Had a really good appetite today, he did. Are you in a hurry, doctor?' she continues, suddenly concerned. 'Are we keeping you from another call?'

'No, no hurry,' I confirm.

It can be a surreal world, this, and one I still cannot get completely used to. You walk into complete strangers' lives at the moment of their deepest tragedies and then extract yourself diplomatically after a quick pronouncement of death and a few platitudes that always seem so hopelessly inadequate.

You rarely ever see them again, and if you do – say, inadvertently in the local supermarket – you don your invisible blinkers and head for the refrigeration zone, or buy things you don't need. Like vodka. Ice. Lime and lemons. And, every now and then, shot glasses.

Should they then discover you in the frozen food section, they tell you that they were so grateful for your help at a time when you felt at your most impotent, your most humble. You look sheepish and squirm a little while they thank you for something you feel you didn't really do, and sigh in relief as they move on.

When the coroner's officer arrives, I take my leave of the grieving Mrs Carter and her mother. The ambulance has been and gone, and we have moved the man's body from the bathroom through to his bed, trying to restore a little dignity to the proceedings.

'Please, Doctor Sparrow, would you mind helping us?' Mrs Carter had pleaded. 'I don't want any strangers to see him like this.'

And, yes, I know it contravenes the rule book. Lucky for her I threw that out many years ago.

All too little, and all too late. It is now half past one in the morning, and already we have had two fatalities on our shift.

Terry is outside waiting, the engine still running.

'We've another call,' he explains, 'back at the hospital. Maybe that'll be it for the night.'

'And maybe tomorrow the world will go spinning out of orbit and crash into the sun,' I respond wearily, 'but somehow I rather doubt it.'

By two o'clock I have seen the patient. At five past two I am laying out the folding bed ready to crawl into my sleeping bag for a few blissful hours of sleep. At ten past two Terry and I are driving out into the atrocious night heading for another hamlet some twenty miles distant, and a house it takes us an hour to find.

At quarter past three Terry is waiting for me as I come out sprinting through the rain with my bags in hand. He has the engine running again.

'Green light and woo-woo time,' he says without expression. 'The other side of Kilkhampton. No details, but an ambulance is already on scene and starting resuscitation.'

'But that's nearly forty miles away,' I remark, aghast. 'In this weather it will take us well over an hour, even if we're lucky, and the patient could be in hospital by then, if they're not dead already. Good God, what do they expect of us? Here, pass me the phone.'

I ring back to base to explain the situation.

'It's not that we mind going,' I say, lying through what is left of my teeth, 'but the weather's appalling, it'll take us an age and the ambulance is already there…'

'They've asked you to go,' comes the answer with a sort of "that's just the way it is" shrug over the airwaves. 'Sorry, but you'll have to do the best you can. Even if your best is…'

I think I hear the word "useless". I also think I hear another word before it.

'So kind, so understanding,' I mutter viciously, my hand over the mouthpiece. 'OK, Terry, Kilkhampton it is. Just remember that our lives are more important than theirs. My life, at least…'

Terry grinned. 'Is equally as important as mine? Hey, I'm driving. I'm looking to save me first.'

On the way out to our previous visit we had hit a large, unexpected puddle hidden in the darkness of a hedge by a sharp bend, slewing for a terrifying few seconds across the road before Terry expertly corrected the skid. On the return journey we slow approaching the same corner, silently complicit in the "I don't think we want to die here" thing. Our hearts rise into our mouths as we round the bend, seeing fifty yards ahead of us a car spinning upside down, sliding to a halt just a few feet from the roadside ditch.

'Jesus,' murmurs Terry as we sit immobilised in our seats for a moment, our headlights picking out the wreckage through the driving rain. 'This is one of those moments when I'm glad you're the doctor and I'm just the bloke who drives a car for a living.'

'But you have the coat,' I point out, although in the event we both get out, oblivious to the rain, and start walking and then running towards the carnage. The road ahead and behind is completely deserted, and to our right we can see the skid marks up the side of bank where the car has slithered up after hitting the flood water before flipping over on to its roof.

The passenger door is towards us. My spirits sink.

The whole top of the car is flattened down level to the bottom of the windows, the boot open and a few bedraggled clothes scattered forlornly across the tarmac. Nobody, nobody could have survived in there, and I wonder how many bodies we are going to find crushed to death inside.

Morrisons

Morrisons

Morrisons

Redeem this coupon with your My Morrisons Card ending:

xxxxxxxxxxxx3750

Valid until:
23/10/21

00710161019

Save

£3

when you next spend £30

Excludes all alcohol in Scotland and Wales, spirits in England. One £money off basket coupon used per transaction. See T&Cs on reverse.

Morrisons
Since 1899

Valassis:
1082 49731

9 926714 463003

620 0195  BL_3250_5791

And then suddenly, miraculously, the driver's door swings open and out crawls the sole occupant, a young lad of around twenty, who straightens up and stands looking down at the decimated remains before us.

'Phew,' he observes sanguinely, glancing across and noticing us for apparently the first time, his face breaking out into a huge grin. 'That was a close one. Can you give us a lift into town?'

It is not the first time we've encountered a bizarre situation on our nocturnal wanderings, once coming upon a car beautifully parked on the outside lane of the motorway with not a soul in sight. Which presents a bit of a predicament. Do you attend to the problem immediately to hand, or continue on to the call to which you are heading? But even this is nothing compared to the predicament once faced by a couple of ambulancemen of my acquaintance.

'It had been a quiet night,' said Richard. 'Hadn't left the station all shift, and then we got a buzz at about four o'clock in the morning. Old chap down near Pipers Pool, in heart failure. The doctor was miles away on another visit, so we arrived long before we knew he could get there. His wife was at the door, and she was so nervous and worried about him. Kept saying "Will he be alright – you will look after him, won't you?" But when we went upstairs we found him dead in his chair in the bedroom, and the poor dear just had no idea.

'We went downstairs to tell her, and I was just about to pass on the sad news when she said "I couldn't bear him to die at home, you know, not when we've lived here so many years together. You won't let him die here, will you? My daughter will be here soon, she'll look after me. Please, please do help him as much as you can."'

'So, what did you do?' I asked, intrigued.

'Well,' said Richard slowly, 'we looked at each other and decided then and there not to tell her. So, we loaded him up and shipped him out to the ambulance to take him down to hospital and tell her later that he died on the way. We're not supposed to, of course, but it was a quiet evening and we reckoned we could be there and back in an hour and a half, two at the most, and she was so grateful, wasn't she, Steve?'

'Grateful was her middle name,' agreed Steve soberly. 'The only problem was, as we were driving down the dual carriageway we came across an accident, happened just a few moments before we got there, and there were two people who had been thrown out of the car, both unconscious and in need of urgent help. We couldn't just drive past, could we, so we stopped to see what we could do.'

'They were both alive,' said Richard, taking up the story again, 'but in a pretty bad way, and we checked with ambulance control who said there were no other vehicles for miles around and could we just do the best we could under the circumstances, which left us with a bit of a dilemma.'

'Which was?' I asked.

'Well,' continued Richard, biting his lower lip, 'it's expressly forbidden to carry a dead body and a live patient in the same ambulance at the same time. We could have been sacked for it, but we couldn't just drive on, could we, and leave the casualties bleeding to death? We just couldn't.'

I could imagine the scene – the still, quiet hours of the night, nobody else around, a corpse in the ambulance, two casualties on the ground in front of them in urgent need of medical attention and a summary dismissal on the horizon for helping both out at the same time.

'So, what did you do?' I repeated, still intrigued.

'Well…' Richard hesitated, 'we – um – decided to improvise. You can't ever repeat this, Mike… we couldn't leave dying people unattended, we really didn't want to be sacked, and we had done all we could and more for Mr Mortimore, so we… um…'

He looked away, briefly.

"We… er … well, we chucked him over the hedge out of sight, loaded up the casualties in his place and drove off to the hospital all lights and sirens blazing, calling a mate in the police to tell him what we had done and asking him to pick up the body and meet us down at Derriford. Which sort of would have been fine, except that when he got to where we told him we had left the body, he … um…'

He ground to a halt, and I waited.

'He couldn't find it,' finished Steve forlornly. 'Until… he realised he was looking at the wrong side of the road. We'd been going west, and he came up the opposite way.'

We drop our itinerant hitch-hiker in the middle of Launceston, at his request, and draw up at the crossroads.

To our left, no more than four hundred yards away, lies the hospital and the ever welcoming bed I so yearn to climb into, and to our right lies the long uninviting drive out to the distant reaches of Kilkhampton and beyond, the call neither of us wishes to go to.

'I think this is just the moment for a phone call,' I say to Terry, 'and I think you could be just the man... not to make it.'

I ring base, and duly plead our position once more.

'Look, about call number 69326,' I begin. 'It's over half an hour since you rang us, and we've only just made it back to Launceston. The weather is unbelievably awful and it's going to take another good forty to fifty minutes from here, even if we're lucky. And there's an ambulance on site, for goodness' sake, and when was this called in, anyway? It's not that we are unwilling to go...'

'Oh, yes, it is,' murmurs Terry in my ear.

'...but it just seems... all a bit pointless,' I finish lamely.

'I'm sorry,' comes the voice at the other end of the radio after a short pause, 'but I've just checked and they still are requesting you to attend. There's a doctor there, though, Dr Callaway. Would you like to talk to him directly?'

'So, there's a doctor, an ambulance and paramedics, we're bloody miles away, but they still want us to attend?'

'Got it in one,' arrives the unwelcome answer.

I sigh wearily.

'Give me Callaway's number, then,' I say tersely.

The apparently needy Dr Callaway, obviously harassed, answers gruff-voiced after what seems to be an eternity. I repeat my question.

'Because I've asked you to come, and I could do with some back-up,' comes the curt reply. The phone goes dead. I think I may have cursed.

'Know this chap, Terry?' I ask.

'Oh, yes,' he nods sagely, 'I'm afraid I do.'

'And your reason for not telling me?'

Terry is quiet for a moment.

'Because I love you, Mike.'

'There was a moment,' I reply after due consideration, 'when I didn't quite believe you there.'

We drive on through the night, exhausted but giggling like teenagers, the weather becoming progressively more awful as each mile merges into the next. Rain crashes down on the windscreen like storm-swept waves on a Cornish shore, even the thunder drowned out by its hammering. Lightning, frequent and vivid, flashes overhead as we duck involuntarily.

Three-quarters of an hour later we are finally closing in on our destination.

'Do you actually know where this place is, Terry?' I wonder.

'Is the Pope a Catholic?' he replies. 'Are Manchester United the finest team in the land? Are you a deeply dedicated professional and I a driver of exceptional skill with a comprehensive knowledge of the local environment?'

'So that'll be a no then, would it?' I say, checking.

'Wouldn't have had a clue,' he admits, grinning. 'But I recognise a blue flashing light when I see one.'

He points ahead through the windscreen to where a police car is moving rapidly through the darkness, before disappearing into the gloom over the brow of a hill.

'And how do you know it's going to the same place as we are?' I demand truculently.

'This is Kilkhampton, Mike,' Terry replies. 'Since when did two things of interest happen here within the same month, let alone the same night?'

We speed up the hill in the wake of the car, and then down into the valley beyond, rounding a corner and drawing quickly to a halt.

'Jesus,' expostulates Terry, leaning forward on the steering wheel and peering ahead. 'Must be every emergency vehicle in the county here, and then some.'

Before us, abandoned haphazardly around the car park, are three ambulances, two paramedics' cars, a couple of fire engines and the police car we have just been following – its door is open, its engine is still running and its lights are flashing eerily in the darkness. People in uniform seem to be milling around everywhere. As I climb warily out of the car I can hear the crackling of several radios, voices raised in desperation as they try unsuccessfully to make themselves heard above the drumming of the rain.

'Here,' says Terry, 'better take my coat. I have a feeling we're going to be here for some time.'

A short, steep drive leads down to a garage where I can see two men in red boiler suits, hopelessness written across their faces and in the droop of their shoulders. I traverse slowly through the darkness to where they stand, blinded by the surrounding lights, not wanting to find what was down there, not wanting to believe.

But there is no escape, and all too soon I round the final corner to find the whole chaotic scene laid out before me.

Beyond the red-suited paramedics lies the body of a maybe seventeen-year-old girl, one ambulanceman standing by her side, drip in hand, while another is crouched over her exposed chest, holding a defibrillator. For a moment they remain unaware of my presence as I stand and watch, taking it all in, feeling my way into the scene before taking a few steps forward into their line of view.

'How long has she been like this?' I ask quietly.

The ambulanceman holding the defibrillator puts one paddle down and rubs his eyes.

'About an hour now,' he responds despondently.

I bend over the pale, cyanosed body and lay a hand on her forehead, cold and still amongst the debris.

'This girl is dead,' I announce simply. 'Why are you still doing this?'

They look at each other briefly, and then back at me.

'Because Dr Callaway insisted,' explains one of them, 'and... and...' his voice tails off into silence.

'Could you maybe put the monitor back on?' I request, watching the screen and the flat line that spreads across it.

'I think perhaps you should stop now,' I suggest quietly. 'This is just pointless, I'm afraid. Is that okay with you?'

'It's fine with us,' acknowledges one of them, while the other shrugs with tacit agreement, 'but...'

'But Dr Callaway insisted,' I finish for him. 'Like Dr Callaway rules the world and all that is within it.'

I take a final look at the young corpse lying before us all, so innocent, so exposed, and so tragically beyond any of our help.

'Where is he?' I scowl.

'In the house,' they answer together. 'Talking to the parents. Rather you than any of us.'

With those words ringing ominously in my ears I make my way back out of the garage and up to the house, heavy-hearted and apprehensive. The hall is in darkness, but I can hear conversation down the corridor ahead of me, voices muted. I take a deep breath and continue forward, turning to the right and stopping at the doorway to the sitting room.

There before me sits Dr Callaway, deep in conversation with the girl's parents and a young lad I took to be her brother.

I cough discreetly. Dr Callaway turns towards me with a look of profound irritation on his face.

'Not now,' he says brusquely. 'Can't you see I'm busy?'

'I'm Dr Sparrow,' I say, 'and I think we need to have a talk together.'

'Not now,' he repeats, turning back to the shell-shocked couple in front of him.

'Oh, yes, now,' I persist, nodding to the room behind me. 'I'm sure the kitchen will do just fine.'

I'm standing in the kitchen, quietly fuming for a reason I have yet to fully understand, when Dr Callaway enters and closes the door behind him. I know him by name, but we have never met and slowly I take in his appearance, trying to gauge the measure of the man before me.

He is dressed in a brand-new mid-green jumpsuit. On his arm, a shiny new exhibit has been recently stitched.

"BASICS Doctor."

Stand back and all hail to a conquering hero.

I can no longer remember precisely what "BASICS" stands for, but I knew the breed so well. I've even tried it myself and it's fun, for a while, until reality and a fit of the giggles takes over when you can't find your stethoscope in the multitude of pockets at your disposal. BASICS doctors drive smartly kitted-out Land Rovers, and I know that some of them do a really good job. Some of them.

It's just that so often when I encounter them they seem to be standing around preening themselves and trying to appear important while the paramedics get on unostentatiously with the job in hand. Just like Dr Callaway, in fact.

And a bit like me, come to think of it.

Callaway, after giving me a 'You've interrupted me when I was being very important' glare for a few moments, decides it is time to put me in my place. 'I was talking to the parents,' he says angrily.

'Really?' I say. 'I would never have guessed, although the fact that the paramedics said, "He's in the house talking to the parents" should have given me a bit of a clue, I suppose.'

Callaway does a bit more glaring. 'I've heard of you, Dr Sparrow,' he says finally, 'and I know you don't think you belong to the real world like the rest of us, but how can you be so facetious at a time like this?'

'Oh, it's easy,' I say, 'I have years of practice, and I can do better than this if I really put my mind to it, but what I really want to know is what the bloody hell am I doing here? There's you, a couple of fire engines, a whole convention of paramedics and assorted hangers-on, and a body in the garage that's been stone-cold dead for over an hour. What am I supposed to be doing – making the tea for everybody, or what?'

'I told you,' he replies, his face beginning to turn an interesting shade of vermilion. 'I wanted some back-up.'

'Okay, so you're a complete prat… but you've got the back-up you wanted,' I say, shrugging my shoulders. 'That poor girl is unfortunately as dead as every dodo, only more so, and it is the saddest thing I have seen for more than a decade. I support you in that. I've told them to stop resuscitation, so please can I go on to my next call now?'

'You've done what?' he shouts, aghast, the veins on his temples standing out so far that I take a step back in case they explode and I get caught in the fallout. The perils of a white shirt on duty.

'How could you, you…' and with that he turns and dashes out of the kitchen, across the hall and out into the night, disappearing round the corner and down into the garage. I follow at a curious trot, and as I re-enter the garage he is there, leaning over the body of the young girl having wrested the defibrillator from the nearest paramedic.

'Don't stop,' he shouts, 'just don't stop. Breathing, someone, check her breathing, damn it.'

The ambulancemen and medics stand there, shifting uneasily from foot to foot. 'Look, what are we supposed to do?' says one of them at last. 'We've got you saying one thing, this doctor saying another… just what are we supposed to do?'

In twenty years of medical practice I have rarely become really angry, but this is my chance to give it full rein. I grab hold of Callaway's collar, yank him up to a standing position with surprisingly little resistance, and say more calmly than I expect to at this point: 'Might I suggest we discuss this outside? Two minutes, gentlemen,' I add, looking across to our assembled audience.

It is still raining out there, and we are getting wet, the wind whipping our words away almost before they were spoken.

'So which planet are you on?' I ask, descending to the language of the school playground, the last place I felt really at home. 'Planet Stupid? Just what do you think you're playing at? She's dead. I am really sorry and I know it must be awful for everyone, but she is still dead and will ever be and nothing you or anyone else can do is going to change it, no matter how long we all sit here and pretend to try and resuscitate her.'

Callaway is struggling to get his words out.

'Because I want,' he begins, running his hands through his hair wildly and tugging at any lock not yet firmly plastered down to his scalp, 'because I want her kidneys. I've talked to the parents, and they think it's a good idea. All we have to do,' he continues desperately, 'is keep going until we can get somebody here to arrange it.' Words fail me – for a millisecond. Maybe not that long.

'You want WHAT?' I shriek.

'You have a dead eighteen-year-old girl in a garage in Kilkhampton at four o'clock in the morning. Half the paramedics in the county are trying to ignore the fact that they are attempting a resurrection even more unlikely than that of Jesus himself, and I have yet to identify a single transplant team waiting in the wings and begging for a recently expired organ.'

I want to punch him. Reality checks in as the girl's mother's sobs echo down the corridor. Their pain is way more important than mine. In fact, their pain is everything, and I am just annoyed. It would be a wake-up call if I wasn't already wide awake.

'You have,' I point out, 'nearly every out-of-hours medical professional queuing up here and begging to be of assistance, yet it hasn't even occurred to you that in an unexpected death in a girl of this age the coroner might just possibly... no, certainly, be wanting to do an autopsy and quite like to have her kidneys himself. And her liver, her blood toxins... her brain, her stomach contents... Need I go on?'

I lean closer and look him directly in the eyes, all the better to deliver the final insult. 'Have you been watching too much *Peak Practice*, Dr Callaway, or what?'

'What you have to do is decide who's in charge here,' I go on. 'You called me in and I'm here, but I'm not standing around waiting to polish your halo while you play games with other people's emotions. You want me to take charge, then fine, I'm here and I'll do it. But you've already been here for over an hour, and you've developed some sort of relationship with the parents. You've landed yourself in a situation you can either now run away from and leave me to sort out on your behalf, or take a deep breath and go and resolve yourself. So, you tell me – which of us do you think should be dealing with the mess you have single-handedly created?'

His face falls, and his shoulders slump in resignation. I climb into the car and say tersely: 'Get me out of here, Terry, if you would be so kind.'

Terry looks across briefly, and away again. 'So, you're right off his Christmas card list, then?' We drive in silence for a while, until he suddenly grins and says, 'By the way, have I got a call for you…'

Twenty minutes later we pull up outside a small cottage deep in the countryside and my heart begins to sink.

'Oh, my God,' I say faintly. 'I've been here before…'

Inside, the darkness lit only by a few dwindling candles and the glow from an untuned television, is a wild-eyed man in his early thirties.

'Hallo again, Clive,' I say, by way of introduction, coughing as an unsavoury smell almost overpowers my senses.

'People think I'm crazy,' he begins, and of course he is right. People do, and I am one of them. But then, strangely enough, both logically and weirdly, maybe that admission on his part demonstrates sufficient insight to show he is not crazy at all. Catch-22 and all that. Maybe I'm crazy instead.

'I've been collecting things,' he continues. 'Bits of myself. People think I'm crazy…'

I breathe a sigh of relief, it's clearly not me that's crazy.

'…and maybe I am, but you're not going to get me this time. I don't want to die, and I've been saving things, bits of myself, my hair and my nails and bits of dead skin. I want to keep all the waste bits of me so they can put me back together if something should happen.'

He points to some pots and pans on the floor around him. 'I've just started to keep something else, too,' he continues, 'something they might

35

be able to use. You can take a look if you like,' and I just know without thinking what it is the smell reminds me of...

Outside, in the car, Terry later told me, he heard a shrill, plaintive cry splitting the night air. Apparently, that was me again.

'Why?' I was calling, loudly and forlornly. 'Oh, why does it have to happen to me?'

# 3
# Groundhog Day – Part I

I have never seen the above film, but feedback from colleagues and patients alike makes me sometimes think I would have liked a permanent part in it.

There will be many of you now scratching your head and wondering 'So what's a groundhog, then?' As far as I can tell, it is a big ugly mole with attitude. I believe the basic tenet of the film's plot is that a man is trapped in some sort of recurring time warp, condemned to relive the same twenty-four hours over and over again, with minor but significant variations on the theme.

This sort of appeals.

I have now reached the age when I feel neither older nor younger than I did twenty years ago, and, as each decade passes, I continue to believe I am worryingly much the same. Sure, another grey hair or two indenting the temples, a few more inches around the waistline and the extra three days it takes to recover from the now much less frequent all-night parties.

No longer will a couple of bacon and egg sandwiches garnished with a double helping of HP sauce and Branston pickle rejuvenate my aching bones. Never again can I wake up with a bottle of malt whisky and two straws, each of them mine, and refloat the kidneys before breakfast. I can now happily forsake ice-cold showers, oat-and-peach-based mucsli and muscle-bound personal trainers clad in tight-fitting Lycra leotards for some comfy pyjamas and one of those lavender neck-warmers from Argos so loved by hairdressers.

While deep inside I still try to pretend to myself I am totally unchanged, unravaged by the passage of time. And even though I've been buying the 'Peter Pan Tablets of Everlasting Youth' from the local homeopathy shop for some considerable time, somehow my body doesn't appear to be listening.

Trapped perennially in my self-deluding cocoon, I could happily convince myself that the years were not rolling inexorably by were it not for one intrinsic but sadly inescapable part of the daily grind – the patients.

It's not even so much the ones that have the temerity to die – or succumb to 'natural wastage', as one of my colleagues refers to it. Nor is it those in the prime of life, such as myself, for they age at exactly the same rate as do I. No, it's the children I hold entirely to blame.

I still continue forlornly to think of everyone in the practice as being the same age they were when I arrived here, clinging pathetically to the hope that if they appear to grow no older, then neither will I. But those patients who were children a quarter of a century ago are impossible to ignore. Try as I might.

'Haven't they grown!' I find myself exclaiming in complete surprise on periodically encountering one of this mystical breed. Or 'Have you traded them in for a new model?' I might say, smiling artfully as the 'new model' shuffles sheepishly from foot to foot, head bowed and looking at their shoes for an outlet, wondering why all doctors and parents are so moronically patronising.

But, of course, when I come to reflect upon it later, it is not just that they have grown, it is more that they have grown older, and so have I. I still have to take a deep breath when I see a seventeen-year-old at the wheel of a car to stop myself saying: 'But they're not old enough to drive – they can't be a day over seven. Maybe eight or nine, if I've missed a year.'

Because that, of course, was the age they were when I first arrived here. Yet stuck irretrievably in the grip of my groundhog mentality, I adhere religiously to the mistaken belief that nothing has changed, and hopefully never will.

But it has. Almost everything has. The first baby I delivered is now twenty-three, the first toddler I treated now has a baby of her own, and that nice roughly middle-aged publican who poured my first 'welcome to the community' pint of Guinness, has now died. Of old age.

I signed the death certificate myself and wanted to weep.

The first spotty adolescent I ineffectively treated for acne has now left university, having qualified as a doctor in his own right, and is rumoured to be a consultant surgeon. More depressingly still, he remains young enough to be one of my own children, as indeed is every other newly qualified doctor from here on in.

And *that* is what makes me feel really old – and getting older.

Foremost amongst my early memories of Lifton were my inaugural twins here. How could I ever forget them?

My first ever twins post-qualification were born in an outlying RAF station to a tiny Scottish lady who by the end of her pregnancy was almost as round as she was tall. She also smoked – at a conservative estimate – a good twenty cigarettes a day, and despite my constant protestations never once managed to cut down. Yet at the end of the simplest of all labours out popped two of the plumpest, healthiest, bouncing baby girls you could ever wish to see. So much for medical advice.

I always find newborn twins absolutely fascinating and I particularly enjoy meeting twins' parents. They are the only people I know who look perpetually more exhausted than their doctors.

The Cardinham twins were born the day I started in general practice in Lifton. I've never been quite sure whether their birth was a celebration of my arrival in the area, or vice versa, but no other twins were born to a patient of mine for another five years. Caleb and Luke, for a tragically short time, were to rule the roost.

Their mother was a rosy-cheeked, cherubic Devonian by the name of Cheryl, four generations of farmers having finally culminated in just the one daughter, whose duty, they all felt, was to prolong their agricultural dynasty. But Cheryl had other ideas, becoming engaged to an Italian, of all things – and, to make matters worse, some several months after conception. The omens were not good.

Her fiancé, Pietro, looked as if he had inadvertently wandered off the set of Francis Ford Coppola's *The Godfather* just long enough to get her pregnant and put a horse's head or two in the neighbouring farmers' beds, before returning to his native land (which he actually did). Sadly, soon afterwards he was gunned down near the Vatican during a long-running provincial ice-cream war between rival manufacturers.

'His family were so proud,' said Cheryl sadly, trying to smile through the tears when we next met, some years later. 'They must have thought that he had been there protecting his family honour, or some such nonsense. They imagined him going down all guns blazing, but I could never tell them the truth, what really happened, could I?'

Apparently, Pietro had gone out to get a couple of 99s from the ice-cream van down the road and got caught in the crossfire between enemy factions, dying instantly. The twins had been left fatherless a couple of months before their first birthday. We all mourned for weeks.

As a rule, the only three reasons I can think of for picking up an infant in the course of my day's work at the surgery are to examine it, to immunise it, or to hand it promptly back to the nearest parent before it is sick on your shoulder. But it wasn't that way with Luke and Caleb.

They were just the most delightful babies, miniature prop forwards in the making with angelically round faces and plump little arms and legs. They did not, I have to admit, actually do an awful lot in the early days, just sitting in their car seats with a quizzical look on their faces, watching the strange and wonderful world that is Devon and Cornwall gradually unfolding before them.

Although truly identical, Luke – the elder by twenty minutes and a lot of sweating and grunting – was a little heavier, and Caleb was marginally the more animated. The only other distinguishing feature between the two was a bright red birthmark on the back of Caleb's bald chunky head, half hidden just behind his right ear, while both of them had some additional webbing between the second and third toes of each foot. Amazingly, amidst all the excitement of their birth, this had remained undiscovered until several days after they had left the hospital, but it was an unimportant oddity and in no need of surgical correction.

You almost never wanted them to grow up. If only they could remain just as they were, a benchmark in time for us all to enjoy as they watched and learned in their delightfully unhurried manner as if they had all the time in the world. Oh, if only that had been true.

Luke and Caleb were a truly bright spot in the often grey and humdrum world of everyday general practice, their visits to the surgery being enjoyed by us all. The staff would jostle for position in the queue round the back of the building to hold one or the other, and even I could occasionally be heard pleading in the periphery of the general melee: 'My turn. When is it going to be my turn?'

We all missed them when they left the practice. Cheryl, we heard in due course, was forging a new life for herself and the boys abroad, her local family having disowned her. We all silently wished her well.

I often wondered what became of them, but then general practice is so often like that. People drift in and out of our lives, and we so often never know if that irritating skin complaint of theirs ever did clear up, or what became of their bloody diarrhoea...

All patients, and their endlessly unedifying ailments, become just a collection of random and unconnected memories in the end.

And then we heard that tragedy had struck Cheryl's life once more as Luke – plump, gorgeous little Luke – contracted meningitis and died with twenty-four hours.

We were never to see Cheryl or Caleb in the practice again.

At the opposite end of the scale, in virtually all respects – age, general appeal, but most importantly standards of personal hygiene – were the Widdecott twins.

They were an integral part of the Widdecott brothers, collectively John, Norman, Edward and Harold, who all lived in a small village just a few miles away from the surgery. More of whom shortly.

We have some interesting village names on our Devon/Cornwall border, although it does not necessarily follow that interesting people live in them. One of them rejoices in the name of Bridestowe, a title dating back to the middle of the fifteenth century.

In those days, hamlets were often named after any attractions they offered beyond the confines of the immediate community. 'Come to Wells and sample our water,' an advertisement of the time might have announced.

Names do change over the centuries, and I understand Bridestowe lost a letter from its original monicker. At the turn of the fifteenth century there was apparently an overly high preponderance of spinsters in the Bridestowe parish, together with a relative lack of able-bodied men to work in the fields.

This, legend has it, led to the village elders putting out signs on their outer boundaries, and advertising on the Middle Ages equivalent of the internet (they sent a horse and rider out to spread the news). 'Brides to Wed,' proclaimed both proudly, later to become Bridestowed, and finally... Bridestowe.

There is little doubt that this is actually true. But then we also have a local village rejoicing in the name of Virginstowe...

One also wonders about the origins of such names as Chipshop – which hasn't got one. But I am reliably informed by Aunty Rita (see book two), who kindly read and offered constructive criticism on the first draft of this book, of the origins of the name. Back in the olden days (i.e. the ones that happened before Rita and I were born) they used to pay the incumbent farmhands with wooden chips that they could exchange in the village post office cum nearest supermarket, for 'goods purchased'.

And then there is Sourton. 'Sour Town' is my interpretation, perhaps at one time a place without refrigeration where the milk always went off, or where maybe the residents walked around chewing a lemon with dour expressions on their faces. And what about Broadwood, which is long and thin and hasn't got one?

Nearest cousin? Broadwoodwidger. What, for goodness' sake, is a widger, and how can we use it to further mankind? Could we maybe eat some in times of famine, or destroy our drain-dwelling vermin with it? The OED has no definition I can find.

Moving tangentially on, how can you explain Germansweek, a small village in precisely the middle of nowhere where people seem to vanish more regularly than in the Bermuda Triangle. After the best part of a quarter of a century here, as far as I know there has never been a ritualistic annual beer festival during which great hordes of Bavarian revellers descend wearing Lederhosen and sporting ever filled beer tankards for seven days of appallingly tuneless singing and other similar debauchery. And even if they wanted to, I'm absolutely convinced they would never be able to find the place, like myself for the first seven years I lived in the area.

I even wondered about my patients' names sometimes. But prudence – and the desire to continue to eke out a paltry living at their and the government's expense – combined to imbue me with an unusual sense of caution when it came to mocking those who were so very sadly afflicted.

Ex-patients, however, are fair game. What, for example, made the parents of the bouncing new baby Cumber call him Colin Urquuat? And is it ever truly forgivable to make anyone travel through life burdened down by the Christian name of Kevin? And how did one elderly man come to have the name 'Gumboots' entered on his birth certificate?

Which brings me back by a circuitous route to the Widdecott brothers, who I am sure each had gumboots superglued to the bottom of their feet. I am equally convinced they would have bathed in them, if they had actually had a bath… and maybe the water to fill it.

They all perpetually wore a jacket that I suspect had once been dark grey, but was no longer, and sported trousers that held a passing acquaintance with a particular shade of green that you only ever encounter in a certain type of farmyard deposit.

On reflection, you never actually saw two of the brothers together at any one time, and there were a couple of local theories regarding this. Firstly, that they only had one set of clothing between them, and consequently three of them hid stark naked within the confines of the village while the fourth ventured out into the community.

'Your turn for the trousers today, Norman,' they might say to each other contentedly.

Or, more sinisterly, was there really only one Widdecott brother left, a master of disguise who collected four pensions each week and had four Meals on Wheels every Monday, Wednesday and Friday?

Who would ever know?

None of their notes in the surgery had a precise address, or a phone number, but just the name of the village. I naturally assumed that they must live reasonably close to each other, as families from their generation so often do in this part of the world. Norman and Edward were the twins and referred to each other as ''im over there', although where 'over there' was could never be precisely determined.

But, as I was later to learn, they did all live in the same house. How scary is that?

Harold, the youngest, was a mere lad of seventy-five, with an expression on his face like a startled rabbit in a thunderstorm. The twins were seventy-nine, and had apparently lived life in reverse. According to reliable sources – which would be Mrs Pilkington at number forty-three – they had apparently emerged from the womb over two hours apart looking more like aliens from entirely different galaxies than identical twins. But, as the years passed, they had grown to look more and more like each other, until they were currently indistinguishable.

'It's allus eating the same food,' Mrs Pilkington would say darkly, 'an' drinkin' the same drinks. Makes you into the same person, 'ere in t' country, mark my words, it does.'

She may of course have had a point, country lore being not always easily explained. But, personally... I think she was barking.

John, the eldest of the brothers, was a sinister, brooding-looking man with pink rheumy eyes and a slow drawling voice that I found both hypnotic and menacing.

'Be seein' you, doctor,' he would say enigmatically whenever he took his leave, and somehow it always seemed a threat, never a promise.

The brothers only ever made occasional visits to the surgery, which at least helped us keep our expenditure on air freshener down to a minimum.

Country people, and farmers in particular, are, I am convinced, congenitally lacking in a sense of smell, them being allegedly so inbred and all. This is, of course, a vital attribute in the battle to make one set of overalls last all year round without actually washing them.

For some reason I could never fathom, none of the Widdecotts would ever sit down in the consulting room. They would always stand menacingly just inside the door, as if to take a seat would have suggested that they were comfortable in my presence, or maybe that I was in theirs. But my then receptionist, Hazel, had a unique theory about this.

'It's their trousers,' she would intone solemnly. 'Have you ever really studied them?'

When men meet new acquaintances, I am reliably informed, they judge them on the firmness of their handshake and the length and texture of their nasal hair. Women, my wife Laura assures me, merely concentrate on the quality of people's shoes.

'I'm not really a trouser man,' I admitted. 'Even though I wear them on a mostly regular basis.'

'The reason they can never sit down,' she continued enigmatically, looking nervously over her shoulder, 'is because...'

When the reception phone rings, it can be a blessing... or a curse. Hazel launched herself at the receiver as if her whole future depended upon it.

'We'll talk later,' she mouthed, holding her hand over the mouthpiece. 'There are dark secrets at large here, Dr Sparrow. Circumstances you cannot even begin to contemplate.'

'Give, Hazel,' I instructed her after a light lunch formulated round a bottle of South American Merlot and some egg and cress sandwiches, and before removing the laxative drip from her arm. 'Or maybe find useful employment elsewhere.'

She glanced suspiciously around the waiting room and held up a finger to her lips.

'It's their trousers,' she whispered conspiratorially. 'They're so encrusted with unmentionable substances they are unable to bend at the knees.'

She even imagined (being, I suspect, stranger than all four brothers combined) that their trousers all stood in a corner at night, and that each brother was lowered Wallace and Gromit-like into his own pair come morning by some sort of Heath Robinson hoist and tackle device. Ridiculous though this obviously was, the trouble was that once Hazel postulated such a theory you were completely unable to get it out of your mind.

Visions of Widdecott brothers flinging themselves off the top of the stairs and coming to earth in the wrong trousers used to haunt me years before the advent of Wallace and Gromit. Consultations with them were bizarre enough as it was. Inevitably, they would amble in and regale me with always the same complaints – Norman, legs; Harold, ears; John, back; and Edward, ''booils' (bowels), feet and 'feeling funny all over'. After ten minutes enlightening me about their totally incomprehensible symptoms, they would then leave before I had a chance to do anything about them, with a 'Thanking you, doctor' left hanging in their wake as the door closed silently behind them.

They both repelled and fascinated me, a relic of some dark earthy past full of primeval forces and pagan rituals that we shall never see the like of again...

... unless you should inadvertently stray into Virginstowe after dusk on the first Tuesday in June in a leap year.

As the years passed, the Widdecott brothers passed too, by one means or another. From this world into the next.

First, Harold died of exposure. Not, as Dr Harper arcanely suggested, because he had dropped his trousers in front of his next-door neighbour's wife and been gunned down in what was left of his prime (which wasn't an awful lot, to be honest) by the potentially cuckolded husband. History records that he had in fact tripped and fallen into an unsuspecting – and totally innocent – subterranean ditch on the way back from the pub on a sub-zero New Year's Eve night, and not been discovered until the following year.

Next went Norman, quietly in his sleep. Although unfortunately he was not comfortably reposing in his bed at the time, but gently slumbering on the last number eight bus back from Exeter on a Saturday evening. Which would have been okay, had he not been inadvertently parked in the depot in his post-mortem state over the bank holiday weekend.

Which left just John and Edward, who survived without incident until circumstances overtook them one dark and bleakly surreal night in the future...

Our district nurse, Lexi, had called in to see Norman (legs) in the first few weeks of starting her new job. Lexi, bless her, had a city upbringing, and her initiation into life in the country had come not so much as a culture shock as a complete revelation compared to her previous life's formative experiences. Every now and then, she would accept her life transformation to be a pleasant one.

'She keeps goats in the kitchen,' she came in expostulating one day, after visiting an elderly lady in one of our rural backwaters, 'and the chickens lay their eggs in her bedroom, for goodness' sake, on her pillow. What sort of practice is it that I have come to?'

'I know,' I reassured casually, 'it's Esmerelda's favourite spot. But if you time your visit for breakfast, you'll get the tastiest egg this side of Bristol.'

'Right,' said Lexi doubtfully.

'Just don't ask where the bacon comes from,' put in Ruth, my receptionist, thoughtfully.

Lexi's face drained of colour. 'I had... just a little this morning,' she said faintly. 'It smelled so good... Where does it come from, then?'

I generally believe in complete honesty amongst colleagues, no matter how painful it may be. But it was too early in her career.

'Tesco's,' I said kindly.


So, having seen Norman (legs), Lexi came into the surgery with an odd expression on her face.

'Mike,' she said, in a bemused fashion, 'I've just been to see Norman Widdecott.'

'Legs,' I nodded knowledgeably.

'I beg your pardon?' she said, looking more bemused than ever.

'Norman, legs,' I explained patiently. 'Harold, ears; John, back; Edward, booils and Norman, legs. They are considering changing their names by deed poll so they can be forever known by their respective complaints.'

'Edward's got a nephew,' added Ruth, on overhearing the conversation, 'called Eccles. Owns the muddiest pair of trousers in the West Country. We call him "Eccles cakes".'

At this point I think Lexi was beginning to question both her sanity and her wisdom in accepting her new post. She made a half-hearted attempt to bring the conversation back to something within reach of reality.

'Have you ever been in the house, Mike?'

'Whose?' I replied distractedly, 'Norman's?'

She looked at me with what I later came to recognise as her 'Are you really that stupid or just very good at pretending?' expression.

'You do know they all live in the same house,' she said, 'a small terrace just behind the old chapel?'

'Actually, I didn't,' I replied thoughtfully. 'I just assumed they each had their own place, close to each other.' Local theory number one about the brothers came immediately to mind. 'Tell me,' I continued, intrigued, 'were three of them stark naked while Norman was wearing the clothes?'

Lexi looked at me as if I had finally taken leave of my remaining senses.

'They don't talk to each other when John's around,' she said after a moment. 'It seems they're either not allowed to, or too frightened of him. It's as if he exerts some sort of evil influence over them.'

She shivered.

'It's really creepy. And they've each got their own cup, their own plate and knife and fork, their own chair, and they cook their own meals, if you can call it cooking, and wash up their own dishes – except they take it in turns to do John's for him. It's like being in a house with a bunch of robots, only not quite so clean or efficient.'

'And did they all have their gumboots on?' I asked curiously.

'As a matter of fact, they did,' she replied, 'even Norman, which made dressing his ulcers kind of interesting.'

'Makes you wonder if they sleep in them,' put in Ruth, who had obviously finished filing her nails but was yet to start on that week's *Hello!* magazine. 'Must catch all the litter and rain in the top, gumboots, if you wear them all the time – potato peelings, old bits of chewing gum…'

I think it was then that Lexi began to develop her nervous tic.

'Is everybody around here a bit odd?' she asked.

'It's not obligatory, Lexi,' I said soberly, 'although it is highly contagious. We were lucky with Ruth, however – she was already rampantly weird when she arrived here.'

'There are no mirrors in my house,' said Ruth mysteriously, before settling down comfortably to read a six-page spread on Elton John's fiftieth birthday party.

In time, of course, Lexi adjusted to life in this rural backwater of ours – and began sleeping in coffins, just like the rest of us.

She breezed in one day, several years later, and announced, 'Mike, would you go and look at some legs for me?'

'Certainly,' I agreed happily. 'Did you have any particular legs in mind, or should I just go and choose a few at random?'

'Gumboots,' she said solemnly.

'Gumboots Norman?'

'Gumboots Norman,' she nodded.

We had a medical student with us at the time, who now looked at us both in much the same fashion Lexi had looked at me in her early days, except the student's look seemed to be tinged with something seriously close to pity.

'I would explain,' I said, smiling sweetly, 'but sadly I don't think you're going to be here long enough to even begin to understand.'

Norman (legs) was suffering. Since the death of his brothers he had been unmercifully bullied by the overbearing John and was quite incapable of breaking away. I sometimes thought that death was his only way out, and that it might in many respects be a blessed relief for him.

It was with a heavy heart that I made my way to their small, dilapidated house and opened the door – we don't knock in the country, as half of the doors would just fall in anyway. I found them both in the gloomy sitting room.

'Afternoon, Norman, John,' I said guardedly.

'And a good afternoon to you, doctor,' responded Norman peaceably, while John just ignored me, as usual. I might as well not have been there, so I ignored him back. Childish, I know, but it sort of made me feel good. And anyway, my mind was diverted by the strange look on Norman's careworn features.

Gone was the startled rabbit in a thunderstorm look he had inherited following Harold's untimely demise. Gone too, the involuntary jerky glances across to the domineering John, as if constantly terrified of incurring his displeasure and later retribution for any imagined slight.

'Are you all right, Norman?' I asked gently.

'Oh, I'm all right, thanking you doctor,' he said almost dreamily, 'I'm very all right indeed.'

There was something odd about the way he said 'I'm' that made me look across at John, who still had not moved a muscle since my arrival. A chill began to settle around my heart, and the silence of that dark little room in the late afternoon sunshine seemed somehow deafening.

I walked across the few steps to where John sat and laid my hand on his shoulder. It was cold and unresponsive to my touch, so I checked his breathing, and his pulse, and his pupils, and then I slowly turned back to the last surviving member of the Widdecott brothers.

'He's dead,' I said, astonished. 'Norman, I'm sorry, but I have to tell you that your brother is dead.'

'Oh, I know that, doctor, thanking you,' said Norman, in the same eerily calm manner of before, 'some three or four hours since, if you must know.'

'What happened?' I asked, fascinated by this unexpected turn of events.

'Well now,' continued the new, revitalised Norman, 'I'm no doctor meself, doctor, but he were sittin' in his chair, like, after lunch, an' I was doin' the washin' up when he gave out this big gasp, clutched the left side o' his chest, like, made to get up 'n' then fell back in his chair jus' where you see him now. Reckon it was probably his heart, wouldn't you, doctor?'

I stood there open mouthed. 'Have you... have you...?' I was fumbling for the words. 'Have you told anyone about this, Norman? The undertaker, or anyone?'

He shook his head slowly from side to side. 'Not as such, no, doctor. Not told anyone as such.'

'Have you... have you done anything at all?' I asked.

I can still cast my mind back, all these years later, to the calm tranquillity of that shabby lounge, an early autumn fire crackling heartily in the grate. If I close my eyes, I can also still recall the slow smile spreading across his face, and hear his words floating across the ether towards me.

'Aye,' he said calmly, 'I've been sitting here, enjoying the moment. Thanking you, doctor. Thanking you very much indeed.'

Norman lived a few more years following John's unexpected demise, having moved soon afterwards into a luxurious private residential home which he enjoyed to the full.

It seemed that John had had money, unbeknownst to us all, and Norman was determined to spend as much of it as he possibly could before he died. He was making a pretty good job of it, too.

I went to see him in his last days, still calm, still peaceful, still smiling.

'I've not long to go, doctor,' he said quietly, 'and I'm ready. I'm off to see my brothers again. I'm looking forward to that.'

'What, all of them?' I said without thinking.

'Aye, all of them,' Norman nodded, smiling peaceably, and raising his eyes to the ceiling. 'Oh, I'm quite sure about that, the three of us up there, all enjoying ourselves in the peace and harmony, for ever and a day, and John, up there with us, watching how happy we be. That'll be his punishment, you see...'

I squeezed his gnarled old hand gently, and rose to leave.

'Be seeing you, Norman,' I said.

'Aye, be seeing you,' he nodded, 'oh, and before you go, would you pass me another of those cigars over there. Haven't quite smoked them all as yet, and I've not so long to go now.'

'My pleasure,' I said, and I whistled softly as I picked up a seriously expensive masterpiece of Cuban craftsmanship. 'Nice cigar, Norman.'

'Take one yourself,' he said, as I bent to give him a light. 'I'd like you to.'

And I did as I was bidden. I have it to this day, maturing quietly in a beautiful antique mahogany humidor bequeathed to me by my paternal grandfather now more half a century ago.

I turned and left his room for the last time, smiling broadly as I heard him gently say in my wake, 'Thanking you, Doctor Sparrow. Thanking you very much indeed.'

# 4

# Lost for Words – Part II

My capacity for being surprised somewhat diminished over the years. A sort of good-natured world weariness set in after a while, and births, deaths, the bizarre, the unreal, the indescribably sad, the downright stupid (like jars of English mustard in unusual places) – the more of these I encountered, the less difficulty I had in providing a calm, measured response.

Yet even I had my moments…

For the benefit of new readers, i.e. those of you as yet unacquainted with my previous two books, I arrived in the small village of Lifton on 1 August 1988. I was fresh – or, to be more accurate, stale – out of the RAF, raring to begin the life of a country GP. Little did I appreciate the realities of what it would turn out to be.

The senior partner, and only other GP in the practice, was Dr Margaret, a lady very similar in demeanour to the Queen, but she soon retired. I was on my own for the next couple of years, until I was finally joined by Dr Roger Harper.

In the weeks prior to Roger's arrival, my long-lost eager anticipation began to return, although for rather different reasons than that of two years earlier. Less work, more time off to spend with my family and – to put it bluntly – the prospect of unloading all the heart-sink patients I had inherited at Margaret's retirement or subsequently acquired on my own.

A heart-sink patient, I should explain, is precisely what it sounds like – a patient whose very presence in the waiting room, or even as a pencilled-in appointment three months hence, causes your heart to sink the moment you become aware of it. Heart-sinks come, I am reliably informed, in four categories:

(1) The dependent clinger: 'Oh, Dr Sparrow, you are just the best doctor I have ever had. I am so lucky to have you…' (I have very few of these, you will undoubtedly be surprised to hear.) Dependent clingers come back at least once a week to be reassured by you regarding their latest non-existent symptoms and complete lack of anything approaching a disease.

(2) The entitled demander: 'I want a second opinion, I know my rights, I do, and I want to look at my notes, all of them, now… how do you know I haven't got a brain tumour without one of those new MRI scans?' 'I don't know if you have a brain tumour,' I would murmur viciously to myself, 'I'm just hoping…'

(3) The self-destructive patient in denial: these are people with real, significant diseases who refuse to accept their condition or comply with your advice, or treatment, or plan of action. They are the ones who stay stubbornly away, only to return when serious, life-threatening complications have set in too late for you to do anything about them.

(4) The manipulative self-medicator: these ones know more about their disease than you do because they have been scouring the internet and have already tried all sorts of inappropriate medications, many of which you have never even heard of.

There have traditionally only ever been four ways to deal with a heart-sink patient – you move, they move, you die or, best of all, they die. To which I now added my own fifth way – transfer them to your new and unsuspecting partner's list.

Inspired by the forthcoming happy event – I walked around whistling for several days until the receptionists solemnly presented me with a petition signed by virtually the entire practice begging me not to – I felt an abundance of goodwill towards my prospective saviour. So great was this abundance, in fact, that it even extended as far as my company cheque book. I asked Dr Harper if there was anything he either needed or would like in the equipment line to ease his passage into this new world of rural practice.

Needless to say, there was.

He had been hoping, it transpired, in his previous den of iniquity – sorry, general practice – to undertake some research into patient fitness levels in some form or another.

'Why,' I wondered out loud, 'when we have enough problems dealing with the sick ones. Who wants to bother with all the others?'

Dr Harper, apparently. He began to explain why…

'That's positively splendid,' I interrupted as he was about to draw his first breath some four and a half minutes later. 'You just tell me what you want, and I'll buy it. Anything, practice expense.'

He duly gave me his requirements, a tinge of disappointment in his voice at being stemmed before he had reached his full flow, and a couple of days later I bought it. I can no longer remember precisely what it was, save for the fact it was something to do with measuring grip strength and cost £463. I can recall the exact sum quite precisely.

I presented it to him, gift wrapped in its original box, on his inaugural day in the practice, feeling so full of the milk and honey of human kindness that I must have wanted to vomit. Then I forget all about it as Dr Harper began the lengthy process of immersing himself into the daily grind of rural drudgery. Year by year, the surgery grew, both in terms of patient numbers and all the subsidiary equipment essential to the disorganised chaos we loosely referred to as practice management.

Five years later, our once seemingly capacious building was beginning to bulge at the seams.

'Time for a clear-out,' I declared reluctantly one day, surveying the debris occupying the no-man's-land between the dispensary and the admin office. 'I suggest we hire a couple of skips for the day and start at one corner of the building – yours first, Roger, as it is by far the messiest – and work our way steadily towards the middle.'

It took a great deal more time – and several more skips – than I had ever anticipated, but eventually the onerous task was completed. Even the fire escape was no longer hidden from view by a pile of rotting carcasses, cardboard boxes and unopened letters from the health authority.

'By the way,' said Roger, as we waved ceremonially to the departing fleet of skip lorries disappearing round the corner of the building, 'I came across this box with some rather useless looking equipment in it under the stairs this morning. Something to do with exercise testing in patients – as if any of ours ever exercise anything more than their vocal cords or anal canals. You had obviously never used it, so I've given it to a friend of mine who's interested in all that sort of drivel. He's doing some research into patients' fitness levels – obviously got nothing better to do with his time. Hope you don't mind?' he added breezily. 'Wouldn't have wanted to waste it, now, would we?'

My mouth opened to speak, but what dark words may have ushered forth will never be known – because, as Dr Harper turned to walk away, he threw over his shoulder, as a parting shot:

'Unlike you, Mike, to waste so much money on an expensive white elephant – can't think why you ever wanted to buy it in the first place…'

You can divide people into an infinite variety of diametrically opposed groups: male/female, adult/child, with hair or without, West Ham supporters and people without a single discriminating bone in their body and, finally, those who adore Devon and Cornwall and those who do not. I am, need I explain here, a still-hairy adult male West Ham supporter who adores Devon and Cornwall.

A love of Devon and Cornwall is not easy to put into words. It could be the pace of life, or lack of it; the moors, brooding and mysterious; the magical private beaches that tourists are unaware of, let alone able to find; the interbreeding between local farming communities.

When I was a child my parents took my sister and me to the same holiday resort for some eleven or twelve consecutive years, sometimes bringing us back as well. We stayed at a place called Scratby, just, I think, to the north of Great Yarmouth, and we would spend two weeks virtually living on the beach amongst the glorious rolling dunes, fair weather or foul. It was the only time we would see the sea each year, whereas in Cornwall there are so many places all but on our doorstep.

As you drive westward along the A30 from Launceston, it is like heading into a foreign land – the deeper you get, the more alien it becomes. I have now lived here for the past twenty-seven years, but even to me, it seems, once you leave behind the last vestiges of the civilised world– you might know it better as Truro – it is as if you have truly entered an unexplored kingdom. Better still, as the peninsula narrows progressively before you, you can by careful observation to the north and south clearly establish where the better weather lies and choose your destination accordingly.

It is a journey of serendipity – follow the sun wherever it may lead, and rest at any moment of your choosing.

There are times when, no matter how hard you try to do what you believe to be right, and no matter how fine and noble your intentions, it all goes horribly wrong and you just have to live with the consequences.

Whatsoever they may be.

Between leaving the RAF and starting my new general practice career down in Devon I had a month or two to kill, not to mention a living to make. As luck had it, Ian, an old friend of mine who is now a GP in East Anglia, was about to travel on a three-month sabbatical to Australia and New Zealand. Catastrophically for him, his pre-arranged locum had contracted an atypical pneumonia. He rang me in desperation late one evening.

'Hi, Mike,' he said, 'I need a really big favour, and if my memory serves me correctly you owe me a few.'

'Your memory serves you wrongly,' I corrected him. 'Remember when…'

We were students in our last year at medical school, all of us struggling with preparations for our final exams.

As the ever-present Sword of Damocles hung lower each day over our heads, we all developed coping strategies in our disparate ways. Some people – inexplicably to my mind – chose to study harder and harder as each day passed, in the deluded apprehension that the more knowledge you acquired, the greater your chances of passing. Some of us chose instead to acquaint ourselves intimately with the previous ten years' papers, trusting in our abilities to successfully predict the forthcoming questions. A few lost and lonely souls, correctly anticipating their complete inability to cope with the academic rigours to come, repaired to our local pub at every available opportunity. You could regularly see us, I mean them, drowning their sorrows in the corner of the bar, umbrellas raised to deflect the torrent of expectation that was to rain down upon them.

'Swotty' Ian belonged to the first of these groups. Whereas I…

But even the strongest and most dedicated of us have our weaker moments.

Four or five days before the first of our written exam papers, Ian made his way unsteadily down to the hall of residence bar in the early hours of the morning, blinking like a dormouse emerging from a particularly long and arduous spell of hibernation.

By sheer chance, I happened to be one of those behind the counter at that moment... not really intending to serve late customers, if I am to be honest, but working instead on my choice of cocktails for the following day.

You have to try them, before they can buy them.

There is obviously a world of advertising out there just desperate for my slogans. I await the calls.

'I need a drink,' Ian confessed. 'And then I need another one really quickly. If I learn one single additional medical fact I shall no longer be able to remember the names of my immediate family.'

There were ninety-five people in our year, and I think most of them must have bought him a gin and tonic. He even managed to drink the first dozen or so...

By three in the morning he was rolling.

The bulk of the previously assembled late-night revellers and sorrow-drowners had by now faded away, but the hard core remained. The bar had run dry, the unattached student nurses had long since returned to their bulletproof, electronically protected and terrorist-resistant quarters, and we were none of us able to clamber over the barbed-wire fences between ourselves and the nearest female student hall of residence.

We staggered off round the corner, therefore, to the tried and tested haunt of the 'Swinging Spoons' – the late-night caravan cafe catering primarily for the local taxi drivers – for a toasted bacon sandwich and a bag of greasy chips.

But life on a night like this does not necessarily cease at this point. We have eaten, and we have drunk, but one thing remains critically missing. The late-night cup of coffee.

There were, if I may put it delicately, women who would, women who might, and women who most definitely would not provide early morning services, all of whom would be tucked up in their beds at this late hour in the medical school hall of residence.

And there was a separate group, unique in their standing. Women you could wake up at any hour of the day or night for just a cup of coffee and a chat, and who would happily provide either or both without complaint.

My best friend Fee, a woman of endless patience and far too nice for her own good, had a room at the far end of the building on the very top floor. I lived at the time in Ladbroke Grove, a forty-minute walk when sober, and at that time a no-go area for taxis – even if you could afford one.

The last Tube train ran at midnight. I didn't always make it.

I swear she kept a spare sheet, blanket and pillow in a cupboard, and unfurled them in preparation when she heard me ricocheting off the walls as I endeavoured to make my way up the stairs. I slept on her floor, and in the morning she made me a cup of coffee. Even her then boyfriend didn't mind, because she was Fee, and she was and still is – forty years later – my best friend.

The major hurdle to overcome on such nights, though, was the need to remember precisely where whose rooms were, and then being able to persuade them to open their door. But we had an indisputable advantage in our favour – most, if not all, were active members of the Christian Union, and it was against their better beliefs to turn us away.

Besides which, should they resort to such wholly uncharitable behaviour, I had a small but significant card up my sleeve – metaphorically speaking – a pass key to all the rooms in the hall of residence. This came courtesy of a small favour I had performed for the previous owner of the key, now departed into the great unknown world of hospital medicine, having finally qualified despite all his concerted efforts to the contrary. 'Oh, my God,' he had recoiled upon receiving the sad news, 'you mean now I actually have to go and *work* for a living?'

After several false starts one night – wrong corridors, incorrect stairs, completely wrong building for one sad soul – we finally arrived at our intended destination. Catherine's room. Catherine, one of the staunchest members of the CU and a devout believer in all things Christian, was unfailingly cheerful and warm-hearted. She was also one of those delightful people about whom it was impossible to find anyone who would say a bad word.

And, more importantly, she had a big kettle, and lots of cups.

'Hi, Catherine,' we chorused raucously from outside the door, rattling the handle vigorously for good measure. 'It's us – John, Mike, Chris and Gig.'

Gig was so named because of his irritating habit of saying, 'Let's get this gig on the road.'

'Any chance of a coffee?'

'Um, no, sorry boys,' came the unexpected response. 'I'm a bit tired tonight, if you don't mind. And anyway, do you know what time it is?'

'No idea at all,' we replied, looking at each other and giggling. 'But it's a bank holiday tomorrow and we... you can have a lie-in, if you like. Come on Catherine, it's not like you – don't be a spoilsport. We're thirsty.'

'No, boys,' she repeated, 'not this time. Please, just go away,' a hint of desperation creeping into her voice.

'Think she means it?' I asked the others, grinning and brandishing the key. We thought for a few moments and then let ourselves in.

'Hi there, Catherine, knew you didn't really mean it,' I said as we stumbled unceremoniously across her threshold. John, you get the coffee, Chris, the kettle, and Gig, you can... you can... what can you do?'

'Search her cupboards for some more alcohol?' he suggested.

'No, get the cups,' I suddenly remembered. 'And you, Catherine, what is it you want? Tea or...'

The words died in my throat, strangled at birth. Catherine was sitting up in bed with the duvet pulled up tightly to her neck, and there seemed to be rather more of her under the covers than I remembered. My eyes travelled uncomprehendingly down to the end of the bed, and the others fell equally silent as they followed my line of sight.

Catherine might possibly have grown an extra little something since we had last seen her, but I very much doubted whether that would have included an additional pair of feet. We gulped collectively, turned without another word and filed meekly out of the door, closing and locking it carefully behind us.

'Oh,' I said, suitably chastened. 'What on earth do we do now?'

There was silence for a moment and then 'Let's go and knock up Samantha,' suggested Gig, 'she's always good for a laugh...'

John, Chris, Gig and I met the next day at lunch in the nurses' canteen, but, gentlemen to the last, we never mentioned the subject again – although we did allow ourselves the odd chuckle or two. Catherine studiously avoided our company for the next week or so, and after that everything was forgotten. Except...

On the way out of the canteen I stopped for a second near the door, where a lone diner was just finishing his meal.

'Nice shoes, Ian,' I murmured, patting him gently on the shoulder. 'Now, whose floor is it that I've seen them lying on recently?'

'Okay, so maybe I do owe you a favour,' admitted Ian, 'and I'm just about to repay it. Here it is, gift-wrapped and covered in pretty pink bows. Rumour has it you're at a loose end for a couple of months.'

'How much,' I asked, 'and for how long?'

'Four weeks minimum – six or eight if you can stand it, standard locum rates, use of the surgery coffee machine Mondays, Wednesdays and Fridays. Please, Mike, I'm desperate. I'm not going to get anybody else at this short notice.'

'Oh, I see, you only rang me because you were desperate, did you?' I said, playing hard to get. 'Not because of my professional capabilities, reliability in a crisis, discretion under the most trying of circumstances...'

'You can have my car,' he said. 'It goes fast...'

'God, you must be desperate,' I observed.

'...and my house,' he continued. 'Bring your wife if you like – or, of course,' he added hastily, noting my stony silence, 'you might prefer to leave her at home. The house is right in the centre of the practice – a minute's walk to work through leafy sun-drenched suburbs, nice class of patient, no riff-raff, no wanted criminals, no on call out of hours... Couldn't be a nicer place for you to earn some of my money.'

'I drink mostly red wine, these days,' I mused, 'but I do like to start the evening with a decent white. Agreed?'

'Agreed,' he sighed in relief. 'Thanks, Mike, you've saved my life. Could you pop round this evening and I'll show you around everywhere.'

I could, and I did. Ian had a large semi-detached house on the edge of the village in which the bulk of his patients lived, a pleasant, light and airy surgery, and a well-stocked wine cellar.

'Easy life you have here,' I remarked approvingly. How did you manage to land this cushy little number?'

'My father was the senior partner,' he grinned. 'Retired at the same time as his partner six months after I arrived here, and left me in charge. I have another partner now, a year younger than me, and I have nice well-behaved patients, two children in the local private school, a mistress in the next village…'

'Do I get the use of the mistress as well?' I asked.

'…only if you give up the car,' he replied without missing a beat, 'and the after-dinner brandy.'

'Brandy and the car it is then,' I shrugged. 'So important to get one's priorities right.'


I settled in quickly and spent a quiet weekend relaxing much of the time in Ian's garden, catching up on some long overdue paperwork.

Monday morning surgery, despite my apprehensions, was a delight – pleasant surroundings, helpful and competent staff, and polite and mostly appreciative patients.

'Yes, I could cope with this,' I thought, 'if I absolutely had to. I wonder if life down in Devon will be the same.'

The rest of the day passed in equal tranquillity, and, as dusk fell, I was back at Ian's home relaxing with the newspaper and a glass of wine when the telephone rang.

'Dr Jameson?' asked the well-spoken but shaky voice of an elderly lady.

'No, I'm Dr Sparrow,' I explained, 'Dr Jameson's away for a while and I'm standing in for him at the moment. Can I help you?'

'Oh, I don't like to trouble you this late,' she continued. 'My name's Mrs Matthews, Jane Matthews, and… oh…,' I could hear her shuddering at the other end of the phone, 'it's my indigestion, it's bothering me so much tonight. I wouldn't normally ring, but my granddaughter – she looks after me – is a bit late home, and I was wondering what I should do.'

'Has it been like this before?' I asked.

'Ye…es,' she hesitated. 'Oh, I'm sorry doctor, I have to admit I've run out of my tablets, it's my fault. I should have ordered some more today, but I'm afraid to say I completely forgot. It's so silly of me. I'm sure that's the problem.'

'That's quite all right, Mrs Matthews,' I reassured her. 'Not to worry, I'll pop round and see you. Whereabouts do you live?'

Her house was only a few hundred yards down the road and I decided to walk, collecting my bag from the car on the way. I let myself in through the back door, as she had directed, and found her lying on a chintzy settee in an immaculately clean lounge. She was rubbing her stomach, in obvious discomfort.

'I'm so sorry to trouble you,' she reiterated as I entered. 'It's probably nothing, but…'

Mrs Matthews, I was to learn, lived with her twenty-year-old granddaughter, Kate, who was also her carer.

'She lost her parents – my daughter and her husband – in a car crash twelve years ago,' Mrs Matthews explained. 'There was nobody else to look after her, so she came to me. I took care of her then, and now she looks after me. She's such a lovely girl, doctor. She should be out there enjoying herself more, but she'll never leave me alone unless she has to.'

She glanced across at a clock on the mantelpiece.

'She's late home from work tonight,' she observed. 'She did ring earlier and say she might be, but it's not normally so dark – probably why I'm worrying so, got myself all worked up about nothing.'

I rechecked her symptoms, examined her carefully and did all those other things keen young doctors do in the early stages of their career, and then settled back in a chair opposite her.

'I think you've diagnosed yourself admirably,' I said with a smile, 'and I have some tablets in my bag that should hopefully settle you down for the night. Now, when do you think your granddaughter will be back?'

'Oh, anytime soon,' said Mrs Matthews, a little colour now returning to her cheeks. 'I shall be fine now, thank you. You must be off back home.'

In the event I sat and waited with her. I had nothing to return to Ian's for, and in truth I didn't like to leave her alone, even though I was happy enough that it was only indigestion that was troubling her. But you never knew...

At around ten o'clock Kate duly returned home – neat, compact, well dressed in a smart grey suit that I guessed had probably cost her a good month's salary, and full of immediate concern.

'Oh, Gran,' she said, rushing over to give her a hug. 'I'm sorry I'm so late. Are you all right? Is there anything I can do?'

'I'm fine,' she said, twinkling in my direction. 'Dr Sparrow here has looked after me splendidly, and now we must let him get back to his home.'

I left the two of them together with an assurance they could ring again if Mrs Matthews failed to settle and strolled leisurely back to Ian's, reflecting on the warmth of the relationship between them. Two generations apart, each with just the one relative in the world to care about. It renewed any faith I might have lost in my fellow humanity.

As I let myself into Ian's I could hear the telephone ringing and I crossed to the hall table to answer it. It was Kate, and as soon as I heard her voice my blood began to run cold in my veins.

'Dr Sparrow,' she said faintly, 'it's... it's Gran. Do you think you could come straight back?'

Jane Matthews was dead in the settee where I had left her.

A matter of minutes after I left the house she had suddenly half risen, clutched her chest, gasped out in pain and collapsed lifelessly back into her settee.

'Oh, my God, Kate,' I said quietly, acutely aware of how ineffective I must sound. 'I honestly thought...'

The rest of the evening passed in a blur – phone calls, the arrival of the coroner's officer and the duty undertaker – and all the time I felt helplessly inadequate. How Kate was feeling I couldn't even begin to imagine.

She stayed mostly quiet and composed, the occasional tear welling up in her eye, and buried herself in simple tasks – making cups of tea for everyone, answering the phone, breaking the news to neighbours who had seen all the commotion outside the house and came round to see if they could help.

Finally, everyone had gone, and Kate and I were alone in the house.

'You'll be needing to get back,' she said in a matter of fact way. 'I'm sure you must have other things to do, and to be honest I could do with a little time on my own to adjust and...'

'Kate,' I began, not really knowing what to say.

'No,' she said, holding back the tears, 'don't worry, please. My boyfriend will be here soon, I won't be on my own for the night. Perhaps we could come and see you tomorrow though, to talk things through?'

'Of course,' I said, 'of course you can,' and then I made my way slowly back to Ian's house for the second time that night, sitting till the early hours in the kitchen, a glass of wine untouched by my side.

Poor Jane, poor Kate. I had let them both down, and badly.

Unsurprisingly, I slept badly that night, and morning surgery the next day was something of an ordeal to say the least.

Lunchtime arrived, the last patient had been dealt with for the time being and still there was no sight or sound of Kate or her boyfriend. I rang the pathology lab at the local hospital, but they had not yet had time to do Jane's post-mortem. I sat for a while chewing my nails. I knew what they were going to find anyway.

Jane had had a heart attack, and despite my best endeavours I had misdiagnosed the symptoms. I went over and over the night before – what had I done wrong, what could I have done that might have made a difference, that maybe would have kept Jane still with us? Up until this point I had been feeling so wretched about the whole affair that the potential consequences had yet to make any impact, but now, to my eternal shame, it began to play on my mind. What if Kate were to complain to the Health Authority, as she had every right to, or the General Medical Council, or contact a solicitor?

One o'clock arrived, and still there was no sign of either of them. I could stand it no longer.

'I'm off visiting,' I announced to Susie, the receptionist. 'I've got the bleep in my pocket if you need me.'

Susie looked up curiously. 'But there aren't any visits in the book,' she said.

'I know,' I replied. 'But this one wouldn't be. I'll be back by three o'clock at the latest for afternoon surgery, earlier if you need me.' I left through the back door, my heart weighing heavily in my chest.

A few minutes later I pulled up outside Kate's door and sat in the car for a short while, taking some deep breaths. 'Right,' I thought to myself grimly, 'time to go and face the music, I suppose. It's not going to get any easier by putting it off.'

Kate opened the door herself, a brief moment of blankness on her face until recognition quickly dawned.

'Dr Sparrow,' she said. 'Come in, please. We were just thinking of coming to see you, we've been so busy this morning…'

I followed her through to the lounge where I had been such a short time before, feeling slightly unreal.

'This is Mark, my boyfriend,' introduced Kate, motioning to where a fresh-faced young man sat on a chair by the fireside. He stood up and shook my hand, which was a little unnecessary as it was already shaking quite a lot at this particular point.

'Do sit down, Dr Sparrow, please,' said Kate, and I perched uneasily on the edge of an armchair, wondering how I should begin. But I needn't have worried. Kate was there before me, and she started to speak.

'We've been up talking most of the night,' she said, taking a seat next to Mark and reaching out for his hand, 'and the one thing we want most is to be really sure about what happened. I shall miss Gran dreadfully, whatever happened to her, but it would just help to know, to understand, exactly what went on.'

I explained simply how I had been called and arrived to find Jane sitting in the seat I was in now. That we had discussed her symptoms, that I'd examined her and come to the conclusion that she had indigestion, and treated her accordingly.

'But I was obviously wrong,' I admitted. 'I genuinely thought…'

'Well, that's what I wanted to know, really,' said Kate, looking across briefly at Mark, who nodded reassuringly back. 'You see… I mean why… why if you thought she only had indigestion did you stay here for so long? She told me what time you had arrived. Why didn't you just go back to wherever you're staying once you had treated her?'

'Because…' I said, taken slightly aback, 'Because… well, she was still uncomfortable and obviously worried about you being a bit late home, and I just… I didn't like to leave her, not on her own. So I thought I'd keep her company until you got back, and she was such a nice lady. I enjoyed talking to her. She was so proud of you.'

'And what would you have done,' said Kate, leaning forward earnestly, intent on my reply, 'if you had thought it was heart pain, and not indigestion?'

'Given her a pain-killing injection and rung immediately for an ambulance,' I said. 'The hospital's not so very far away, is it, and the ambulance would probably have been here within a quarter of an hour or so. And then…'

'I thought so,' Kate nodded, closing her eyes for a moment. 'And then Gran would probably have died in the back of the ambulance on some lonely road in the dark, or frightened and alone on a casualty trolley in a corridor somewhere down in the hospital… she always hated hospitals…'

'We wanted to thank you,' put in Mark, as Kate fell silent, 'for what you did.'

'But…' I began.

'Staying with Gran to make sure she was all right until I got home,' continued Kate. 'I know nothing about you, Dr Sparrow, and very little about medicine, but I'm sure you did what you thought was the right thing at the time. And even if you turned out to be wrong about what the real problem was, you did what we both would have wanted you to. Gran didn't die cold, and alone, and frightened in some strange, unfamiliar place. She died at home, in front of her own fire, with me holding her hand. It's all we could have ever asked for.'

I could feel a lump rising in my throat.

'So, both of us, Mark and I,' finished Kate simply, 'and Gran too, if she was still here, would like to thank you for what you did. Being wrong maybe in your eyes was being very right in ours.'

I looked at the two young people in front of me, holding each other's hand for comfort as they struggled with the awful shock life had just dealt them, and yet thanking me for making an incorrect diagnosis. I opened my mouth to reply.

But I was lost, lost for words, and nothing would come out.

Somewhere out there is the real Kate, who may one day read this and know this is she. I hope, Kate, that you have found the happiness you deserve. You taught me a lesson that day I have never forgotten.

Practising medicine is not always about being right, or about being defensive when you are wrong. It's about doing the best you can, as often as you can, and taking the time to look after your patients as human beings in their own right.

# 5
# Everyone Needs a Jason

I suppose, in a cerebral Inspector Morse kind of way, that general practice exhibits the art of detection in its own unique calling.

Our patients bring us their collection of signs and symptoms – we refer to them as 'big clues' in those meetings the public are excluded from – and pick our way through the multitude of red herrings and false trails before announcing solemnly, 'It must be a virus.' Some patients even lie to us so well, and so blatantly, that you can't help having a sneaking admiration for them.

In my early days at Lifton our patients were more of an Arthur, Ethel and Cynthia outfit – and that was just some of the men. Old country names and values were dominant. Indeed, rumour had it that one long-established farming family who unwisely called their eldest daughter Kylie had their crops burned, their living room carpet hoovered, and their kitchen floor washed and sterilised by angry, unforgiving neighbours.

I can only assume, then, that Jason had slipped in unnoticed on our list one day when our practice manager's attention was otherwise diverted.

A ferrety, whippety-looking sort of chap with short, dark hair and an adolescent beard on a thin, chiselled face, he had bodybuilder's muscles beneath his ubiquitous Liverpool football shirt. To my eternal surprise he somehow managed to hold down a job, making quite a reasonable living, but he was forever trying to play the system.

A typical consultation with Jason might have gone something like this:

He swaggers in, generally without having troubled the reception staff for an appointment, sprawls into the nearest chair and sticks his chin out truculently.

'I want a certificate,' he says.

'Certainly, Jason,' I agree. 'A certificate to establish that life in you is not yet totally extinct, a certificate of freedom from parasitic infection, a certificate to…'

He gives me a withering look.

'A sick note,' he says scornfully, my childish sarcasm having apparently failed to amuse him.

'Right, Jason,' I say briskly. 'And what is it that is actually wrong with you – this time?'

I am maliciously pleased to see him squirm uncomfortably in his seat.

'Well, nothing at the moment, but with all them sick people and their germs in the waiting room, and you running over half an hour late…' (It was a classic Jason trick, this, trying to turn defence into attack with a few carefully chosen words, without worrying too much about how accurate they might be.) 'Who knows what 'orrible infliction I could be coming down with in the next few days. No, I want one for a week last Thursday.'

'Hmm,' I consider thoughtfully. 'A week last Thursday. And was there anything actually wrong with you then?'

'Yes,' he says triumphantly. 'I had guts ache, couldn't stop going to the loo, neither. And sick, I was sick, in an' out of the bleeding bathroom all day, all night an' all the next day too,' he finishes defiantly, as if daring me to contradict him.

'And you didn't go to work?' I ask.

'Course not. I was too ill, weren't I?'

I look back through his notes.

'But you didn't come in to see me, Jason, did you?' I say reproachfully. 'Or Dr Harper – you didn't even ring us, or request a visit. Were you just being thoughtful, as ever, knowing it was our busiest time of the year?'

'Well, 'ow could I?' he fires back truculently. 'Cos I was on 'oliday in Majorca at the time. Couldn't just get on a plane and fly back, given my state of ill 'ealth, now could I?'

The clarity of his logic is inescapable.

'But,' I begin, trying to find my way out of the quagmire, 'you didn't go to work because you were on holiday, not because you were ill.'

'That's exactly it,' he says animatedly, 'it's just what I mean. Cos I can't have my holiday proper if I'm ill, can I, and I can claim those days back on the sick. So you can give me a note, can't you? A week will do,' he adds generously, 'cos you can't go back to Majorca for just the two days, can you?'

I sit back, biting my lip and regarding him long and hard.

'It's a tempting offer, Jason,' I admit, 'but the answer is no. You cannot have a certificate from a week last Thursday for pretending to be too ill to enjoy a couple of days on your holiday.'

He shrugs nonchalantly.

'Okay,' he accepts. 'Worth a try though, wasn't it? I'll just have one for this week then.'

'But you're not actually ill at the moment, Jason,' I pounce, 'are you? You've admitted so yourself.'

He coughs dramatically.

'But I think I'm going to be, Dr Sparrow. All them bugs and viruses in the waiting room you've let me be exposed to – I think I've got a cold coming on.'

Jason was a keen footballer, and a good one, too, if inclined to be a little over-exuberant in the tackle. I heard he once went an entire fortnight without a single booking or sending off, which was either a vicious rumour or coincided with a long spell of bad weather making the local pitches unplayable.

He was undoubtedly very fit, so I was somewhat surprised on returning from a fortnight's holiday to find a clutch of forms from the DHSS – Department of Health and Social Security to you, Department of Haggling Silly Servants to me – waiting ominously for me in my overburdened in tray.

He had applied for Attendance Allowance, Disability Living Allowance, Mobility Allowance and a Blue Badge for parking. I half expected to find a claim for Maternity Benefit in there, or a Cold Weather Payment (despite the fact it was late spring), but I suppose there are limits even for the Jasons of the world.

There is a popular belief that all these allowances are allocated according to a degree of need, based on the severity of illness or disability the patient might be suffering from at the time. This is, of course, abject rubbish. It depends purely on their ability to lie shamefacedly and without compunction when it comes to filling out the forms.

The worthies at the DHSS must have had their own scale of assessment, based on a points system with credits given for imagination, intent to deceive, sheer affrontery and, I can only assume, the direction of the wind at the time. Jason's offering was a masterpiece of misinformation, and by the time I had finished reading it I was filled with so much compassion I wanted to rush round to his house and give him the money myself.

'Do you need help getting in and out of the bath?' asks one question.

'Yes, or I worry I might get stuck in there and drown,' Jason had written. You had to admire the boy.

'How far can you walk without pain?' goes another.

'Most of the way to the kitchen,' he had inscribed. 'But not every day.'

'Do you need a walking aid?' inquires a third.

'Not now, thank you,' Jason had responded with startling honesty. 'Because I've already got one.'

And there was more. So much more, so movingly written, that I actually began to doubt my initial cynicism. Had something unaccountable happened to Jason during my absence? Could I have totally misjudged him?

Was the world really flat after all, and were countless sovereign nations falling off the edge into oblivion day after day?

Coincidences, I repeat, happen, and happen again. That's why they are called coincidences.

It was Saturday morning surgery, and Jason's wife was on the phone. Their young son was ill and she was asking for a visit. Normally I would have mouthed the usual platitudes – liquid paracetamol, lots of fluids and tepid bathing, get the mother-in-law round and ring back if you are concerned when the out-of-hours service will have taken over and I am safely out of here for the weekend – but today I realised was an opportunity.

At the back of the surgery I had an escape hatch – sounds grand, but it is actually just a rear door from my consulting room opening up on to a small flight of concrete steps down to the car park. Here I sit in moments of quiet contemplation with an illicit cigarette, the *Telegraph* crossword and the sounds of the village echoing up from the valley.

I can hear the early kick-off at the Rec, hounds baying in the distance as they move in for the kill, fledglings chattering excitedly as they edge closer to their inaugural flight, hearts in mouth. One of my favourite moments of the week. I inhale slowly and relax.

Time to make a move.

Jason's two-year-old was teething, and had nappy rash. Not maybe the most urgent house call I have ever made, but as my last-but-one destination of the day before returning home I shrugged metaphorically and resolved to make the most of it.

'And where is Jason?' I asked casually as I prepared to leave, another life saved, another abandoned soul redeemed.

'Oh, making the most of the day out in the village somewhere,' said Alison, his wife. 'It's Saturday. We try to make the most of our blessings. Can you see yourself out?'

I could, pausing briefly by the front door to collect a memento. Not normally known for absconding with my patients' personal possessions, and more likely to leave something of my own behind (stethoscope, car keys, more than once one of my children), on this occasion I felt it somehow appropriate.

Work was finished for the day. Play was just about to start.

Jason's sister, a character in her own right, had an equally unconventional approach to consultations. She rang me one summer afternoon, sounding breathless.

'Can you give me the morning after pill, Dr Sparrow?' she asked, giggling.

'Yes,' I replied wearily. 'When do think you'll be needing it?'

'In about ten minutes,' she sighed. 'I'll send my mum round to collect it while I'm resting…'

I drove down to the Rec, where a hotly contested football match was drawing to a close. There, in the thick of the fray, was a mud-bespattered Jason, hurling himself uninhibitedly into the action. If there was a disability on the field of play, and Jason had it, he was clearly intent upon passing it over to a member of the opposition.

The final whistle blew and the teams trailed off with mixed emotions. Jason was almost level with me before he realised my presence, stopping and staring at me with a calculating expression on his face.

'In this hand,' I said lightly, waving the left one, 'I have your disability forms. And in this one,' the right now coming into its own, 'I have the walking stick you are apparently unable to manage without. You left it in your hall, by the front door.'

You had to admire the man. He did not even flinch.

'Thanks, Doc,' he said, taking it from me. 'I'll be needing that now.'

He clutched it to him as if his life depended upon it and limped off towards the changing rooms. Even I could not fail to be impressed. The man had a certain something – no, not morals, if that was what you were thinking – but an unquestionable degree of panache.

There is a deep-lying quarry some ten miles outside the practice perimeter, where on sunny afternoons I still occasionally walk my dogs. Gertie, née Gertrude, a black Labrador/collie cross now approaching eleven and feeling her age, sleeps most of the day, but gambols around like a spring lamb when the back door opens and the boot of "Freddie" the Freelander beckons. Dotty (Dorothy) delights in the kennel name of 'Penadlake Puffin Billy (ACS)' – no, I don't know why either – and is a pure-bred black Labrador whose intellect is sadly deficient. She just lollops around looking for discarded food from indolent teenagers. Whoever it was that said one of the saddest facts of life is the number of horses and dogs we outlive had it spot on. Apart from the horses.

The quarry is down a well-hidden country lane and is surrounded by some ineffectual barbed wire. A dilapidated sign at its entrance wearily announces: 'Danger. Keep Out'. Which, as far as the local children were concerned, might as well have read: 'Free jelly and ice cream. Do come on in'.

There had, over the years, been the odd fatality here. A lost child playing innocently on some precipice above a terminally rusted Austin Cambridge, a lovelorn ruminant searching endlessly for her errant calf, and the prospective Conservative candidate who presciently said, 'It's so lovely here. Do you think I'm too close to the edge?'

Gertie sat panting at my feet. It was a long walk back, and I feared I had brought her too far. Dotty was gleefully worrying a half-buried jam doughnut, tail wagging in delight. I perched sadly atop a recently built cairn, rain-washed stones carefully positioned on an ancient burial site. I was between marriages and the children were beyond my reach – there's nothing like a bit of wallowing in your own misery.

I drew my late father's pipe from an inside pocket, rubbing the dark burgundy stem against my sleeve. I don't do maudlin, but for a brief moment it felt that everything I had ever had was gone. The bottom of the quarry was calling like a host of sirens with the sweetest song I had ever heard. It was time to make some decisions.

Suddenly, my peace was shattered. Far above my head I heard a crashing through the undergrowth as a car burst into sight, executing a beautiful mid-air arc in the slowest of motions before somersaulting down the hill, its bonnet catching on an outlying ledge as the rest of the car plummeted down to the floor of the valley. It lay prostrate in an eerie silence, dust rising in the afternoon haze.

I stood up, aghast. And as I watched, rooted to the spot in dreadful apprehension, I recognised the disintegrating vehicle with an unnerving jolt. It was Jason's, and I just knew that when I scrambled down the scree-ridden hillside to the spot where it lay, smoke pluming from the battered exhaust pipe and the petrol tank just waiting to explode, that I would find his spreadeagled body across the steering wheel, unconscious, his life draining away.

I careered down the hill, slipped on a rotting fern and collapsed into oblivion as my temple caught the outcrop of a huge limestone boulder perched on the edge of the precipice. Darkness descended upon me.

If you ever saw *Peak Practice* on ITV back in the nineties, you will have observed the following, without perhaps appreciating their full significance.

Firstly, all the doctors appear to really like each and every one of their patients, striving their utmost to do the best they can for them before repairing to the pub to bond meaningfully over a pint or two of cider. Secondly, only one of their charges ever gets seriously ill during any single episode. Thirdly, the partners have so little do on a daily basis they spend half their lives roaming the major hospital corridors explaining to their more qualified consultant colleagues how to do their job just that little bit better than before.

Oh, if only it were so.

I awoke with a start on Sharp Ward, an acute orthopaedic short-stay bed unit, wondering where I was, how I got there, and what my name might be. A young orthopaedic registrar hovered by the side of my bed, consulting his notebook. I swear he had yet to reach puberty, or even develop all his own teeth.

'I hear you were there,' he said in admiration, scratching his head. 'Amazing escape – falls 200 feet down a ravine, and barely a mark on him. Unbelievable.'

'But he's alive,' he went on, 'and no bones broken. It's a miracle, an absolute bloody miracle – just a bit of whiplash and a couple of abrasions on his back. Lucky to have only that, if you ask me.'

'Where is he?' I asked.

'Waiting outside to see you, when you're ready.'

'And how are you, Dr Sparrow?' I shot weakly after him as he sped down the ward and disappeared from view. 'Thanks so much for asking.'

I sank back on the pillow, my head swimming. There was something lurking at the back of my mind, a memory hiding just out of sight. I closed my eyes and drifted back to sleep.

I was dreaming. Sirens were sounding and helicopters circled ominously around me. An ambulance grew wings and flew off into the heavens, leaving me hanging from the back door, hospital gown flapping in the wind. My ex-wife drew up in a hot-air balloon and promised she would save me, before disappearing in a puff of smoke and cackling like the evil witch…

That's when it turned into a nightmare, and I woke up.

Jason was sitting quietly in a chair next to my bed, a curious look on his face and a stiff neck collar holding up his chin.

'I'll be needing them disability forms proper now, then, Dr Sparrow,' he informed me with a smug smile on his face. 'Lucky to be needing anything at all, I suppose.'

'What happened?' I said, trying to clear my head, 'I just remember… I just… If only I could think… There's something I can't grasp, something that will come to me in a moment.'

'They tell me they found you there,' Jason said slowly. 'One of your dogs standing guard by your side, howling until they got close enough to see you, and then baring her teeth and snarling at them as they tried to airlift you out.'

Gertie.

'They're both safe, in the police pound in Launceston,' he reassured me. 'You can pick them up as soon as you leave. Which is what I'm doing now. Me and the wife and kid, we're going to try and make a new start, up north with her family. Something like this happens, and, well – it kinda makes you think, doesn't it? Be seeing you, Dr Sparrow. Have a good life.'

I watched him walk away, uneasy. Jason's car, that valley, my slip down the side of the precipice and the last thing I saw before I blacked out. The last thing I could recall. It was suddenly so clear.

'Jason,' I called out, as he was about to disappear from sight. 'Jason – I think you need to come here and talk to me before you go. I think you need to do that right about now.'

He stopped and stood rigidly, his back still towards me, and then I could see his shoulders sag under the weight of his knowledge. He turned and walked back, until he was standing by my bedside, an odd look in his eye.

'I've just remembered,' I said simply.

Jason, Mrs Jason and son of Jason moved away shortly afterwards, as he had said. I was never to know where, and as the years passed by they slipped from my mind.

Everybody does, in the end. Apart from the few that don't.

'You'll never find me,' he said, 'because you'll never come looking. I've been your patient for nearly twenty years, and you delivered my son, and saved his life when another man would have walked away and sent for an ambulance when it would have been too late. And you'll never send anyone after us, because you are too good a man to do that. Like I said, Dr Sparrow, be seeing you. But in another life, maybe.'

And then he was gone, and I was left alone with my memories.

Kate, our perfect health visitor in the days when we still had one attached to the surgery, called in to visit while I was waiting to be discharged.

'I was in the area,' she said nonchalantly. 'Not a special trip, or anything, but…' She reached into her bag. 'Pork pie and smarties,' she announced. 'Still your favourites? And I can drop you off at home, if you like, I'm on my way back to Launceston in half an hour or so.'

She regarded me shrewdly.

'Headache, Dr Sparrow? Bit of a moral dilemma you're not quite sure what to do with? Anything a large gin and tonic would be unable to resolve for you?'

She glanced surreptitiously round the ward and then handed me a bottle of what appeared to be Pepsi.

'Disguised as a health-giving tonic,' she said sotto voce, 'but with the kick of a Dartmoor pony.'

I took a sip, and gasped. She was right. But then she always was, about everything.

'Hey,' she continued conversationally, 'have you been to the Waterfield's recently? I was there just this morning.'

I shook my head, and then wished that I hadn't.

'Not for a while,' I admitted.

'Well, I think you should do,' she said, grinning, 'while you can still get in through the front door. My God, the rubbish in that place. I bumped into Colette there, the one your previous health visitor warned me about before she took that sudden retirement. Colette asked me if I would like to see her paintings.'

'Paintings?' I said, surprised. 'I would never have thought of her as being much of a collector.'

'And you would have been right,' Kate said. 'Remember those painting by number sets we used to yearn for when we were children…?'

'Yes?'

'Collette's still got them all. "See," she said to me, "you paint all the number ones red, and the number threes blue…"'

'She doesn't get out much these days, does she?' I mused. 'How old are her children now?'

'Nine, six, and thirty-three – that would be Eddie, her husband,' she explained. 'But I didn't have to look at his paintings because he hasn't yet learned to recognise numbers.'

We sat and giggled together for a few moments, reviewing the latest entries in our 'Ugliest kid in the practice' competition, and our 'Patients most in need of a wash' category.

'You know, Mike,' she said, 'you do "complicated" better than any GP I have ever met, but sometimes the mundane is beyond you. What's on your mind?'

I was back in that quarry, Jason's car hurtling over the edge, and powerless to intervene. It was a truly chilling moment. Death about to happen before my eyes.

All my training, all my instincts, all my vocational urges compelling me to respond… and then I fell into oblivion.

But not before I saw Jason slip out from behind a rock, cross the floor of the quarry and drape himself inside the wreckage of his car. I swear I could see his disability forms in his hand.

Kate dropped me off at my front gate and waved goodbye.

'Paul and I are leaving at the weekend, Mike,' she said. 'We're taking a Winnebago across America for a couple of months before we move back to Surrey. Sorry, I didn't quite know how to tell you. You're sure you'll be okay?'

'I'll be okay,' I promised. 'Thanks for the lift.'

I stood and watched her drive down the road. Everything changes, but then everything stays the same.

Life in Lifton moves on inexorably. Serendipity rules. And you never know what is just around the corner, waiting for you.

Ten years later I was visiting an old GP friend on the outskirts of Birmingham, who was still practising despite a lifetime of drudgery and fighting the odds. I was on my way back from a 'Big Boys' medical convention, a meeting of the good, the great and the powerful in our profession. I had taken with me a dustpan and brush and I had offered to help clear up when it was all over.

I knew my place.

I hadn't seen Ken since we qualified so many years before, and I was feeling unaccountably emotional and nostalgic. Maybe I was just getting too old and soft for all this.

There, in the waiting room, sat Jason, walking stick in one hand, DHSS forms in the other. Next to him sat Mrs Jason, her leg in plaster, and Jason, encased from his neck down in voluminous crepe bandages.

I wandered into my friend's consulting room, between appointments.

'Hello, Ken,' I said in greeting. 'Long time no see. But... about your next patient...'

# 6
# Home Delivery

It was Jessie, my dog's fault, to be honest. In fact, I held her entirely to blame. Without her, I would never have been there in the first place...

Jessie (a forerunner to Gertie and Dotty) had a tendency to laziness and was not always that interested in physical activity. I, on the other hand, relished our evening walks together in the bitter cold and pouring rain of the midwinter – I'm being ironic here – after sweating over a hot couch in the surgery. It was a matter of pride, as we stood shivering in the darkness on the doorstep, not to be the first one to back out.

We would stand there, the pair of us, regarding the driving rain with distaste and draw a collective deep breath.

'Well,' I could imagine Jess saying with a sigh, 'he'll be so disappointed if I don't take him out tonight. But just down the road to the corner and straight back – no loitering. Agreed?'

'Agreed,' I would have replied firmly were I a registered dog interpreter. 'It's bloody freezing out there.'

You just never know how your day is going to pan out. What starts off as a routine, midweek, humdrum formality, can so quickly spiral out of control, no matter how careful you are. No matter how much you think you know what is going on.

One of the greatest skills of medicine is triaging. In other words, assessing which of your patients is most in need, and which could be deferred to a later time or date. It is especially difficult to do over the phone. We all do it each and every day, but we are human, and fallible, and are never always going to get it right. Not even me. And I like to think that I am good. In fact, more than good, mostly better than the rest. You know that thing about pride…

I have to tell you that it is true.


'I have Mrs Allsop on the phone,' said Mandy. 'She would like to talk to you. Her husband is apparently having severe chest pains. You want to speak to her or summon an ambulance, or should I put in a call to your lawyers?'

'You wouldn't know who they are,' I countered feebly.

'I've worked for you most of my adult life,' she responded. 'I know everything about you. Line two. Pick it up, Michael. You need to deal with this now, whether you think it is important or not.'

I know when I am beaten.

'Hallo, Mrs Allsop,' I said, trying to hide the weariness in my voice. We had been here several times before. 'What's happening?'

'Geoffrey has had a pain in his chest, dear.'

Geoffrey, I knew, was eighty-six years old with a heart complaint, a huge hiatus hernia and an addiction to clotted cream which he would lavish on anything ranging from strawberry cheesecake to an M&S Christmas pudding, even in mid July. I kind of thought they might all be linked. I am pretty sharp that way.

'So, how long has he had it?' I enquired. 'A couple of minutes, approaching an hour, more than a fortnight, or just over three years since he was first diagnosed with angina, give or take? And is it the same pain he had when you called in the other week, which turned out to be indigestion and was relieved by a little bit of belching and some over-the-counter antacids?' (I may not have said all this out loud.)

'Oooh,' she said. 'It's so hard to say. I'm not really sure.'

'It would really help if you could be a little more specific,' I encouraged, 'so I can judge how to respond.'

There was a long pause at the other end of the line, and then…

'Quite some time, dear,' she replied. 'Quite some time.'

'I need,' I explained as carefully as I could, 'a little more information. Where is the chest pain, exactly?'

Another long pause.

'In his chest, dear.'

'And what sort of pain is it?' I persevered, 'Sharp, persistent, intermittent, radiating to his left arm…?'

'I'll ask him,' she promised. 'Geoffrey,' she called out, 'what is your chest pain like, and how long have you had it?'

Wouldn't you just know it?

'I think he's had it quite some time,' she replied eventually. 'Probably since his birthday.'

'And when was his birthday?'

'The same as all of us,' she said, sounding confused. 'He has one every year.'

I sighed in resignation. She had done it again.

'I'll visit later this afternoon,' I suggested. 'Doesn't sound too urgent at the moment. Just ring back if anything changes before then.'

Jessie was pining.

Whiskey, a newly acquired long-haired Jack Russell with insecurity issues, was at the vet's for the day having her nails done. (Well, that's how I sold it to her. For 'nails' read 'anal glands' and 'tooth stuff'.) I had called home at lunchtime to find Jessie on her own, sitting forlornly by the front door, waiting for some company. She stood up and wagged her tail enthusiastically as I entered, a pleading look on her face.

'No,' I said resolutely. 'I'm working. I've got visits this afternoon, and anyway I said I wasn't taking you out in the car again. Not after last time.'

Her upper lip trembled.

'No,' I repeated. 'And it's no good looking at me like that – it was my best stethoscope.'

She lay down on the floor in front of me, resting her head on her paws and doing her best woebegone look. And doing it well.

'No,' I said again, but I was beginning to weaken. She sighed, and, if I didn't know better, I would have sworn there was a tear in her eye.

'Oh, all right,' I relented grudgingly. 'But this time you'll have to sit in the back.'

So she sat on my lap in the front, as usual. It was the only place in the car where she wouldn't get travel sick and I had sort of got used to it by now, as long as she didn't wriggle around too much, or too often. It was just when she got excited that I would find driving a little difficult, particularly when she sat bolt upright and I had to try and get some sort of view of the road by peering over or round the head bobbing away in front of me.

Visits duly completed, there was still an hour or so to kill until evening surgery. It was a beautiful day, still and cloudless, and Jessie caught my eye. I knew that look. It was her 'How about a quick walk, dad, while the sun is still shining?' beseechment. 'Sort of now, before it gets cold and dark and wet and you change your mind when all I want to do is go home and lie underneath my blankie. Please?'

We stopped the car on the moor and stepped out into the late afternoon sunshine, Jessie foraging ahead with excited little snuffles and whimpers. There was a small cottage just down the road and, as we drew alongside it, a wild-eyed man in his early thirties rushed out of the front door and stood in the road before us in some disarray, clutching his head in his hands.

'My wife,' he said frantically, 'she's having a baby.'

'Congratulations,' I said kindly. 'Just got the news, or...' eyeing him thoughtfully, '...celebrating the conception?'

'What,' he stared, momentarily perplexed. 'No, she's having the baby *now,*' he continued, hopping up and down on one foot rather like Dr Harper does when he's just about to throw something at one of the receptionists. 'What shall I do?'

'Call the midwife?' I suggested helpfully. 'Take her to the nearest hospital? Get a few friends round for drinks and cigars?'

He grabbed hold of my arm frantically. 'You... don't... understand,' he said through gritted teeth. 'She's having the baby now. Right now, not later, but now. In the next few minutes. I think I can see the head. The midwife is on her way, but there's no sign of her yet.'

'Ah,' I said, finally getting the point. 'That sort of having the baby. The "now it's about to come out" moment. Well done, both of you.'

A variety of alternatives were flitting through my mind. Turn and make a run for it... feign a sudden heart attack... pretend I was carrying something particularly contagious in my back pocket...

'I know you,' he said suddenly, recognition dawning. 'You're that new doctor down at Lifton surgery, aren't you? Thank goodness you were passing. Please, can you come in and help?'

So that was it. Stuck.

Every doctor's worst nightmare is a woman in labour, miles away from anywhere, and not a paramedic, fireman, midwife or taxi driver in sight when you need them. No Chinese takeaway for a short-term E-numbers fix. No Starbucks, no travelling van selling bacon and brie paninis with a large coke to go. No Tom Cruise abseiling from a helicopter above the cloud line with Angelina Jolie in tow, saving lives before the opening credits.

It was down to me.

'Oh, shit,' I breathed silently, and started walking into the house.

'She's upstairs,' he said, as if the 'Oh, my God, I think I'm dying' noises could have come from the scullery.

'Best take a look then,' I affirmed, with a great deal more confidence than I felt.

His wife, sweating profusely, was on all fours, bent over the end of the bed and naked from the waist down.

'I've brought the doctor, love,' said Gabriel, who had introduced himself on the way in.

'Gosh, that was quick,' she grimaced, before smiling weakly in my direction. 'Not the most dignified of greetings, I'm afraid. How come...'

'I was out walking my dog,' I explained. 'Um, I'm sorry, I've just been introduced to your perineum but I'm afraid I don't know your name.'

'Judy,' she said, wincing sharply as another contraction hit her. 'Delivered any babies at home recently?'

'Not so many this week,' I admitted, thinking privately 'or this month, or this year...'

In fact, the last time I had been in this position, a woman in labour and me all alone to deal with it had been at medical school all those years ago (see book one). The memory still lingers, I guess probably even more so for her than me. I shuddered involuntarily, and then took a grip on myself. Like it or not, I was all Judy had, and it was time to get on with it.

Gabriel was right – he could see the head, or at least the top of it.

'Judy,' I said gently, 'this is probably the last thing you want to be doing right now, but I need you up on the bed, I'm afraid, on your back.'

'Oh, God,' she groaned. 'Can't I just give birth like this. People do, don't they?'

'You can,' I said honestly, 'but I can't. I need you on your back, Judy, if I'm to help. I'm a GP, not a midwife, and I'm not used to people giving birth that way. And besides, I have disc trouble – I don't think my vertebral prolapse could take it.'

'On my back it is, then,' said Judy, giving me a sudden smile. 'Best give you all the help I can.'

'Gabriel,' I said, spotting him hovering around nervously, looking for a piece of furniture to fall over, 'could you give her a hand? I've just remembered something. I'll be back in a moment.'

I dashed back down the stairs, out of the door and ran to the boot of my car. By sheer good fortune I had in there a fully prepared delivery pack which I had borrowed from Tavistock Maternity Hospital a couple of weeks earlier for an intended home birth that later ended up in the maternity unit, and which I had thankfully forgotten so far to return. I grabbed it, together with my doctor's bag, and sprinted back to the cottage, not a moment too soon.

Judy was grunting loudly, and the head was about to emerge. I tore the delivery pack open and knelt beside her on the bed.

'Steady,' I said, 'steady, Judy. The baby's head is just there, almost ready to come out...'

She let out a big scream, and then a bigger one. I'm glad I'm a man.

'Told you,' I grinned. 'There you go, Gabriel, your baby's head, go on, take a look. Now, Judy, pant for your life and don't push for a moment. I need to check everything's okay.'

'I am panting,' she grimaced.

'So's Gabriel,' I observed, slipping a finger round the baby's head down to its neck, and then freezing for a moment. 'Oh, my God,' I breathed silently, my blood running cold. 'Oh, bloody hell...'

The cord was wrapped tightly three times round the baby's neck, and meconium – dirty fluid because the baby had opened its bowels while still in the womb, a sign of distress – was gushing out of her. Of all the things we none of us needed...

'Gabriel,' I said tersely, 'I need those clamps over there, and the scissors,' nodding towards where the instruments lay scattered on the floor following my less than entirely tidy unwrapping of the delivery pack. So much for my sterilisation technique. 'Quickly, Gabriel, please.'

'Is something wrong?' asked Judy faintly.

'No, everything is fine,' I lied. 'I just need to deal with the cord for a moment. Relax, if you can. It will be okay.'

'Just what I tell my clients,' said Judy, 'when I'm wondering what on earth to do next.'

'Clients?' I asked, trying to keep her mind off what I was doing down at the business end of proceedings. 'What is it you do for a living?'

'I'm a solicitor,' she said. 'Personal injuries and medical negligence my specialities. And I'm good at my job…' Time to insert the scissors. 'Oooh, that hurts.'

'Sorry,' I apologised, thinking, 'Now she tells me.' Not only had I never delivered a baby at home on my own – and to a solicitor, for goodness' sake, who might just have some vague idea of how to sue – I had never had to deal with a cord wrapped three times round the neck. Not even in hospital with all the appropriate back-up available – support staff, resuscitation equipment, more experienced doctors than me and personal counsellors for when it all went wrong.

People who knew what they were doing.

Somehow, and to this day still I am not quite sure how, I managed to clamp the cord in two places, squeeze the long-handled scissors between my fingers and divide it, gently unwinding it from the baby's neck and releasing it on to the bloodied bedclothes.

'Okay, Judy,' I said, as steadily as I could – which wasn't all that steadily – taking a deep breath and muttering a silent prayer, 'next contraction that comes along, let's push this baby out. I need it out on the first attempt. The first, you understand.'

She caught the tone in my voice but Gabriel, thank goodness, remained blissfully unaware of what was going on.

'It's okay,' she said, somehow managing a small smile, 'I don't really do medico-legal work…' I managed a weak smile back. '…but I have lots of friends who do.'

'I'm out of here,' I threatened emptily. 'Call an ambulance, 999, and tell them the passing, off-duty GP who was just walking his dog has given up due to a total lack of ability and competence. Tell them I gave it my best for a couple of minutes and then wimped out…'

She suddenly went quiet on me.

'Judy?'

No panic. Well, just a little bit. Not out of my depth at all.

'Judy, stay with me. Stay with me, please.'

She was exhausted. Another contraction came, and went, and the baby moved not at all. I was beginning to feel desperate.

'Judy,' I said, grasping her hand and looking her directly in the eyes, 'I need this baby out – you need it out, we all need it out. This time, whatever it takes...'

The next contraction seemed to take a lifetime to arrive, and then it was upon us, all too soon. With a final agonising scream Judy gave an almighty shove, collapsed back on the pillow and out came the baby, slowly, miraculously, into my hands.

But the baby was blue, and lifeless, and still, and my heart froze.

The seconds expanded into hours as I looked down at the baby girl lying motionless in front of me.

All that meconium, cord three times round its neck... it was no surprise she wasn't crying, or moving, or even breathing. And I had no drugs, no intubation equipment, no oxygen... no paediatrician, no special care baby unit... no anything. Nothing.

Nothing to help me at all.

It is a wonderful thing we have, the cerebral cortex – the brain, for the less medically educated – and how it reacts under the greatest of duress.

At this time of extreme crisis, a tragedy in the making, I thought not of all the lectures I had attended, or the medical books I had read, or the ward rounds I had sleepwalked through or even the deliveries I had been involved with during my obstetrics training.

I thought instead of James Herriot.

I glanced quickly round the room. Judy was semi-conscious on the bed, overcome by her exertions, and Gabriel was standing in a state of complete shock by my side, the sheer awfulness of what was happening yet to strike home to him.

'Gabriel,' I said urgently, conscious of the need to get him out of the room as soon as possible, 'I need hot water, immediately, and lots of it – there's a bowl in the kitchen, isn't there, I saw it on the way in – and towels, three or four of them. Maybe five. Preferably white. Quickly, please, there's not a moment to lose.'

Gabriel, bless him, shot off unquestioningly. Which was just as well – had he asked me what the hot water and towels were for I had not the least idea how to answer, apart from hastening his exit and giving me a moment to think.

It had struck me completely out of the blue. Like so many people I had read and thoroughly enjoyed the James Herriot 'It Shouldn't Happen to a Vet' series of books, and one of the stories had sprung unexpectedly into my mind. On a late afternoon visit the great man himself had delivered a litter of puppies, one of which failed to start breathing. Although I could no longer recall why he had done it – maybe on a whim, or perhaps employing some old-fashioned wisdom from a venerable predecessor – he had picked up the tiny body by its paws and swung it round and round his head like a hammer thrower, until it finally began to splutter into life.

Newborn babies are slippery things. Easy to drop, and not all that bouncy. I looked at the limp and unresponsive body of Judy's daughter, prayed as I have never prayed before, and started swinging, as if our lives depended on it. Which, when I look back after all these years, is exactly what the baby's life did.

When the community midwife arrived some twenty minutes later, I was sitting outside on the grass, smoking a cigarette and still shaking.

'They're all inside,' I said, motioning towards the door. 'Upstairs. I've left them together for a moment.'

'And you are?' she inquired, a little frostily for my liking.

'Exhausted,' I said simply. 'Emergency midwife, so to speak. I just happened to be passing.'

She pushed past me without a word and disappeared inside.

'God, I could do with a drink,' I thought.

The midwife returned in a more conciliatory mood.

'She's beautiful,' she said. 'Feeding away as blissfully as anything. Did everything go okay?' she added curiously, 'only you look…'

'Jessie,' I exclaimed with a start. 'Oh, my God, what on earth has happened to her? My dog,' I added hurriedly, as the midwife was looking at me as if I was stark staring mad. 'I was out walking her when we stumbled into this.'

I stood up and began calling frantically, heaving a sigh of relief as Jessie trotted happily round from the back of the house, licking her lips appreciatively.

'I see you managed to clear up and take everything downstairs,' said the midwife. 'I thought I might just go and take a look at the placenta.'

Jessie had now arrived by my side, and was wagging her tail vigorously, grinning from ear to ear. A trail of blood ran down her nose and dripped on to the path.

'I think you might be a little too late,' I said slowly.

Jessie and I got into the car, and I was just about to start the car when a thought struck me. Geoffrey and his chest pain. I had better visit on the way back to the surgery.

The sky was blue, the birds trilled away happily in the spring buds of the forests and the sun shone down on all humanity with a benign air. Jess and I had had a good day and I drove down the country lanes with a song in my heart.

Mrs Allsop was waiting for me at the door of her picture postcard cottage.

'It's so kind of you to come, Dr Sparrow, but you needn't have bothered. Geoffrey is fine now. I'm so sorry to have called you out.'

'Well,' I said, 'now that I'm here...'

Geoffrey was in bed, comfortably arraigned in soft white pillows with a pink printed duvet tucked under his arms, a book by his side. Mrs Allsop followed me up the stairs and stood by my side.

'So,' I said, regarding the peaceful but very dead figure of Geoffrey with some concern, 'how long... how long has Geoffrey been like this, Mrs Allsop?'

She looked me squarely in the face.

'Oh, I think, quite some time, dear,' she answered, seemingly unconcerned. 'Quite some time...'

Charlotte, who is Judy and Gabriel's daughter, must be in her early twenties by now, although I haven't seen her for several years. The family moved away from the area some time ago, together with Alex, a son born to them in far more peaceful circumstances a couple of years later.

A week after Charlotte's birth Judy came into the surgery, cradling Charlotte in her arms.

'I thought you might like to see the result of your handiwork,' she said. 'I never got a chance to thank you properly.'

Charlotte was perfect and nuzzled happily into my shoulder.

'It's strange,' continued Judy, looking at me curiously. 'I don't remember too much about the birth. I was so exhausted, it all seems like a dream, but I had this peculiar feeling that I saw Charlotte flying around the room like a bird in a cage, looking for the way out. It's odd, isn't it,' she added thoughtfully, staring intently at my face, 'the tricks your mind can play on you?'

'Yes, isn't it?' I agreed absently, changing the subject rapidly. 'Oh, look at her face, bless her. Doesn't she look just like her mother?'

# 7
# The 100 Club

Students came at staggered intervals around half a dozen times a year from Bristol Medical School, to spend time at the practice learning exactly why being a GP is a less than ideal career option. They stayed with either my partner or me for the duration. Mostly they were very keen, enthusiastic and knowledgeable, but the occasional one was in need of some gentle guidance and redirection, which is where I feel I am probably at my best. Poacher turned gamekeeper, in my later and wiser years.

At the Sparrow household we had been graced by the presence of Ruth, a pale and not very interesting hermit who emerged blinking into the daylight from her room only when mealtimes beckoned. She would eat as if a pack of hyenas were waiting in the wings to scavenge her remains, and scuttle away again into the shadows once the last mouthful was in the process of being swallowed, and before we could endeavour to engage her in what we grown-ups have always referred to as polite conversation. We also had Damian, who made a runner bean look short and fat and was, I suspect, in reality a used car salesman with an amphetamine habit, and Alex, who was so child friendly we used to send him out on the practice school runs.

There had also been Claire, who bounced around like a teenage Tigger on energy drinks; Sophie "The Gore Queen" who just loved the messier bits of the day; "Perfect Peter", who rather frowned down his nose at us as if our lifestyle was too louche for his liking, but later wrote a charming letter saying how Lifton had been the best attachment of his entire training; and Rahul, a second-generation almost geekily intelligent Indian from the north of England, who became my daughter's godfather.

'So, Rahul, tell me,' I asked towards the end of his stay. 'Do you consider yourself English or Indian?'

There was a pause before his reply, at which point I wondered if I had inadvertently offended him.

'I consider myself Mancunian,' he said dryly. 'Next question?'

Now we had Mark, tall, dark-haired, so clean-cut you could have sliced bread with him, and good-looking enough to have the fifteen-year-old babysitter looking all gooey-eyed and dreamy every time he came into the room.

It was lunchtime on his first day and Mark and I were out doing the usual rounds – branch surgery, home visits, rounding up the odd itinerant sheep and listening to *Test Match Special* on Radio Four. Possibly – no, probably – the best thing ever on the airwaves. England versus Australia, the Ashes, Headingly 2001… and England, beggaring all possible belief, were actually winning.

Mark was a keen cricketing fan.

'Ah, Headingly, 1981,' I reminisced. 'The glorious Botham years… I nearly got thrown out of medical school, thanks to him.'

'Really?' asked Mark, intrigued. 'How come?'

'I was down in Devon, due to drive back that evening for the Professor of Surgery's most important ward round of the term and on my very last warning. "Miss it and you will die," his secretary had warned me solemnly. "Disembowelled at dawn, very probably, and without the benefit of any sort of appeal… or an anaesthetic," she added darkly.'

'"I'll be there," I promised fervently, "come what may. No matter what unexpected twists of fate may intervene, no matter what obstacles may befall me, no matter how deep the river, how high the mountain, how long the…"'

'"Shut up, Mike," she sighed. "Just be there. For all our sakes. Please?"

'And I would have been, Mark, I honestly would, but just before tea, when England were in a pretty hopeless position and almost bound to lose, a young bowler called Graham Dilley came in to bat with Ian Botham and they both started smacking the ball all over the place. It was magical, enthralling. I sat watching, utterly spell-bound, and poured myself a drink – just the one, I promised myself, and then… well, just one more. And then Dilley scythed one through the covers, Botham straight-drove a ball to the boundary, nudged one over the slips and I was gone. Unfortunately, so was a considerable amount of the bottle of whisky I had with me.'

I sighed, all misty-eyed at the memories.

'If I get up early tomorrow, I thought, I can have a shower and a cooked breakfast and still be ready for the first ball of the day. I'd worry about what was going to happen when I finally got back to London. And they won, against all the odds – the stock market had closed for the first time in its history because of a test match, so many of the traders were watching. And now, almost twenty years later – my God, that's getting perilously close to a quarter of a century – it still feels that it was worth every hour, every minute, every second of all the trouble I got into. So, go home, Mark, and watch the cricket. It might be a day you will never in your lifetime witness again.'

'I couldn't,' he said simply. 'I'd feel guilty. I'm supposed to be here working.'

'So,' I reflected seriously, 'disobeying an order on your first day here, then…'

'You really mean it?' he said, his eyes brightening.

'Good God, no,' I said sardonically, 'not when we've got an enema to perform, followed by a pustule to die for.'

Mark went back and watched the cricket as any self-respecting student should, with a couple of beers and an unopened textbook lying next to him on the settee. I returned home and listened to his account of it long after the final wicket had been taken and victory was ours.

Mark thoroughly enjoyed his time with us, absorbing information like a newly bought sponge. I always enjoyed having students in the practice. You can learn so much from them.

'So what would you do about with Mr Fripp's cholesterol level?' I asked him.

'Give him some drugs to reduce it?' he suggested.

'Really?' I answered, transfixed. 'You can do that these days, can you?'

'You are joking,' Mark said, looking across at me as if he was the first ever tourist at Jurassic Park. 'You are joking, Mike. Aren't you?'

When I first came to Lifton, an inexperienced GP just out of training and not completely confident in what I was doing, the practice had two patients both over a hundred years old.

Edith, in the now-no-longer-existing residential home next door to the surgery, was a quiet, demure lady of 102, petite and uncomplaining. George, in a Social Services-run accommodation in Tavistock, was a rumbustious ex-mariner with an eye for the fairer sex and still-wandering hands whenever he got the opportunity. I sort of warmed to George, though, and he retained a twinkle in his eye to the very end.

The first patient Mark saw on his own was Mr Bagshot, a delightful chap of ninety-nine who always spurned the offer of a home visit and walked the mile and a half down to the surgery whenever he needed seeing, and the mile and a half back again, uphill all the way.

'And he'll be a hundred in two days' time,' Mark reminded me. 'He's amazing. Had a pacemaker fitted nearly twenty-five years ago and has had hardly a day's illness ever since. You just don't see people like this in Bristol.'

'He is pretty unique,' I agreed. 'His wife, Gwen, died about six months ago – and she was nearly ninety-five – and he looked after her all on his own for the last few weeks. I came up to see him the day before she died, and she was sleeping peacefully in the chair in the corner, a quiet, white-haired, genuinely old-fashioned lady. After almost seventy years of marriage he was still looking at her adoringly.'

'Oh, she may not look much to you these days, Dr Sparrow,' he told me, 'but she was the finest rabbit killer I ever did meet.'

'Really?' I said, taken aback, 'somehow she doesn't look…'

'Used to crawl up to the rabbit holes on her stomach,' he reminisced through rheumy eyes. 'A rabbit always leaves its burrow in the same direction, and she'd carefully inspect the ground around the hole for paw marks before laying her trap with infinite precision. Finest sight I ever saw was Gwen, cigarette in her mouth, gun over her shoulder and a brace of rabbits swinging from each of her hips as she made her way back across the fields to the house. Never went hungry in those days, though we were poor, poor as church mice.'

He sighed, lost in the memories of their past.

'I hate to see her like this, Dr Sparrow. Do you think it will be long?'

'It's funny,' I said to Mark, 'I've been doing this job now for over twenty years, but I still tend to look at people as if they've only existed from the time I arrived here. To me Mrs Bagshot was a meek, little old lady who liked her privacy, and yet she had all those years of rabbit slaughtering that I knew nothing about. It's humbling, somehow, and genuinely moving... God, I'm beginning to sound like I have some vague depth of human feeling.'

I sat back for a moment in silent contemplation.

'Pass the tissues, Mark,' I said falteringly. 'I think I can sense a moment coming on.'

He narrowed his eyes and fixed me in a stare across the desk, clearly trying to make up his mind. And then he grinned.

'Now I know you're joking,' he countered. 'So, do you have any more patients like them?'

'Not quite like the Bagshots,' I said, reflecting. 'But yes, I have had others. For the first seven years I was here I had at least two patients on the list at any one time who were over a hundred. There was George, 106 when he finally died in one of the local residential homes, and still chasing any woman, available or otherwise, who came within reach. Never caught any though, unless they had their back to him and were hard of hearing. Only man I knew that had his Zimmer fitted with wheels and a turbo-charged motor.'

'So what happened to him, then?' asked Mark. 'Died of old age, I suppose.'

'Good Lord, no,' I replied. 'Got his catheter bag caught in the motor of his frame as he was chasing a mere ninety-three-year-old along the corridor. He was catapulted down three flights of stairs and ended up dangling from the balcony on the second-floor landing with the catheter wrapped twice round his throat. "Death by misadventure" confirmed the coroner. Only person I ever heard of to have his cause of death written up as "Strangled by his own catheter".'

'You're making this up as you go along, aren't you?' said Mark dubiously. 'It's just like Freshers' Week at medical school, everything designed to make you ill at ease and then they reveal it's only a hoax after all. This is your Lifton version of an initiation ceremony, isn't it?'

'Oh, Mark,' I sighed. 'You're a good student – in fact a very fine one – but you still have so much to learn. Practising medicine in country life is not anything like the sanitised version you've been brought up on so far. You've been spoon-fed "real facts" from the day you first entered the door by people who have rarely if ever stepped out of a hospital environment. This is the real world down here, warts and all. And people don't always tell you the truth around these parts. They conceal things for a whole variety of reasons, some good, some bad, and often give you the version of events they think you want to hear.'

'You're making it sound like a minefield,' he observed, looking rather uncomfortable at the prospect.

'No, it's more unpredictable than that,' I said, smiling to defuse just a little the message I was attempting to put across. 'Part of my job as I see it is to make you question everything you encounter, and evaluate it carefully and clinically, never taking anything at face value. Because those are the skills you are going to need as you move up in a world you will find more hostile each and every year you venture further into it. It's a jungle out there, Mark. I'm just trying to teach you some survival skills.'

'You're going to tell me some more stories now, aren't you? Ones where I won't have a clue whether they're really true or not.'

'Now you're beginning to understand,' I nodded. 'So let's start with Edith Gilbert.'

'Make-believe or real?'

'You decide,' I continued, remembering back to my early days and my utter confusion at what I had inherited. 'She lived in the old house next door but one to the surgery, that large building you can see as you turn right out of the car park. It was a residential home then, and a good one, but ended up being shut down by "Health and Safety" officials due to its failure to comply with fire regulations. She hadn't been seen by a doctor for twenty-five years until the day I had to go round and certify her death.'

'Twenty-five years,' expostulated Mark, 'and you're telling me she hadn't been seen in all that time, when she lived next door? I don't believe it. What on earth did you do? Order a post-mortem, I suppose.'

'Well, no,' I shrugged, a gentle smile playing around my lips. 'I may have been a little green around the ears when I arrived here, but by this stage I was learning a thing or two. I checked through my predecessor Dr Margaret's records and photocopied the death certificate she had already issued in 1966. And then I went to take a look at the body.'

'How did she look?' asked Mark, perplexed. 'I don't understand.'

'Just the same as she had when she died all those years ago,' I explained kindly, 'before she was embalmed and put back in the same bedroom she had shared with her late husband. The home had been claiming her State Pension, Attendance Allowance, Disability Living Allowance and Meals on Wheels for more than a quarter of a century and sharing a percentage of it with Dr Margaret. And that's just the one patient – think how many others like that we could have out here.'

'That's insane,' he breathed, rubbing his eyes in disbelief. 'You've got to be kidding me.'

'Hey, welcome to the wild rural outback,' I said, 'with so few of us here as the latter-day sheriffs. And, be honest with me, what would you have done? Stand back and turn a blind eye to your conscience, or blow the whistle on one of the most respected local doctors of a previous generation?'

Mark sat back and pursed his lips.

'I can't believe you're being serious,' he said, shaking his head. 'I really can't. Things like this don't really happen, except in the pages of the Sunday tabloids. And yet, somehow... What did you do?'

I leaned forward and rested my head on my hands.

'Blackmailed them all,' I said deadpan. 'Twenty pounds per week, per patient... There's a lot of them out there, Mark, and the living out here is not quite as good as you might think it to be.'

'You're joking again,' he repeated. 'You *are* joking... aren't you?'

But of all the centenarians I have ever come across, the one that lingers longest in the mind is Jimmy.

Jimmy, when I first met him, was already 102 and had long white hair. Deaf, belligerent and Scottish – not normally an attractive mix – he was undoubtedly fascinating to listen to, and great company when on form. I was never quite sure what he had done with his life, but at a hundred years plus, I guess it must have been quite a lot.

'Gave up smoking when I was eighty-three,' he would bellow cheerfully to anyone within earshot, and quite a few who thought they were safely without. 'Nearly twenty years ago. Sixty a day, I used to smoke, and gave up overnight.'

It was what he attributed his long life to. That and copious amounts of single malt whisky.

'My God, how did you manage that?' I asked, impressed, the first fifteen times I heard it. 'I wish I had your willpower.'

'Do you buggery,' snorted Jimmy, raising a glass of whisky in salute. 'Had a stroke after a late night out with some friends and couldn't for the life of me remember what a cigarette was for. But my God,' he admitted from the very depths of his soul, 'what wouldn't I give for one or two of them now, before I die...?'

As Jimmy's 103rd birthday approached, his health began to deteriorate. He was still at this stage living just down the road from the surgery with his great-niece and her husband, who were managing well beyond the call of duty. One day, however, came the inevitable phone call.

'I'm sorry, Dr Sparrow,' said Elaine tearfully, 'we've tried and tried but we just can't cope anymore. I so wanted to keep him at home until he died.'

Memories of the Edith Gilbert story I had concocted for Mark flooded into my mind. 'Well, if you could just hang on for a couple more weeks,' I wanted to say, 'until we get the paperwork sorted. Attendance Allowance for you, the Meals on Wheels, the State Pension and the Motability car for me. It could work for us both. What do you reckon?'

But I didn't. Of course I didn't.

In the event I admitted Jimmy to Launceston Hospital the next day, three weeks before his birthday. Each morning we expected news of his death, each day he somehow clung on to life. He was mostly semi-conscious, occasionally rousing to take some fluids or a spoonful of liquidised food. Elaine and her husband, Tony, religiously took twelve-hour shifts to sit by his bed, holding his dry and withered hand, and mopping his brow whether it needed it or not.

'She'll be here,' I heard Elaine say early in the second week after he was admitted, repeating it over and over again. 'Just hang on, Jimmy, don't give up. She'll be here,' a silent tear running down her cheek. 'She'll be here. I know she will.'

'Who's "she", Elaine?' I asked later. 'Who is it that you're waiting for?'

Jimmy, it transpired, had another great-niece out in Australia, Eliza, the last of his living relatives save for Tony and Elaine.

'She's trying to get back here for his birthday,' Elaine explained. 'Or I suppose, if I'm being realistic, to get back here before he dies.'

Just hang on, Jimmy, we all prayed. Just hang on...

For the last two weeks we kept Jimmy alive on a drip, a prayer and a concoction of drugs that would have killed an elephant. Each day he somehow maintained a tenuous hold on life, neither dead nor really alive, until the weekend before his birthday the following Tuesday.

'I'm really sorry, Elaine,' I admitted, as I visited the hospital to see Jimmy for probably the last time, because I was, unusually, going away for the weekend. 'We've tried so hard, but he hasn't regained consciousness for the past ten days. I've no more drugs left to give, no other miracles to produce. If only we had had a little more time.'

The day of Jimmy's 103rd birthday duly arrived, and I awoke with a sense of foreboding. Eliza was due finally to arrive that day, sometime towards the end of the morning. So many miles, so sadly too late. I went to work with a heavy heart and yet have to confess that by lunchtime, after yet another busy surgery, all thoughts of Jimmy and his niece had passed from my mind.

At two o'clock the call came through from the hospital. It was Sandy, the sister in charge.

'It's Jimmy,' she said, a catch in her voice. 'He wants to know when you'll be up here for a drink.'

All but comatose for a month, Jimmy awoke for his 103rd birthday just twenty minutes before his great-niece Eliza walked through the door expecting to hear news of his death. The whole ward was celebrating, staff and patients alike.

I made it there towards the end of the afternoon, and Jimmy – half blind, almost completely deaf and hitherto beyond comprehension – greeted me like a long-lost brother.

'You'll no doubt be wanting a whisky with me, Dr Sparrow,' he insisted. 'Mike, Michael – ye'll forgive me for using your first name?'

'I'll forgive you anything, Jimmy,' I agreed, accepting a tumbler of amber liquid and saluting the man, the achievement.

'Here's looking to 104,' said Jimmy, winking mischievously.

Jimmy died the following morning, after probably the best party the ward had ever had, and I like to think he died happy. In fact, I know he did. Eliza, his great-niece, came down to see me at the surgery later that day.

'I don't know what it was that you did,' she said 'but I'd like to thank you for keeping him alive so long. But in truth, I don't think it was just you that did it.'

'I don't believe it was either,' I agreed. 'In fact, I'm not even sure what it was that I did, apart from chuck every bit of medicine I had available at him in the hope that something might just help. I guess there are some things we'll never be able to explain.'

'It's been so many years since I've seen him,' she went on, 'so many stories I've never heard, and I've blamed myself for that. Always said to myself I was too busy to find the time... I will never do that again, with anyone. Jimmy taught me that before he died. But yesterday, with whoever's blessing it was to give us both that time together, I think I finally caught up with all his stories. I would so much like to thank you, Dr Sparrow, but most of all I would like to thank the God I have never before believed in, until this day.'

I have no explanation for what happened, no simple answers to give. There was maybe a determination in Jimmy to survive until Eliza's arrival, come what may, and his apparently comatose state was just his way of conserving strength until the great day.

It may have been the sheer bloody-mindedness of the nurses who cared for him day after day, night after night, willing him to last those final few hours. Or it may of course have been the sheer skill, dedication and professional expertise of his GP – but somehow I rather doubt that. I don't think it was anything to do with me at all.

But who cares? I would rather just accept there are forces in life we will none of us fully understand, and be grateful for that.

Jimmy, on his 103rd birthday, had had the day of his lifetime, and which of us could ask for anything more?


Mark was exhausted. It had been a long week for him, though just a normal one for ourselves.

'How do you manage it, day after day?' he asked as he prepared to leave for the weekend. 'It seems to be more difficult than house jobs, and everyone always dreads those.'

I sat back and tried to rationalise. 'I think,' I said seriously, after several minutes of deep thought, 'there's probably only one explanation. We're just heroes and heroines, each and every one of us. See you on Monday.'

The next day, Saturday 1 March, the sun rose to greet Mr Cedric Bagshot's 100th birthday, but unfortunately Cedric did not rise with it, having died in his sleep sometime during the night before. Nobody could be sure precisely when. It was my weekend off and it was not until the Monday morning, when I returned to work, that I heard of his death.

'Poor old Mr Bagshot,' said Tess, my receptionist, 'so near and yet so far. Ninety-nine years and 365 days, and all because it's a leap year. It just doesn't seem fair, somehow.'

'Then we'll all pretend we got the date wrong,' I said. 'No one's going to argue with me, and the coroner will never know if we don't inform him. We'll make sure we get Cedric's telegram from the Queen and make sure it's buried or cremated with him.'

Tess gave me a long look, obviously trying to decide if I was delusional or unusually empathic.

'Somewhere deep inside you,' she said slowly, at last, 'are the last vestiges of a decent human being.'

And then she ruined it all.

'I promise not to tell anyone.'

'His body's down at the undertakers,' put in Sally, who had been upstairs making coffees. 'They rang first thing this morning before you both arrived – hadn't had a chance to tell you yet. He's for cremation – the funeral's this Friday – there's a bit of a rush on because his daughter is undergoing chemotherapy and they're not quite sure how much longer she has – and they've asked if you could do all the paperwork by the end of the day. At the latest. Leon, the head undertaker...' (sounds slightly surreal, doesn't it? Leon, the head undertaker; Peter, the hands; Gerard, the heart, liver and lungs...) '...is on holiday as from today but said he is happy for you to liaise with Nigel, his locum. I've promised him I won't let you forget, like the last time. You do remember the last time, don't you, Dr Sparrow?'

I did. The body in the boot of my car at an unknown airport (more of which later). I shuddered.

'I won't forget,' I swore faithfully, and I really meant it this time.

The next couple of days came and went, as they generally do, running assorted children from one venue to another, receiving unexpected though very welcome guests, spending an evening at the pub that went on longer than anticipated. Just your average couple of days in the maelstrom of life in rural general practice as we know it. So visiting the undertaker's somehow sort of slid unobtrusively from my mind, which I'm sure you can all understand.

Wednesday morning dawned. The late Mr Bagshot remained still unvisited until a desperate phone call from Nigel, the locum undertaker, jogged my memory.

'I know you have this habit of cutting things fine, Mike,' he said, 'because Leon warned me about you. But there are limits. Old Mr Bagshot is being cremated tomorrow and you haven't signed the forms or removed the pacemaker. As I'm only a stand-in, I'm not allowed to do it.'

'Not a problem,' I promised. 'I'll be there by lunchtime, and I'll have a student with me. He can take it out for you – be good learning experience for him.'

'Mark,' I said, turning towards him. 'This is your task for the morning – and make sure we don't forget it. I'm trusting in you now.'

'I'll do my best,' he affirmed. 'Not that I expect it will make the slightest bit of difference, from what I've seen of the way you work. It would probably take the Four Horsemen of the Apocalypse to tie you down to something specific.'

But we made the visit to view the body, and he was of course as dead as had been reported, lying in state in the chapel of rest. I filled out all the requisite forms, sent Mark down to do his bit with the body, apologised profusely to Nigel and grovelled my way out of the funeral parlour. But there was something nagging at the back of my mind, something I had forgotten to do. I brushed it aside. If it was important, it would come back to me later when I wasn't thinking about it. And if it wasn't... I could live with that. Because mostly I could live with anything.

As we were driving out of the car park my mobile phone rang – an event in itself, as I so rarely switched it on, always claiming as my excuse for being uncontactable the poor reception in our area. My staff swore I knew exactly where the coverage ceased in each and every part of the practice and that I only turned it on the moment I was across the line of no signal. But ring it did, and for once I was able to answer it.

John Deacon, the parish clerk, sounded like he was having a heart attack. Mark and I sped off as fast as we were able, hoping desperately that the paramedics would have arrived there before us.

I rarely attended funerals in those days. But for Cecil I felt it was important. We had history together, over twenty years of it. And as he had been the first patient Mark saw after arriving at the practice, he asked if he could come to. Morning surgery over, we made our way to the crematorium, some twenty miles away.

'That was so dignified,' said Mark thoughtfully, as we filed out into the sunlight after the service. 'Not that I'm much of a funeral goer, you understand, but it wasn't quite what I'd expected. The nicest thing, I think, was that it was so obvious the vicar had really known him. You felt like he was talking about a real person instead of just reading out bits of information somebody else had given him.'

'I know what you mean,' I agreed, 'I remember the vicar coming round to discuss what he was going to say at my ex-father-in-law's funeral. He was struggling to know what to say, because he had never actually met him. "Was he a patient man?" he asked my mother-in-law, obviously looking for one of those nice but bland things people say about the dead. "No," she replied slowly, staring him squarely in the eye, "I don't believe you could say he was patient."'

Mark grinned.

'But it does so much make a difference,' I continued. 'When my mother died, three or four months ago now, the vicar who took the service had known her for nearly twenty years. He'd "retired" and moved to one of the neighbouring villages, but he came back specially for the service. My father's funeral had been one of the first he had done after arriving in the parish back in 1981, and he had married my sister – to someone else, stupid,' I added, as Mark looked a bit confused – 'so he knew all the family, and talked about my mum with great affection. It makes all the difference.'

We walked down the path, nodding here and there to a few fellow mourners, and reached the car.

'Well, Mark,' I said, 'that's one man and one funeral you won't be forgetting in a hurry, isn't it?'

'Certainly is,' he agreed, a rueful smile on his face. 'I don't know how you do it sometimes, Mike, when you've known people for such a long time. Doesn't it ever get to you when patients die, or when you have to do things like that?'

'Yes, occasionally,' I admitted. 'I'm not completely inhuman, you know. But you learn how to deal with it the hard way on the wards, where all manner of sharp edges get rubbed off you, and I've been at it for nearly twenty-five years by now, don't forget. Fat lot of good I'd be to the rest of my patients if I spent all my time openly grieving about the demise of the last. But, yes, I suppose in Mr Bagshot's case I'm glad you were here to do it for me. Thanks – I owe you one. Any lingering problems?'

'No,' Mark shrugged. 'It was just a bit macabre, that's all. It wasn't so very difficult once I got down to it.'

We got in the car and prepared to drive off.

'What did you do with it, by the way?' I asked.

'Do with it?' Mark looked blankly. 'What do you mean?'

'The pacemaker,' I said, the first hint that there might be a problem just raising its head above the parapet. 'You did remove it, didn't you?'

'Yes, course I did,' he replied, and I relaxed visibly. 'Just as you said, it came out easily. A quick incision through the skin of his chest and out it popped, then a short tug on the wires – that is what you said, isn't it, how you told me to do it?'

'It is,' I agreed, 'so can I have it, Mark? I need to arrange its return to the cardiology department as soon as we get back to the surgery. They are valuable commodities and they reuse them whenever they can.'

'Well...' he hesitated. 'I... um... removed it as you said... and I don't think you told me that.'

'And?' I said faintly. The hint of a problem was now all the way over the parapet and running full tilt into the firing line.

'...and... and I... tucked it down in the coffin beside him,' Mark explained. 'Was that not quite what you had in mind?'

We both turned and looked back across at the crematorium, basking quietly in the early afternoon sunshine. It was an idyllic, peaceful country scene, enough to grace the lid of any chocolate box. Sheep bleating in the background, birds soaring overhead, trees bowing gracefully in the wind as if acknowledging the passing of a good man.

'Oh, shit!' I exploded. 'Oh, bloody hell and back. Out of the car, Mark, quick...'

'RUN,' I bellowed to the startled congregation as we burst into their midst, 'Run for your lives...'

And they all started running in front of us, not a single one of them knowing why, until behind us the crematorium burst into flames with a deafening explosion, and bits of debris began to rain down around our heads.

'Well, at least he should be well and truly cremated,' I said, looking at the dust on my hands. 'No need to go and scatter the ashes, either. Pacemakers, Mark. Pacemakers and crematoriums just do not mix…'

That last bit about running for our lives might not have happened, but it is in fact possible for an unremoved pacemaker to cause damage to the crematory chamber itself, which fortunately for me didn't happen on that occasion.

# 8
# Not on My Watch

I don't wear a watch. In fact, I haven't for over forty years.

They just don't work on me – possibly this has something to do with my disruptive magnetic aura, but more likely it's because 'You never wind it up', as my father used to say wearily. For my eighteenth birthday he bought me a far more expensive watch than I knew he could afford.

'It's automatic,' he explained patiently. 'That means you don't have to wind it up. It works off your kinetic motion.'

It broke the following week. I lost it a fortnight later.

I have, at various times, had three other watches in my possession. One, my pride and joy, was my late father's gold watch, which I once loaned to old George Brown, an elderly patient and long-time family friend, for a funeral he was attending while his own watch was being repaired.

George was a meticulous dresser.

'I can't go with a bare wrist,' he said wistfully. 'It's just not the done thing.'

Unfortunately, he was still wearing it when he attended his own funeral a couple of weeks later, while I was holidaying abroad. His family had always known he wanted to be buried with his gold watch on, and buried wearing a gold watch he was. It just happened to be my father's, instead of his.

My other two watches I still have. One of these arrived courtesy of a bequest from my maternal grandfather, who left £100 to each of his five grandchildren, which was quite a tidy sum nearly forty years ago.

'Ask him what kind he wants, then go and buy him a watch,' my grandfather had told my mother. 'If you can get it between my death and the funeral, there's a fair chance he might turn up on the right day and at the correct time. Make sure it's shockproof, waterproof and any sort of proof they do these days.'

Never left much to chance, my grandfather, although he was a touch absent-minded. He is the only man I ever knew who had his three-piece suits insured against catching fire if he should inadvertently put his still-lit pipe in his pocket, which he did on a regular basis.

And as for my other watch...

My first job in medicine was that of a junior surgeon.

After a difficult start, due primarily to a lack of competence and knowledge, I had graduated to the point where I now knew what a hernia was; that having haemorrhoids was generally less painful than having them cut out; and that every surgeon who removed what proved to be a normal appendix lied through their teeth about it. 'Nastiest case I've ever seen,' they would nod sagely. 'Only just got to it in time.'

Of general medicine, I knew not a thing.

In beds two and three on the male ward were, respectively, Mr Jordan and Mr Edwards. Each was still the proud possessor of one leg – Mr Jordan his right, and Mr Edwards his left – and each was in for assessment of their remaining lower limb and potential further amputation.

Both were understandably very apprehensive about such a prospect and the resulting implications. They waited in trepidation while the consultant and his registrar failed to come to a decision, not because – as far as I was concerned – it was clinically complicated, but because of their general indifference to the outcome.

It just did not seem to occur to them that the two patients were agonising over what they themselves regarded as a simple academic exercise. It was cruelty by insensitivity as far as I was concerned, and it made me angry. Finally, they reached a decision, and I was dispatched to relay the news.

Mr Jordan was to undergo further surgery, they said, and Mr Edwards was reprieved. I broke the news as gently as I could, reflecting on how they never told you about these sorts of moments at medical school, which was maybe just as well.

But worse was to follow. At the end of that day the registrar stopped me just as I was going off duty.

'Better prepare that leg for theatre tomorrow before you leave,' he said off-handedly.

It was late, I was tired and hungry, and suddenly very, very angry.

'It's not a leg,' I retorted sharply, 'it's Mr Jordan's leg, it's his right one and the only one he has. They are patients, you know – living, breathing, feeling people, not lumps of meat.'

There was a sudden silence, and I thought for a moment that even the registrar had a conscience buried somewhere beneath his supercilious exterior.

But then he said, 'No, it's the left leg we are taking off, definitely the left. And that's Mr Edwards, is it?'

I nodded, scarcely trusting myself to speak.

'Run along and break the news to them, then,' he added carelessly. 'All part of your learning experience.'

I can still remember approaching Mr Edwards' bed, and the look on my face must have spoken volumes. I don't quite recall how I told him, but I remember only too clearly how I felt. In the end, in his own quiet, dignified way, he was all but consoling me, like a grandfather his grandson after a particularly painful experience.

The operation next day went well, if 'well' is a word you can use in such circumstances, and Mr Edwards recovered without incident until the night before he was due to be discharged home. The phone call came at three o'clock in the morning.

Mr Edwards was in heart failure, and fading fast.

I rushed on to the ward, trying desperately to remember what little I had paid attention to during my training, and slid to a halt at the end of his bed. He looked ghastly.

The nurses, who had been working feverishly up until my arrival, stood back temporarily, awaiting my instructions.

'Well, Mike,' said the staff nurse quietly, 'what do you want us to do?'

I looked at Mr Edwards, his life draining rapidly away in front of us. This was the man who had comforted me when I gave him devastating news, who without a shred of self-pity and not a single complaint for the past three weeks had shared with me the ups and mostly downs of a junior doctor largely out of his depth. And here was I, not knowing how to cope.

'I don't know,' I said forlornly. 'I don't… I'll ring Zalides.'

Zalides was the senior medical house officer, an engaging Greek who was a couple of years older than me and a lifetime more experienced. Nobody knew whether Zalides was his first name, his last, or just a nickname.

He was just – well, Zalides, and his room was down the corridor, around the nearest corner. He was also off duty, in bed, and asleep. But Mr Edwards was dying, and I couldn't let him do that, whatever the personal cost to my pride.

Zalides was a godsend. I phoned him.

'Give him diamorphine, Stemetil, Lasix, aminophylline… do you want me to come?'

'You're off duty,' I said helplessly. 'Yes, please.'

The phone clicked dead, and in no time he was by my side – fully dressed, hair neatly brushed, as immaculately groomed as if he had been expecting my call for the past three-quarters of an hour and wanted to look his best when it came.

'I'll talk you through it, Mike,' he said, 'but you have to do it. That way, you'll be ready for the next time.' And he was so right.

We threw the medical textbook at Mr Edwards for the next twenty minutes, Zalides directing quietly from the sidelines and me taking centre stage. When we had done all there was to do, Zalides tapped me gently on the shoulder.

'Nice work, Mike,' he said easily, 'and now, if you don't mind, I'm off back to bed. As for you, don't stand there looking at him – it might make you feel better, but it just makes everyone nervous, as if you're waiting for something to go wrong. Go away for half an hour and then come back. Give me a ring if you need me. Otherwise,' he grinned, 'I'll see you in the morning. Just not too early, if possible.'

And with a casual wave of his hand he was off, sauntering back down the corridor as if he had taken a gentle stroll round the park before retiring to bed.

Thirty minutes later I was back. Mr Edwards was out of danger, drowsy but fine. The following morning, after a couple of hours' uneasy sleep, I stood by his bedside once more.

'They tell me you saved my life,' he said with a croak in his voice, 'though why you bothered with an old man like me I'll never know.'

'I get paid for it,' I said straight-faced. 'And anyway, it wasn't me. I had help.'

'Ah, the good Dr Zalides,' he nodded, struggling to sit up. 'Yes, he's already been in this morning – told me not to believe any false modesty from you, and that you barely needed him at all, really. He says he thinks you'll make quite a good doctor, one day.'

'He's Greek,' I shrugged. 'He lies well.'

A few days later Mr Edwards had fully recovered from his ordeal and was discharged home. It took me a week or so to catch up with Zalides, due to alternating shifts, and I thanked him for his help and compliments.

He studied me seriously.

'I meant it, Mike,' he said. 'You're not the first houseman to be standing alone in the middle of the night with a situation they didn't know how to deal with, and you certainly won't be the last. The difference was, instead of struggling blindly along on your own and getting it wrong, you swallowed your pride and asked for help from the best man available. Me.'

He winked self-deprecatingly.

'Not everybody does that, you know.'

Several months passed, and my last day in the post arrived. Zalides had left some time before as part of the usual amorphously shifting mass that was the lot of the junior hospital doctor in those days. Now it was my turn to move on.

I was walking down the main corridor, heading for my car and then who knew where, when I heard footsteps clattering up behind me and a breathless voice calling 'Dr Sparrow. Dr Sparrow'.

Working on the theory that it was probably me they wanted, and as there was nowhere immediately available to hide, I stopped and turned round. Before me stood a large, perspiring lady in her mid sixties that to my knowledge I had never before seen in my life.

'Oh, Dr Sparrow,' she wheezed. 'I'm so glad I caught up with you. I've been meaning to come in for ages, but you never get around to it, do you, and then Arthur had an appointment in outpatients today and when I asked at reception they said it was your last day and they thought you had left but then I saw you, by chance really, and I thought I was going to miss you so I ran as fast as I could, which isn't very fast these days because I'm not as young as I was and I try to diet, I do, but it's not as easy as they make it seem on those Weightwatchers' adverts, is it, and I hardly eat anything, only cream cakes on Sundays and special occasions, but you don't want to hear about that and anyway, here you are and this is for you and thank you, thank you so much from Arthur and me, if it wasn't for you he wouldn't be here now, you were *so* kind to him, and I have to go now because Arthur's tired and although he's okay and life is good to us he still needs his rest, and I hope you like it because we owe you so much and goodbye and thank you, thank you, thank you for everything you did for both of us.'

And then she was gone, while I was still trying to digest everything after the opening 'Oh, Dr Sparrow' and marvelling at her lung capacity. It was just that I had no idea who she was, or what was so wonderful that I had done for Arthur.

I glanced down at the package she had thrust into my hand during one of her 'thank you, thank you' passages, hoping that the decapitated head of the surgical registrar would be resting in there with 'All part of the learning experience' tattooed on his forehead.

Inside was a small card inscribed:

'With grateful thanks from Arthur Clement Edwards, watch and clockmaker by Royal Appointment. False modesty or no, this is just for you, not the good Dr Zalides. With thanks from us both for saving my life.'

I lifted out the card and stood, open-mouthed, staring at the watch enclosed. It was, and still is, a prince amongst watches, and for six months I felt unworthy of wearing it. I have it still, sitting in pride of place on the bookshelf in my study and I can look at it now and think that maybe I deserved it a little bit.

Because, after all – I did ring Zalides.


Charlie Bickle was a reclusive, rather mysterious chap embedded in the folklore of the village. He lived alone down a rarely frequented country lane just a couple of miles from the surgery.

Some hermits are notoriously rich misanthropes with short arms and deep pockets, leaving millions of pounds to deserving charities on their demise.

But Charlie – Charlie was broke, with no visible means of support and nothing to leave to anyone save for his body and the problem of its disposal. He had no family of his own, but there was a 'niece' called Mabel, who had adopted him as an honorary uncle after milking his cow out of compassion while Charlie was asleep in his pigsty.

She had visited him regularly with her kaleidoscopic family and was Charlie's main lifeline to the outside world.

'I tried to get him to accept Meals on Wheels,' she told me once, 'but he said that wheels were the work of the Devil, and if God had expected him to use them he would have attached one at each corner of a cow.'

Mabel's family made the Larkins look like the epitome of middle-class conventionality, but they were unfailingly good-humoured, honest quite a lot of the time, and always prepared to help others whenever they could – especially if they could help themselves at one and the same time.

When Charlie finally died the task of arranging his funeral fell by default to Mabel, who promptly decided to opt for a burial (cheaper) and then look around for other ways they could make savings.

'So they rang me,' said the Very Reverend Paul, struggling to contain the belly laugh that threatened to rupture the stitches of his recent gall-bladder operation, 'and asked me if it would be alright…'

His shoulders heaved, and there was a long pause while I went to look for some tissues.

'…would be alright to prepare the grave themselves?'

'And was it?' I asked eventually, after sponging him down for a spell.

'Couldn't think of any reason why not,' he gasped between bursts of oxygen, 'so I said "Fine, if that's what you would like" and thought no more of it, until today.'

I was intrigued. 'So how did they know where to dig?'

Paul fell off his chair and rolled around the floor for a while, while I summoned the emergency services.

'Oh, I shouldn't,' he said weakly, every now and then. 'I really shouldn't…'

When he had finally recovered – a large gin and tonic and a thorough dousing with the emergency fire extinguisher later – the story came out. They hadn't, of course, known where to begin their excavation, so had wisely asked the local grave digger.

'I'll leave a post out for you,' he had said. 'At the back, near the south corner. Just keep to the left of the tree.'

'It depends, of course,' said Paul drolly, pretty much all laughed out now, 'which side of the tree you're standing as to which side is the left.'

On a quiet summer's evening, the sun setting tranquilly in the valley and with no one around, they inserted their spades and began to dig. And a very nice hole they produced too – beautifully straight walls and just the right size for Charlie's home-made, biodegradable coffin.

There was just one problem. They had dug it in the wrong place.

As they reached the bottom of the pit, they also reached the junction of the grave next door, and, if Paul was to be believed – and I wasn't at all sure that he should be – the remains of another body tumbled through the walls and came to rest at their feet, left hand upturned, fingers arched and pointing to the heavens.

'And did they know who it was?' I asked curiously.

Paul nodded, using up the last of his few remaining faculties.

'Apparently so,' he said, 'but they're not saying for fear of upsetting the relatives. They just filled the hole back in and crept quietly away, covering it with a tarpaulin to try and reduce the smell. They came to me this morning to ask if they could try again, but in a different place.'

I looked at Paul long and hard.

'Is this a wind-up?' I asked.

'Oh, no,' he answered, starting to laugh again with just a hint of self-admonishment that he could find such gravity in the least bit amusing. 'At least, I don't think so.'


I was undecided on whether or not to believe Paul, to be honest. Even for rural Devon this was a little out of the ordinary, but then you just never knew…

My curiosity was soon relieved as the first patient of evening surgery was Mabel herself, with two of her sons. She was clutching a small brown paper bag.

'How are you, Mabel, boys?' I greeted them. 'Interesting times, I understand. What can I do for you?'

'You've heard, then, Dr Sparrow, have you?' she asked, biting her lower lip.

'I have indeed,' I replied.

'I'm all of a quiver,' she went on. 'Such a shock it was, too, us digging away all right and proper like, and then there he was, just rolled into our hole as sweet as you please. But I'm all right, now, me and the boys, we're fine, thank you. And it's more what we can do for you, really, than the other way round.'

'Go on, Mam, give it to him,' nudged Sam, the older boy.

'Yes, go on, Mam,' urged Jed, his younger brother.

Mabel passed across the brown paper bag ceremoniously, crossing herself quickly as she did so.

'Well, it's like this,' she said hesitantly. 'The body we... we... well, came across, if you know what I mean...'

I think I know what you mean, Mabel,' I said slowly, peering into the bag. Something solid and gold met my eye.

'It was old George Brown,' she said quietly, and then finished off in a hurry, 'and we was wondering if you might be liking your watch back?'

# 9

# The Rule of Evelyn

We stood outside the church, clapping our arms round our shoulders to keep warm.

'Six days of sunshine and now this,' murmured one of the mourners in my ear. 'Would you just take a look at that...' and he pointed down to the wooded valley where a bank of driving rain was heading towards us, blotting out the last glimpse of blue sky, the final vestiges of sunlight nestling in the grassy fields.

'Time to go inside,' I agreed, as the first big, fat drops of rain began to fall. And then the heavens opened, hailstones bouncing up the hill to the church through a dark vale of trees, forming a thin white veil across the overlong grass surrounding the graves in a matter of seconds.

'Welcome back to Coryton, Evelyn,' I thought wryly, looking back down the lane for a sight of the hearse before diving into the church for cover.

'Dr Sparrow?' asked a grey-haired man in a long dark coat I didn't recognise – the man that is, I'd seen the coat many times before – 'Are you giving the address?'

I nodded.

'We've saved a place for you,' he continued, gesturing towards the front.

'Looks like you saved three-quarters of the church,' I whispered. 'Where is everybody?'

A dozen or so people were standing huddled together behind the rows of pews, rubbing shoulders with the bell-ringers. While the sides of the church were filling up rapidly, the main tract in front of me was all but empty, as if a fox had parachuted down into a hen coop and scattered the occupants to the four corners of the field.

'Reserved for the family,' he whispered back. 'They've not arrived, as yet.'

'I knew she had a lot of relatives,' I said, 'but how many can one woman have, for goodness' sake?'

'Ninety-four at the last count!' came the answer, 'and the whole ruddy lot of them running at least twenty minutes late.'

I took my place just inside the entrance and stood there, looking round the small but dignified church, nodding with recognition at the odd face here and there. And this being Devon, there were a lot of odd faces to nod at. I felt as I had all week, like a bit-part actor having walked inadvertently on to the wrong set, and then the church doors swung open as the bearers came into sight just in front of me, sweating with exertion after their struggle up the path from the lane forty yards below. They shuffled their feet backwards and forwards, manoeuvring the coffin inch by inch into the narrow aisle at right angles to the entrance.

'They're not going to make it,' I heard a voice say in hushed tones behind me, followed by a subdued giggle and a 'Ssssh...' And then suddenly they were round, the coffin fully in, and the reality of it began to hit home.


For seven or eight years after the new surgery opened, we were blessed with Evelyn.

She lived in the flat above the treatment room which had been built for a caretaker cum message taker, and Evelyn was both of those, but so much more. Back in the Dark Ages, long before the advent of mobile phones and the out-of-hours co-operative cover, I had worked for two and a half years single-handedly, on call every day, every night and every weekend.

It was a nightmare. I was away from the surgery each night and most Saturdays and Sundays, but I was tied to my telephone, and my bleep. Jokingly I used to say there was a piece of string, fifteen miles long, nailed to my door and tied firmly round my waist, and when I reached the limit of its extension there I had to stop, within the confines of the practice boundaries.

The flat above the new surgery remained stubbornly empty while I wondered what I should do with it, not trusting anyone with the responsibility that would entail.

Until, that is, Evelyn happened upon the scene.

She was running a farm with her son out in Coryton, one of the more rural areas of the practice some eight or nine miles from the surgery. Her husband had died suddenly a few years earlier, sadly uninsured, and his sisters – who were joint partners – had taken their share of the money and run, leaving mother and son to struggle on unsupported, often beyond the point of exhaustion.

The inevitable finally happened. Farming was hitting one of its many terminal downslides, and after a bad year with the lambs they could struggle no more. The farm had to go, and with it their home, their security and the last of their money. All future prospects of independence disappeared at a stroke, or so it seemed.

It was just so easy.

Empty flat above the surgery… homeless Evelyn…

They were just made for each other.

We sat and watched as the bearers laid the coffin to rest, singing the first hymn in what felt like a trance.

A well-groomed man I vaguely recognised read a passage from the Bible in thoughtful, measured tones before retaking his seat. The church fell quiet for a moment, apart from a stifled cough, the shuffling of feet and an air of subdued expectancy, and then suddenly I realised it was me they were waiting for.

I moved out into the aisle, my heart pounding, and walked slowly forward, the distance to the lectern seeming to stretch further and further away with each step I took. My feet felt heavier and heavier, and all I could think of was the Monday morning, five days previously, when I turned up to work and pulled into the car park at the rear of the surgery like any other day for the past seven years.

There was only one car there, that of Jack Sharp. He dropped his young children off each day on his way to work, for Evelyn to look after. Because Evelyn – as Rowan, my late practice nurse, once described her – was the 'Rolls-Royce' of childminders.

The children were still strapped in their seats, poking each other and laughing as only little ones can do, with Jack nowhere to be seen. I suppose I must have noticed the fact without acknowledging its significance, as normally he would have taken them round to the front of the building and up the steps to the separate entrance to the flat. But none of this registered as I sat for a moment, listening to the end of a news item, until I became aware that Jack was standing outside my car door, pale-faced and shaking. I wound down my window.

'Mike,' he said, his upper lip trembling, 'there's no easy way to tell you this, but I'm afraid I've just found Evelyn upstairs in her bed in the flat. I think... I think she's dead.'

There are times in your life when you struggle to take in what you hear, or what you can see with your own eyes. I rushed up the stairs, and a matter of seconds later I was standing by Evelyn's bed, pulling the quilt gently across her body in case she should be cold, before standing and just looking, unable to believe what I could see.

'Oh, Evelyn,' I said, 'what on earth are we going to do now?'

Jack had stayed outside with his children, leaving me alone for a moment. Eventually I had to walk back down the stairs and make the phone calls I was dreading.

The rest of the morning passed in a blur of activity.

Each member of staff, all of whom were friends and colleagues of Evelyn, had to be met with the sad news as they arrived, and then quickly readjust to the daily tasks ahead. Patients flooded through the door as usual, unknowingly, their own agendas pre-eminent in their minds. For what could we tell them?

'Sorry, there's a body upstairs we all care very much about. We are deeply upset, and don't know how we are going to cope with the next few hours. Any minute now the undertakers will be here, taking her away, while we struggle to come to terms with our grief. Please bear with us if we find some of your complaints trivial and unworthy at this difficult time.' We might then have taken a deep breath, and sighed, dewy-eyed, 'We thank you for your understanding.'

We might have done that, but we didn't. We just buttoned down, straightened our shoulders and got on with the job in hand.

Next came the police, followed by the undertakers. There was a surreal moment as they were carrying her body down the back stairs. They were puffing and panting from the effort, for all the world as if one or the other of them might succumb to a coronary themselves, when Rowan burst into my consulting room: 'It's Lucy... she's out in the waiting room. She has an appointment with you in a couple of minutes.' Lucy was Evelyn's granddaughter.

In the shock of the situation no one had noticed. Rowan called her into her room and broke the news, and I came in a few moments later. What could you say? What could you possibly say...?

And then Evelyn's daughters turned up, and a little while later her son.

'I was all right till I got here,' said one of them, a catch in her voice, and I had to turn away for a second, unable to speak.

And all the while patients had come and gone, and somehow we all found a way through, but none of us can remember a single person we saw on that most awful of days.

The quicksand parted and I moved from slow motion to fast forward, standing all too soon behind the lectern, looking out at the sea of faces before me.

The moment had arrived. I shuffled the cards on which I had written a few notes, and took a deep breath.

Please let me get through this without breaking down, I prayed silently. Everyone waiting, everyone watching. I started at a stutter.

'There are two things that fill every GP with dread,' I began, hoping they wouldn't think that I was taking this too lightly. 'Monday morning surgery on a cold wet winter's day, and being asked to say a few words in public...'

Please don't let it fall flat in front of me, I was begging silently, or else how am I going to get through the next few minutes without choking.

'...but this is for Evelyn, so here I am.'

The sea of faces stared at me sympathetically, and a woman in one of the side pews gave me an encouraging smile. Poor soul, she was probably thinking. Needs all the help he can get.

I took another deep breath, and then had a mental vision of Evelyn looking over my shoulder, smiling with that 'Well, get on with it, then' look on her face. I clutched at the lectern ever tighter and got on with it, just as she would have wanted.

'Evelyn, as you all know, died in her sleep at the surgery on Sunday night. I'm sure that we've all been wandering around in a state of shock and unreality this week – she has been so much part of our lives that it just doesn't seem real without her.

'She came to the surgery some seven to eight years ago now, and has been an omnipresence ever since. She was there when we arrived in the morning, and there in the evening when we went home. I hadn't realised until yesterday that Evelyn was actually born in Lifton, when a patient told me how, as a little girl, she used to leave her bike at her house after cycling into school.'

I looked up from my notes and was reassured to see a few nods and smiles of remembrance from people who had known her so much longer than I had. Whether this was quite what they had expected or not, it seemed to be striking a chord, which was all I had wanted.

'I was talking to Kathy, Helen and Ralph (her children) yesterday,' I continued, beginning to feel a little more confident. 'They asked me to speak this afternoon and I asked them if there was anything they would especially like me to say. "Anything you like," came the answer, "but don't for goodness" sake get anything wrong – don't, whatever you do, say she liked the W.I., because she didn't. And make sure you turn up on time for the funeral. She would never forgive you for being late."'

I felt secure enough to try a little humour now and turned to where Evelyn lay in her coffin, just to my left. 'Well, Evelyn, at least *I* wasn't late,' I said.

I could see a few more smiles in the congregation and took heart.

'Having Evelyn around was like having a surrogate mother, grandmother and favourite aunt all rolled into one. Rowan, our practice nurse, was reminding me last night of the day I walked into the surgery sporting a beard after being away for a couple of weeks, and how Evelyn looked at me in that way of hers and said, "Well, that will have to go for a start."

'I can still remember the look on her face when I turned up at the surgery wearing my earring for the first time, and I have it here today – no, I'm not wearing it,' I admitted, patting my breast pocket, 'I wouldn't dare.' There was a ripple of laughter.

'If Evelyn was here now, she would be standing with her hands on her hips and saying "Haven't you got a black tie? Could you not have brushed your hair? And look at your shoes – how about a bit of polish on them, just this once, on this special day?"

When I read a passage from the Bible at my mother's funeral, my voice was rock steady, but my right leg was trembling uncontrollably now.

'I shall miss her not standing there in the mornings with that look of benign tolerance on her face, asking "And what have you been up to this time?"'

'I can't think of any other occasion when I would choose to repeat this in public, and I shall probably regret it in about five minutes' time, but one of my favourite memories of Evelyn dates back a couple of years to a particular morning when I had been out to some friends the night before...

'As that evening wore on I developed the feeling you sometimes have after a couple of drinks, when no matter how enjoyable the surroundings and the company, what you yearn for is your bed. Mindful, however, of the lateness of the hour, and the infinitesimal amount over the drink-drive limit I undoubtedly was, I decided to borrow my host's push-bike and cycle the seven or eight miles home.

'The surgery was about the halfway point in the journey, and as I reached the turning to it off the main road I had the distinct feeling that this was about as far as I was going to get. I cycled round to the back of the building and let myself in, propping up my borrowed bicycle against the corridor wall.

'I rang home to explain what had happened and, relieved to have found some sanctuary, raided the linen room for a couple of blankets and a pillow and settled myself down in Rowan's office for some sleep.'

I was wondering all the time if this was an appropriate story for a funeral and stopped to look around the church. Everywhere there were nods of encouragement and reassuring glances, even if some of them were of the "I've no idea where all this is leading, but please carry on anyway" variety. I ploughed on.

'The next morning, of course, down came Evelyn as usual, sees a strange bike in the corridor she doesn't recognise, opens the door to Rowan's room where I have yet to properly surface, and turns and rushes back up to the flat to ring my home.

'"Is Michael there?" she asked, "only I think a tramp has broken into the surgery."

'"Um, no," came the answer, "but I think you'll find it's not actually a tramp..."'

'So, Evelyn walked downstairs again, opened the door to Rowan's room once more and stood there in the doorway, hands on hips. "Michael Sparrow," was all she said, shaking her head and disappearing back up to her flat.

'But five minutes later she was back again with a mug of black coffee and a bacon sandwich, grinning all over her face. And that,' I said, 'is the Evelyn I have known and loved for the past ten or so years.'

'She told me that story about you,' Jane (Jack Sharp's wife) told me some time later. 'She said she always looked upon you as the errant son she was sometimes glad she never had.'

The atmosphere in the church was relaxed, almost happy, everyone lost in their own memories of the Evelyn we had each known. It was time to draw to an end. I cleared my throat and gathered myself together.

'There were three things in Evelyn's life that were important to her,' I went on. One of them was gardening.

'She came to me one day, a year or so after she had moved in, and asked if she could have a little patch of the grass we euphemistically called the surgery garden in which to grow some flowers. And, as any of you who have been there will know, that "little patch" became bigger, and bigger, until she took over the whole thing, tending it as lovingly as she would her own.

'So many weekends I would come in and find her, often out in the rain, weeding and planting and just enjoying what she had created. Rowan picked some daffodils the other day to put in her room. "But only the broken ones," Helen and Kathy told me. She would never have dared to pick any others.

'Another of Evelyn's great loves was unquestionably children. Evelyn and children just belonged together; they had this natural, indefinable affinity for each other. I don't have any idea how many little ones she looked after in her life, firstly as a registered nanny, but most of them will now be grown up with children of their own. I suspect they felt about her as my two, whom Evelyn looked after on numerous occasions, certainly did.

'Over they would come to see me after Saturday morning surgery, taking one look in my direction before saying "Hi, Dad. Is Evelyn in?

Can we go up and see?" and then rushing up the stairs without waiting for an answer. I would go up maybe an hour later and there the three of them would be, spreadeagled across the floor playing Ludo, Snakes and Ladders or Mousey Mousey, all perfectly at ease in each other's company.

'"Oh, Dad!" they would exclaim, "do we have to go home *now*? Couldn't we just stay for another ten minutes?"

'And you could repeat that story a thousand times over, so many children, so many parents echoing the same sentiment.

'But Evelyn's greatest love, of course, was her own family. From exasperation to adoration, her family were a constant theme in her life, her primary reason for being. The last time I saw her was a week ago today, going upstairs as I so often did for a chat, and there she was, surrounded by her granddaughters and cooing and chuckling over the most recent arrival, her first great-grandchild. I have never seen her so happy as in that moment.

'Last Saturday, the day before she died, Evelyn was out at a family celebration, loving it as much as she always did, each and every minute. I'm so glad that was one of her last memories, and I hope it will be your abiding memory of Evelyn. A woman at peace, who had found her niche in life and gloried at being there.

'If you wanted to advertise for a replacement Evelyn, how would it read? "Wanted – mother, aunt, grandmother, gardener, friend, surrogate everything." It would take half a dozen people to fill the vacancy, and they would never occupy it so well.

'If I had a glass I would raise it, but I don't need one to say what we all feel. To the memory of Evelyn…'

It all seemed so quiet as I gathered up my notes, replaced them carefully in my pocket and walked slowly from the lectern back to my seat, oblivious of all those around me. I had got through my address with a dry eye and no lump in my throat, and I was grateful to have had the chance to say goodbye in a way I hope she might have appreciated. But I could not keep the tears away in the short walk through the rain to the graveside, or the walk back down to the car.

No more Evelyn with her cups of black coffee and bacon sandwiches. No more Evelyn with her exasperated affection and her 'What on earth have you done now?' expression when I came in with an 'I really wish I hadn't done that' look on my face. And no more Evelyn for my children and so many others to rush up the stairs to play old-fashioned board games with.

Evelyn Mary Trant, the Rolls-Royce of childminders, mother, grandmother and favourite aunt rolled into one, I miss you, your children miss you, we all miss you still.

There is a footnote to this sad tale.

As the first anniversary of Evelyn's death approached, we decided at the surgery that we should mark the day in some way. After a discussion between Rowan and myself, it was agreed that we should close the surgery for a half-day, bring all the staff in for the afternoon and spend the time tending Evelyn's garden.

I was away for two spells of a week in the month leading up to the day, and it was on my mind when I returned from my second break to finalise with Rowan what we were going to do exactly. That Monday, however, was a shocker, one of those days when you hit the ground running and never seem to stop. By seven o'clock in the evening I was exhausted, and I realised that I hadn't eaten all day.

Rowan had left by the time I finished. I almost rang her at home, but I decided I should go home as well, followed by a drink, a meal and some sleep as soon as I could possibly manage it. Tomorrow would do to talk about it, but I mustn't forget, I thought. There were only another eight days to go, and if we were to close for the afternoon we had to give the patients due warning.

The next day duly dawned, but it wasn't until halfway through the morning that I got a chance to have a word with Rowan. 'I've been thinking about Evelyn,' I said quietly. 'I thought we should discuss next week, and what we should do.'

She looked at me for a moment, and then took me by the arm. 'Yes, Michael,' she said, 'we must. Come with me up to her flat for a moment…'

It was a year to the day and I was making my way down to the church, flowers resting beside me on the passenger seat. The clouds were gathering, the wind whipping up, and I drove slowly along the narrow country lanes, mindful of the overhanging branches dangling by a thread from the trees lining my route.

It had been an odd day thus far. The morning had passed in the usual blur of activity and I had scarcely given Evelyn a thought. Then at lunchtime I had gone to see Muriel, an old friend of hers who had just returned to Launceston Hospital for convalescence following major surgery in Plymouth.

'I haven't cried for a whole year,' she said, the tears welling in her eyes. 'But today...'

'I know, Muriel, I know,' I agreed. 'But you'd better stop it now or you'll have me going as well.'

I reached the short lane leading directly down to the church and turned into it. A few yards in front a barrier of red tape met my eyes. For this was Devon, March 2001, and we were in foot and mouth territory.

I could see the church tower just peeking out over the brow of the hill. So near, and yet so far. I picked up the flowers, got out of the car into the howling wind and, stepping resolutely through the red tape, set off down the hill. Foot and mouth be damned – this was Evelyn we were talking about.

Fifty yards down the road I came to a sudden halt. An enormous tree, one of the largest I had so far seen, had fallen across the lane and was blocking it completely.

'I'll climb over it,' I thought grimly.

Five minutes later, with torn and muddy trousers, I realised that climbing over it was not going to happen, and I trudged forlornly back to the car.

Kathy, one of Evelyn's twin daughters, lived less than half a mile down the road, so I decided to drive there instead. There were several cars outside the house and Kathy's sister, Helen, and a couple of Evelyn's grandchildren were inside.

'I thought I'd bring some flowers,' I said as Kathy answered the door, 'but there's a tree down on the road and I can't get through to the church.'

'Come in,' said Kathy. 'We haven't been down there ourselves yet – and anyway, it's so windy we decided to keep the flowers here for a day or so. If we took them down now, they'd be blown back here before we were.'

'I had thought we might close the surgery for the afternoon,' I explained forlornly, after telling them the story of my day, 'and get all the staff to do some gardening. Your mum would have liked that.'

'Yes, she would have done,' said Helen, as Kathy nodded in agreement, and then they both burst out laughing.

Rowan had taken me up the back stairs to Evelyn's flat and opened the door.

I had stayed out of there for most of the past year, just occasionally venturing in and wandering aimlessly around. It was empty now, with only memories to fill the space that had once been Evelyn's, and a sense of sadness always came over me whenever I entered. I followed Rowan through to the bedroom where a vase of daffodils rested on the floor.

'I picked them at the weekend,' she said. 'I didn't want the flat to be empty, It's today, Michael, not next week. The anniversary is today.'

The following weekend, the tree having been cleared away, I drove back out to the church by myself and sat by the graveside, remembering.

'Well, Evelyn,' I said. 'It's been a long year and we all miss you still. But I have to tell you that I got the wrong day and didn't make it down to the church with your flowers even when Rowan reminded me which day it was.'

I stood up to go, a picture in my mind of Evelyn standing in front of me with her hands on her hips, looking at me in that way that she so often did.

'Oh, Michael,' came a soft voice on the wind. 'Whatever are we going to do with you now?'

# 10
# Lost for Words – Part III

In 2001, the year I was in at medical school held its twenty-first anniversary reunion.

This was the second reunion, having held a similar event ten years previously, eleven years after we all qualified. It was meant to have been a ten-year reunion, but this is St Mary's we are talking about, and it was only a small matter of twelve months late.

I have to admit that much of what transpired during the former event remains an alcoholic mist, save for a brief interlude in the early hours of the morning when the bar of the country house hotel we were staying in temporarily ran out of drink.

'Big wedding next door,' said the barman, nodding towards the adjoining suite, 'and an awful lot of champagne they had delivered there this morning. Can't believe they'll have got through it all – might be worth a try while you wait for me to get back.'

It was indeed worth a try, but a try is as far as we got. We mingled unobtrusively – or so we thought –with what remained of the guests, moving inexorably closer to the as yet untouched bottles until they were just within our grasp, and then…

'Friend of the bride, friend of the groom, or part of the overflow from next door?' asked a large, unpleasant-looking middle-aged man barring our way.

'Er, friend of both,' I said, caught rather on the hop for a moment.

'Name them,' he demanded – not unreasonably, with the benefit of hindsight. 'Either of them.'

'Well, we're… sort of new acquaintances, really,' I replied. 'Not wholly on first name terms, as yet, but looking forward to a long and happy relationship. Nice talking to you, but we were just about to replenish our glasses, as it happens.'

'Not in here you don't,' he said grimly. 'And before you get any funny ideas, take a look around you. There's an awful lot more of us than there are of you, and quite frankly we don't want you in here. Now get out.'

'Yes, get out,' chorused a few others nearby.

We looked at each other and shrugged nonchalantly.

'Well,' reiterated John, 'it was worth a try. Could we not just toast the happy couple before…'

'Out,' repeated the unpleasant man. 'Before we throw you out.'

We beat a hasty retreat down the corridor, stopping outside the door of our bar.

'Wait, listen,' said John, holding a hand up to his ear. 'Did you hear something?'

'No,' I replied, 'nothing out of the ordinary.'

'Are you sure,' asked John, pointing at a couple of objects attached to the wall. 'Are you really sure you didn't hear somebody from next door shouting 'Fire'?'

'Not at all sure, now I come to think of it,' I said slowly, reaching for the nearest of the two fire extinguishers. 'Better to be on the safe side, don't you think? Wouldn't want the wedding presents to be burned to a cinder, or anything like that, now would we?'

'Absolutely not,' agreed John, fingering his fire extinguisher lovingly. 'We wouldn't want that at all.'

'And they would be so grateful,' I added, 'were we to save them all from a fatal conflagration.'

We turned tail, took a deep breath, and charged back down the corridor…

Our second reunion was a more sedate affair, though in truth I suspect that more alcohol was drunk than on the previous occasion. We were just ten years older and couldn't charge around as much.

Of our original year, qualified in 1980, somewhere between a half and two-thirds had turned up, many of whom I had not seen since the first reunion. There were even some people I had not set eyes on at all since leaving medical school. Thank God.

The main event was to take place on the Saturday night. But for those of us who lived further away – the venue being just outside Silverstone – and those who just had too much time on their hands, arriving for a preliminary knees-up on the Friday before seemed de rigueur.

'I can't believe it,' my then other half reported to her parents a few days later. (I refuse to name her because she is not worthy, but she did accompany me to that reunion.) 'They haven't seen each other for a decade or two, and the first thing they talk about is who has been divorced the most times, and who is dead.'

Come the second night, all the usual suspects are there – Polson, my old Circle Line colleague; 'Skid' Kelleher; Langford… now with too much weight on him to ever fit in a two-seater soft top for a five-legged race; and 'Shortknees', my ex-flatmate, who had flown back from Australia especially for the occasion. Twenty years since we had last met, and he was looking more like Jools Holland than Jools Holland ever did.

Once we had checked on the essentials – who was no longer with us, who had run off with whose wife, who'd been struck off for kerb-crawling in Central Birmingham – it was time for the platitudes and general bitchiness.

'You haven't changed a bit,' we would lie to each other, 'but, my God, have you seen how much weight Simon's put on. And what happened to Davison's hair. Is that a wig or what? Last time I saw her she had more hair under her arms…'

The best moment of the weekend for me, however, came when a couple in their mid forties wandered into the bar and began their slow, circuitous route re-engaging with old friends. Eventually they navigated their way towards the last of the free champagne, which was coincidentally located just a matter of inches from my left elbow.

'Hello, Mike,' came a voice I hadn't heard for the best part of a quarter of a century. 'How are you?'

And there was Fee, the only person I know who you could describe as truly 'nice' without making it sound like an insult. I'd always imagined her doing something gentle and innocent, like waving fluffy toys at cherubic newborn babies, or commiserating with well-off middle-aged ladies when their third facelift hadn't quite come up to expectations.

'So, what have you been doing with yourself these last two and a half decades?' I asked, making idle small talk to divert her attention as I made an ungainly lunge for the single remaining glass on the waitress's tray. When all I really wanted to do was give her a great big hug.

'G.U.M. clinic,' she said with a grin.

'G.U.M.?' asked she who will never be named. 'What is that?'

'Genito-urinary medicine,' I explained kindly, acknowledging her educational difficulties. 'Catering to the disorders of the reproductive system. Specialist in sexually transmitted diseases... Clap Clinic,' I finished. 'How lovely for you, Fee,' I said. Must have been what you always wanted...'

There is, to my mind, no simple answer to the question as to how we should refer to such a branch of medicine. And, with the greatest deference to Fee, what sort of doctor is it anyway that wants to spend large chunks of their day examining other people's diseased genitalia. Surely there are only so many urethral discharges, so many fulminating ulcers that any one person can take?

There is, I think, a film starring Jimmy Cagney called *Where Angels Fear to Tread*. And I may of course be wrong, but I seem to recall its central tenet was that even violent criminals have areas where they would consider it unwise to venture.

I think we doctors should be the same. That long wiggly tube from the appendix round to the rectum, for example. Surely no doctor wants to be up there for any great length of time, and yet there's a whole branch of medicine dedicated to just that subject. They shelter under the euphemism of 'gastroenterologists', which sounds terribly grand but can be loosely translated as 'people in white coats who stick long bits of cold metal up your anal canal, while trying to tell you it's all in your best interests.'

The quickest way I know of clearing a busy outpatient department is to wander out reflectively amongst the assembled congregation waving a sigmoidoscope – a mere one and a half feet of rigidly shiny cold steel – stroking it lovingly and saying, 'Phew, that was a close one. Nearly lost it in the last patient – had to put a foot on each buttock while I was trying to pull it out. Happens every now and then. Now, who is next?'

But at least gastroenterologists have a little variety in their lives – every once in a while they get to shove those long metal things down your neck and into your stomach instead. What possible defence can a proctologist muster, though, as a troglodyte who spends his entire life immersed in other people's rectums. Would you want to shake hands with one, or have them invite you to dinner? Of course you wouldn't.

At least us GPs only insert inanimate objects into other people's orifices as a matter of necessity. Or so I have been led to believe.

A critical part of our academic syllabus as students was to attend the 'Special Clinic' – as in Fee's later area of expertise – on three consecutive Friday afternoons; male side, female side, and contact tracing.

In the latter, they endeavoured mostly fruitlessly to establish the original source of any particular outbreak of herpes, or gonorrhoea, or indeed any presenting discharge from the bits of our body we mostly shy away from exposing to the general public.

On my first visit of the three, by luck or design I had been allocated to the male side under the tutelage of Dr Almiri. He was, I have to say, a man not afraid to get to grips with the subject in hand on a surprisingly intimate basis. Like most rugby or football players who have shared a communal bath on a weekly basis – even if we didn't have a game, some weeks – I am not entirely unfazed by the sight of the male reproductive organ.

I was, however, somewhat unused to the vision of a middle-aged Eurasian man in a grubby white coat directing a seemingly never-ending succession of mostly not very clean young men to drop their trousers in front of him, and then grab hold of the offending article in a concerted attempt to milk what discharge he could from the very end of it.

If, as newsreaders say before a subsequent sports programme, you do not wish to know the result, look away now, and rejoin me later in the chapter.

I sat, rooted to the spot, watching Dr Almiri examine penis after penis after penis, and it was only after an hour into the clinic that it hit me. Not only was he not wearing any gloves, but at no time during the entire proceedings had he thought to wash his hands.

'Jesus,' I thought. 'What sort of place is this?'

But there was even worse to come. Dr Almiri had scarcely spoken to me all afternoon, and I had spoken even less back. One penis, after the first hour and a half, was looking pretty much like any other, even those with scabby abscesses and little black crawly things running like headless chickens all over the floor once the good doctor had inadvertently shaken them off their erstwhile home.

But I was coping, or so I felt, even offering a word of encouragement to a patient here and there...

'Dear God,' I expostulated at one point to the good doctor. 'Even if you were a woman, why would ever you want to touch *that*? Oh,' I realised, just a little bit too late, 'you just did.'

As the afternoon progressed, I became more and more inured to the steady progression of disease-ridden appendages parading in ever increasing numbers before my eyes, and I was no longer concerned that Dr Almiri's hands remained unwashed and ungloved. I would cope, I thought – only two and a half Fridays to go and all in the cause of my future career. But there is a breaking point for us all.

Three-quarters of the way through the clinic, Dr Almiri sat back in his chair and surveyed the pile of notes on his desk.

'No more than another hour or two to go,' he observed. 'Time for coffee and something to eat.'

I watched what he then proceeded to do, first in curiosity, then distaste, and finally sheer repugnance. He reached his unwashed hands into the left drawer of his desk, took out his sandwiches and proceeded to eat them.

That was more than enough for me. I left without another word.


Nearly twenty years later, and for a reason so far removed from the above story it seems almost inexcusable for the one to follow the other, I again found myself unable to speak.

It was a cold, wintry Monday evening, and I was again on Kernowdoc duty – another shift with the Cornish-wide co-operative that consisted of a happy band of like-minded GPs who covered the out-of-hours emergencies on a day-by-day basis. We had been driving and visiting for nearly three and a half hours, and were just returning to our base at Launceston Hospital for a break and hopefully a drink, when the bleep burst into life once more.

'Chest pain,' reported Colin, the driver, with a sigh, 'St Giles… why is it always somewhere we've just driven through? And it says ASAP.'

He stopped and spun the car expertly, heading back in the direction from which we had just come.

'No time for some coffee and to catch the late news first then?' I suggested hopefully, as he sped off down the road. 'Oh, well,' I continued, 'let's just hope the ambulance gets there before us and has dealt with it by the time we arrive. Why don't you pull up in that lay-by over there for half an hour or so, and say we've had a puncture or hit a stray flock of sheep, or something.'

'Because the only available ambulance is on the way back from Derriford,' said Colin. (Derriford was the nearest major hospital, some thirty miles away in Plymouth.) He then slewed the car in a handbrake turn round the next corner so violently that I closed my eyes and began to pray for the first time since I drove my father's new Saab into our gate-post one Christmas morning while he was looking out at me through the living room window. 'It won't be here for a good thirty minutes,' continued Colin. 'Still want to stop for a cup of coffee?'

'More than ever,' I admitted. 'Rather that than deal with a life-threatening emergency all on my own. I wouldn't want anyone thinking I was competent.'

'Not competent,' Colin reassured me, 'just available.' He increased his speed and put the green flashing light on.

We found the house in St Giles without difficulty and pulled up outside, despite my suggestion that we should drive round the block a few times in the hope that we might encounter some off-duty paramedics in the immediate vicinity, maybe taking their dogs for a walk.

'It's all yours, Doc,' said Colin.

'Yeah, thanks, Colin,' I replied. 'And you're sure you'll be okay all tucked up nice and warm in the car without me to keep you company?'

'I'll struggle through,' he promised. 'And anyway, I need to be here in case…'

'…the telephone rings,' I finished for him. 'Where would I be without your moral support?'

I entered the house with a bag in each hand, wondering, as so often before, what I might find in there. A slim little girl with short dark hair met me in the dimly lit corridor.

'I'm Jenna,' she said simply. 'My dad's in the sitting room,' pointing to a door to my left. 'Are you the doctor?'

'Yes,' I said, trying a smile of reassurance.

'Please help him,' she said in a small voice. 'I think he's very ill. Please don't let him die. He's all I've got left – my mum died, you see, last year, of leukaemia. Please don't let him die too.'

'I'll try my hardest, Jenna,' I promised, and made my way into the sitting room. I stopped for a moment at the door, taken aback. Little Jenna, probably not much more than ten years old, had a father who looked to me to be in his mid sixties, and unlikely to get through to the next decade.

There are times, thankfully not all that often, when you encounter a patient that you just *know* is in the throes of having a heart attack. Stephan, Jenna's dad, was cold, grey, pallid and sweating, clutching his chest and breathing what may well have proved to be his last. I threw both my bags open and started looking for drugs I had at least some half-forgotten idea what to do with.

Please, God, let an ambulance turn up soon, I prayed for the second time that night, fumbling for an ampoule of diamorphine (heroin, as you may know it, a potent morphine-based painkiller that also can help with the fluid-filled lungs that often result from a heart attack). I also took out prochlorperazine (an anti-sickness drug to counter the nauseous effect of the diamorphine), furosemide (a diuretic which also helps rid the lungs of unwanted fluid) and a cylinder of oxygen – not for the patient, but to quell the panic that was rising in my breast.

I drew all the drugs up together in a syringe, attached the needle, and then I hovered, indecisively. 'Muscle or vein?' I thought desperately. Injecting into a vein acts more quickly but runs a greater risk of side effects if you have overestimated the dose, whereas inserting it into the muscle of the backside gives a slower but steadier release of the drugs into the system.

Stephan gasped, clutching his chest again in acute spasms of pain, and in an instant my mind was made up for me. Side effects or no, he wasn't going to be alive if I didn't act quickly. I tightened a ligature – well, one of my shoelaces, I couldn't find the tourniquet in my panic – round his arm, thanked God he had easily accessible veins and slowly injected the cocktail of drugs I had mixed. And all the time I was wishing I had a mobile cardiac care unit on the way there, that I had a couple of calmly efficient paramedics beside me to give their advice, that the patient didn't look so absolutely bloody awful.

His head began to sag forward on his chest.

'Don't go to sleep on me, Stephan,' I said sharply. 'Don't you dare to go to sleep now.'

He raised his eyes briefly to mine, opened his mouth momentarily to speak and then suddenly collapsed sideways.

'Don't do this to me, Stephan,' I shouted. 'Don't do it to your daughter...'

'The diamorphine,' I thought urgently. 'Had I given him too much? Had I inadvertently killed him while struggling to save his life?'

The sitting room was suddenly quiet. Stephan wasn't breathing, and had gone blue, and very, very cold.

I took a deep breath and counted to five, an instinct from my old training.

'They'll either be dead by the time you reach them,' a wise old registrar had taught me in my early years as a houseman, 'or alive and you won't need to do much beyond receive the accolades. Failing those two things, shout loudly for some back-up and look for somebody to share the blame with.'

I counted to five again. Nothing had changed, and Stephan was looking bluer by the second. It was time for desperate measures...

I thought about running away, but there were too many witnesses, and then I gathered my senses, stepped forward, and slapped Stephan firmly on the cheek. His head jerked sharply to the side, and for a minute I thought it might fall off until he gasped briefly and opened his eyes.

'That's my boy,' I breathed, slapping him again for good measure as he threatened to relapse into a coma.

Three minutes later the paramedics burst through the door and I shed my first tear of relief. Stephan was now sitting up unaided (although by no means out of the woods), his colour returning to normal and his breathing much less laboured.

'How is it going?' asked Marcus, the senior paramedic, who I knew of old.

'A bloody sight better than when I arrived,' I said, 'but he's not a well man, Marcus. Can you get him into hospital as quick as you can?'

'No problem, Mike,' agreed Marcus, efficiently unpacking his equipment and swinging smoothly into action. 'I remember this chap – took him in once before nigh on a year ago, and to be honest I never thought he'd make it then.'

He peered forward suddenly, staring at Stephan's face. 'What's that red mark on his cheek?' he asked. 'Looks a bit like... well, a bit like finger marks,' he added quietly, giving me an odd glance.

'It is finger marks,' I admitted, adding an explanation of what had happened.

'Interesting resuscitation technique,' he murmured appreciatively, raising his eyebrows. 'Interesting, but apparently effective, by the look of it.'

'As far as it goes,' I agreed. 'Best I could do on my own, Marcus. It's over to you lot, now. Don't screw up my good work, will you?'

'Do we ever?' he grinned. 'In fact, what good work of yours could we ever have made a mess of...' he added, considering carefully, '...because what good work of yours have we ever encountered?'

In a little under ten minutes Stephan was loaded into the ambulance and safely on his way to hospital.

I watched for a moment as they drove down the road into the darkness of the night, and then made my way back towards the Kernowdoc car.

'Dr Sparrow,' came a small voice by my side. 'Sorry to bother you, but my dad, is he going to be all right?'

Stephan's daughter... my heart sank.

In all the haste and worry I had been so caught up in, I had to my shame completely forgotten about her.

'Jenna, I've done the best I can,' I said gently, 'and he's in good hands now, the best I know. We both have to pray for a while...'

I looked back at her as Colin and I drove away, a forlorn figure standing outside her front door, waving goodbye. Her mother was dead, her father on the way to what for her was probably a far distant hospital and likely to die before the night was out, and all she had to comfort her was the next-door neighbour, an arm wrapped protectively round her shoulder. Tears were running down eyes as yet too young to understand all the consequences.

'Thanks for looking after my dad,' she had said. 'Thanks for everything you did…'

I sat quietly in the car all the way back to the hospital, a lump in my throat, and unable to speak.

Yes, you've guessed it.

Lost for words.

# 11
# Groundhog Day – Part II

A few days after the funeral of Norman (legs), I was sitting quietly at home, having breakfast – it was actually lunchtime, but, like morning surgery after a bank holiday, I was running a little bit late – when my other half wandered in with the midday post.

'Anything interesting?' I enquired disinterestedly, as she proceeded to open the ten per cent that wasn't junk mail before standing still for a moment, looking at one particular delivery.

As I was looking at a more important delivery at the time – England were playing Sri Lanka at Lords – I initially paid scant attention, but I paid a little more when she said in a slightly strange (but normal for Cornwall) voice: 'How would you like to go to the opera?'

Assuming she must be talking to the cat, the only other active life form in the house at the time, and probably more likely to answer in the affirmative, I ignored her completely.

'How would you like to go to the opera?' she repeated.

'Why?' I asked, primarily because it seemed a less inflammatory response than 'I wouldn't' or 'Can we watch the next five hours of the test match in complete silence?'

'Because your life is a cultural desert,' she replied with compelling accuracy, 'and I have two free tickets in my hands.'

I am not a prejudiced man. I have been to the opera before – once, in Cardiff, with Welsh people – despite my professed opinion that opera was full of fat people from other countries singing about things I wasn't interested in, in a language I couldn't understand. I fell asleep in Act

Two, wondering why on earth Mimi's tiny hands should be frozen in the middle of a centrally heated auditorium full of more hot air than a dozen Krakatoas exploding in unison.

'And why would anyone want to send you two free tickets to the opera?' I enquired.

'No reason at all,' she replied sweetly. 'The letter was addressed to you.'

I reached out a hand for the envelope and studied its contents carefully.

'Verona,' I mused out loud. 'Isn't that somewhere on the Circle Line, a bit further to the west of Covent Garden?'

I'd seen that look on her face before. She shrugged her shoulders and patted me on the hand with slightly more force than I felt necessary.

'You are a sad man, Michael Sparrow,' she said. 'Sad, and geographically ignorant. That would be Verona, as in Italy. Europe, north of Antarctica.'

'Is that Italy as in pasta,' I asked, 'with cheap Lambrusco and lots of angry people shouting at each other in the street?'

'Cultural,' she repeated slowly, 'desert.'

You can keep Venice, as far as I am concerned. It's just London with dirty water, after all. And I know they say that if you sit outside a café in Paris long enough then sooner or later everyone you have ever known will walk past you, and that's fine by me, because I won't be looking. I have, however, sat in the Piazza Bra – yes, seriously – in Verona, watching all the passers-by in their expensive attire and designer shades, walking coolly down the promenade, and then walking coolly back again, for no better reason than they want to, and they can.

Verona is in fact a wonderful place. Our hotel was in a back street – there don't appear to be many front streets – a narrow pedestrian lane lined by five- and six-storey buildings reaching up to the sun, and not a smelly canal in sight.

'We've got a balcony,' screeched Lucy, the six-year-old, joyously.

'Everybody has,' I murmured cynically, but in truth, I rather like balconies myself.

The strains of a violin wafted in through our window with the sunshine. 'Sherlock Holmes,' we chorused together, and everywhere we went there was music – classical, operatic, and not a Spice Girl in sight. It was actually rather wonderful.

We were just two minutes' walk from the arena, and the opera. Imagine opening your front door, strolling round the corner to a new branch of M & S, and then leaving the food hall only to stumble into a Roman amphitheatre located just between C & A and Mothercare.

And what an amphitheatre. As dusk began to fall a tangible air of excitement bubbled up from the streets, and seemingly from nowhere crowds began pouring into the square, thousands upon thousands of them. And yet the queue was so orderly, as the companionship of expectation and anticipation made fellow travellers of us all. It was the most enjoyable such wait I can recall, and I once queued overnight in the late seventies to buy tickets for a Bob Dylan concert.

As you enter through the gates of the amphitheatre you suddenly understand it all. It is a truly staggering spectacle. The vast arena, the fading light, the row upon row of candle-lit terraces and the stars budding like early roses in an exceptional spring. It was just totally, uncompromisingly, magical.

We found our seats with ease and sat drinking in the atmosphere, watching and waiting, and hoping that those moments would go on forever. As a hush settled like a comfort blanket over the excited crowd, Phoebe, my other half, turned to me and said quietly, 'It's wonderful. But what on earth do you think we're doing here?'

With the opera tickets had been a compliments slip from a firm of solicitors in London. I rang them for an explanation, and got no explanation at all, so I asked for two extra places for the children, which arrived promptly the next day. Then came the flight reservations and the coach tickets from Exeter to London. The latter were first class and gold-embossed with the promise of a full English breakfast.

'Only tourists and ladies with blue rinses take coaches,' I sneered unconvincingly. 'I like to drive.'

'But you can have a caffeine-free drink on the coach,' came the immediate response, 'or even two, if you wish. And the kids will be dropping their crumbs on somebody else's floor, for a change, and if they get travel sick...'

So we became tourists, and took the coach. A brilliant idea of mine.

But we still had not the least idea whatsoever why we were there. Until the unassuming man in the dark grey suit in the seat to my left tapped me gently on the shoulder at the end of Act Three – just as the giraffes and elephants were entering, a pivotal moment – and said in a tone I found faintly unsettling, 'Good evening, Dr Sparrow. So glad you and your family could make it.'

We wandered back from the opera in the early hours, through the narrow, lively streets, still drunk with the spectacle that is *Aida*. It had just about everything – people who sang, people who danced, people who did acrobatics and people who just wandered about in a staggering array of theatrical costumes trying to avoid tripping over the light fittings. They even had horses, half a dozen magnificent white stallions high-stepping majestically into the arena.

And there was other stuff, although I might have made some of it up for the children. 'What a pity it was the alligators' night off,' I said as we made our way out through the majestic doors, and such was the aura of the place that for once they believed me. For a while. We watched them now, dancing ahead and full of the sparky energy that extreme fatigue so often brings, Phoebe walking quietly by my side.

'I take it the man in the grey suit next to you was the reason for us being here,' she said at last.

I nodded silently.

'So what is it they want you to do? What is it they're asking from you?'

I shrugged. 'To go for a drive in the country,' I said.

'Well, that should be somewhere within your capabilities,' she said encouragingly. 'Just.'

I felt another 'just' coming on. I am so perceptive.

'Just as long as you are the passenger. You don't drive so well in the mornings. Not that you drive all that well in the afternoons, or evenings. Or weekends. Just make sure you sit to the left of the driver.'

I had nearly two seconds of gloat.

'Okay, it's Italy, I may for once have got it wrong. To the right, or maybe… in the back. With cushions and some fizzy water.'

'Oh, I can cope with that all right,' I said. 'It's the getting out at the other end bit that bothers me.'

The next morning dawned clear and still and I woke early, drifting out to the balcony as the sun rose. The city slumbered on as I sat there, watching, waiting and wondering what the coming day was to bring.

When I saw the black limousine rolling noiselessly down the street, I just knew it was for me, and somehow the 'getting out at the other end' bit assumed even greater importance. I stepped back into the cool of the room and collected my jacket, all the while aware of Phoebe's eyes watching from the darkness as the children slept on.

'Time to go,' I said, rather more lightly than I felt.

'You're really going?' she said quietly.

'I'm really going,' I confirmed.

'Despite the fact that you don't know where you're going, who you're going with, or what you're going for?'

'Despite all that,' I agreed. 'I'll look at it as a sort of magical mystery tour – it'll probably be a coachload of blue rinses from Harrogate Women's Institute on tour with the women from the Lifton Golden Circle.'

'I do believe you are quite dumb,' she said, walking across the room and straightening my collar absent-mindedly, 'but you might as well be tidy and dumb.'

She looked at me in silence for a few moments. 'There, you'll do,' she added. 'Try and come back in one piece, if you're going to come back at all. It would be time-consuming trying to find a replacement for you if anything goes wrong.'

The limousine was cool, dark, and very, very long. Could mislay an entire party of schoolchildren in here for a week, I thought. Out of the door stepped the driver, a squat, square-shouldered, powerfully built man with pockmarked skin, a dark suit and a pair of the most impenetrable sunglasses you could ever wish to see. I didn't mind not seeing his eyes, to be honest. I thought they might be pockmarked as well.

He opened the door for me courteously enough, but in fact he could have been as rude as he liked and I wouldn't have argued at all. I took a deep breath and stepped in, waving my hand behind my back to the upstairs balcony where I knew Phoebe would be watching. I didn't look up, because I knew if I had it would have been the moment I started running, and I would probably still be running today.

I sat in the back of the car appreciating the sheer unadulterated luxury of the leather upholstery. We rolled gently off and the driver slid the connecting window noiselessly to one side.

I waited in trepidation for the resulting hail of bullets.

'Coffee is in the pot, and beer there is in the fridge,' he said in heavily accented though not unfriendly tones. 'Beside you on seat your daily paper – you read *Telegraph*, no? My boss say you are to relax and enjoy journey – take about two, two and some hours. You must knock if you want something,' and the window slid just as noiselessly shut again.

I do read the *Daily Telegraph*. I picked it up, unnerved, and did my first double-take of the morning. It had that day's date on it.

We drove up high into the hills, the sun pouring down on us. The scenery was magnificent, but rather lost upon me as I sat back in my seat, reflecting. What in God's name did I think I was doing? Why, oh why, hadn't I headed straight back to the airport and jumped on the first available flight out of town?

We finally drew up outside a pair of imposing gates set several yards back from the road. They had more metal in them than most Cornish tin mines. My driver, who had remained silent since his opening words two hours ago, now spoke a few unintelligible words into his mobile phone and the gates rolled smoothly open.

Money, I thought perceptively, this place is awash with the smell of money.

We passed through the entrance to a long, immaculately kept drive winding around the side of the hill, before drawing up several minutes later in front of an imposing five-storey, multi-turreted building with spectacular views back across the valley. This place wasn't merely redolent with the aroma of money, I corrected myself, it was creaking under the weight of its wealth.

I stepped out of the car, lost in admiration – okay, immersed in total jealousy – and was led through an opulent entrance hall into a cool, expensively decorated sitting room at the back of the house. Patio doors opened on to a vast lawn where several children were splashing excitedly in a subtly hidden swimming pool under the watchful eyes of a couple of beautifully tanned adults with beautiful figures.

'You are to wait here,' instructed my chauffeur, in a manner that brooked no argument. 'If you would please.'

I pleased. If he had instructed me to hang upside down by my toenails from the picture rail I think I would probably have thought it a really good idea to do just that. He glided out of the room with a surprising

143

lightness for a man of his bulk, and I was left suddenly alone, wandering around the room admiring an array of exquisite antiques, ancestral portraits and expensively mounted family photographs. Photographs...

I studied them intently. Perhaps in one of them there would be a clue to the reason for my presence. There was one person I thought I recognised, standing prominently to the front of several of the photographs, but it was just a hint of familiarity. I shook my head in frustration. I just couldn't be sure.

My ear was caught by the excited shrieks of a couple of dripping children rushing across the lawn towards the house, towels draped round their shoulders. I stepped out through the patio doors on to the terrace as one of them tumbled over on the ground before me, wincing and sitting up in discomfort, holding his foot.

'May I see?' I asked, bending down towards him.

I was in Italy, and this was an ten-year-old boy on the ground in front of me – but he would understand English, wouldn't he? This was a continental child, for goodness' sake.

And he did, too, holding up his foot unquestioningly for me to take a look at. But then I am a doctor, am I not? Our respect and authority transcend all international boundaries...

'Ouch,' I said sympathetically, inspecting a small cut in the webbing between his first and second toe. 'That must hurt.'

Time stood still for a moment, my heart suddenly racing as I held his foot in my hands. Now, I thought, I understood who had brought me here. But the why and the what? Something told me I had to be careful. Very careful indeed.

'I see you have met each other, Dr Sparrow,' came a calm voice over my shoulder in perfect English, with just the trace of an accent.

'We have indeed,' I agreed, turning to find an immaculately dressed man in his mid to late seventies moving effortlessly across the room towards me, 'but to date I have met only his big toe and a bit of his ankle. We have yet to be formally introduced.'

He frowned imperceptibly, and then relaxed.

'Ah, the English sense of humour,' he said, advancing further into the room with his hand held out. 'I should have remembered.' There was a smile on his face, but his eyes remained reptilian-like, cool and still beneath hooded lids. This, I thought warily, was a man to take heed of.

'My name,' he continued, 'is Luigi. I am a...' he coughed discreetly '...a businessman, as you would say in your language. It is my pleasure to meet you. And this,' he said, gesturing towards the young boy, 'is my beloved grandson. Say hello to Dr Sparrow, Luca. He has come a long way to find out if you are who we all hope you to be.'

'Hello, Dr Sparrow,' said Luca, grinning cheekily. 'It is nice to meet you, even if I don't know what on earth Grandad is talking about.'

'Run along now, Luca,' continued his grandfather indulgently, 'and get changed out of those wet clothes. But be back down here in five minutes, and make sure your mother is with you,' he added.

Luca ran off obediently.

'He's a fine boy,' observed Luigi, 'but is he the boy that we think he is?'

'I'm afraid I haven't the faintest idea what you are talking about,' I said, a good deal more calmly than I felt. In truth, though, I was beginning to add two and two together, and had made them almost into three. 'Perhaps you would be kind enough to explain what I'm doing here.'

'Indeed,' he said, motioning me towards a chair by the open patio doors. 'Do take a seat. Perhaps you would care for a drink?'

'Yes,' I nodded, thinking that actually I would care for several, 'a glass of wine would be most pleasant.'

'Lineage,' said Luigi unexpectedly, raising a bottle of wine in my direction. 'This will do? Good. Lineage,' he continued while pouring, 'is of the utmost importance in my family. Luca is the eldest son of my eldest son and will inherit all that I possess in the event of my death – which will be sooner, you must understand, than you might think from my apparently healthy outward appearance. My eldest son...'

For the first time a trace of emotion flitted across his face, but it was gone in an instant.

'...my eldest son was killed in an unfortunate accident shortly after Luca was born. I did not meet Luca myself until he was nearly one year old, but now...' he shrugged. 'As you can see, he lives here with his mother and the rest of my family in some degree of comfort.'

I cast my eyes over the opulence around me. If this was 'some degree of comfort', I wondered what he would have thought to be luxurious.

'It does look fairly comfortable here,' I agreed, risking a little sardonic wit. His eyes narrowed slightly, and I started checking his beautifully cut clothing for signs of gun-shaped bulges. Maybe sardonic wit was best avoided for the moment, I thought.

'I had three sons,' continued Luigi, walking across the room and handing me a glass of wine, 'and in my family everything passes to the eldest son. If he dies, which of course he has, it passes to his eldest son, if he has one, but to no other child of his. If his eldest son, my grandson, should die before I do then it passes to my second son instead. My second son...'

He sighed, as if uncertain how to proceed.

'But Luca is alive and well,' I said slowly. 'He's not ill, is he?'

'No, he is not ill,' Luigi replied. 'But it is vital that we clarify for once and for all if Luca is actually... Ah, my dear,' he broke off, turning at the sound of footsteps approaching. An expensively groomed lady in her early thirties appeared at the door, Luca by her side. 'Come, join us. I believe you already know my daughter-in-law, Dr Sparrow.'

'Hello, Dr Sparrow. Mike,' she said, advancing elegantly across the floor and extending a beautifully manicured hand, 'we meet again. I'm sorry about all the "cloak and dagger" secrecy in bringing you here – a bit like a second-rate spy story, isn't it? But Luigi wanted to be sure, and he didn't want you to come with any preconceived ideas about it all. You don't,' she added shrewdly, 'seem all that surprised to see me.'

'The photographs,' I shrugged. 'I knew there was someone in there I recognised, but I just couldn't quite place you. You've changed, rather a lot – on the outside, at least.'

'Wealth has a habit of doing that to you, one way or another,' she said easily. 'We've become rather used to it, Luca and I.'

'Ah, Luca,' I said. 'I recognised the webbing on his feet after he stubbed his toe on the ground just outside here and I took a look at it. Luke... Luca... It's all the same, isn't it? Hallo, Cheryl. How have you been?'

We drove back out through those impressive gates in silence, Cheryl and I, making our way down the hillside towards Verona and the real world, which were still thankfully waiting for me.

'Why didn't you just contact me?' I said at last. 'It would have been so easy, and I would have done whatever it was that you wanted.'

'I know that,' she said, giving me a wry smile, 'but don't you think he would have known that too? You had to be put on the spot and have it thrown at you out of the blue. Any other way and it wouldn't have worked. You've seen the house, and the estate... wouldn't you want to preserve that for your son, if you could? And he's a good boy, even if I do say it myself. He has his grandfather's commitment to honour and duty, an English sense of humour and a Cornishman's honesty, endeavour and love of pasties – for whatever that's worth. But I know him – he'll do a lot of good for our adopted home and country, in time. I have great hopes of him.'

'And what would you have done if I'd got it wrong?' I asked. 'So much hanging on the equivalent of the toss of a coin.'

'But you didn't,' she said simply, squeezing my arm gently. 'Did you?'

'I had two grandchildren,' Luigi had said, his face a mask of inscrutability. 'Twins born to my son over ten years ago. And one of them died before he was even a year old...'

'I remember hearing about it,' I said. 'We all do...'

'...but which one?' continued Luigi, almost unaware that I had spoken. 'My family have only Cheryl's word for it, and whatever my feelings for her I know what I would say and do if I were in her position. But you – you were there, when they were born. The midwife,' he shrugged, as if it was of no importance, 'she is dead. The health visitor is gone – somewhere, anywhere, but you... you remain. You will know, and I need you to tell me.'

'Tell you what?' I asked, buying for time.

'They were identical,' he continued, a look of pain on his face, 'in every way but one, so I believe. They both had webbed toes, and you have seen that. But there was something else, was there not? Something that only their doctor might still know about?'

I sat quietly for a moment, looking from Luigi, to Cheryl, to Luca. So much resting on my next few words. I took a deep breath.

'There was something,' I admitted. 'Something that would no longer be easily visible.'

'Aaaah,' breathed Luigi, his eyes suddenly alight. 'I knew it. I always knew that there was. And you must tell me now... it is imperative of you.'

I glanced quickly across to Cheryl, who remained impassive.

'Luke... Luca, as he is now,' I said slowly, 'was the elder. Both the boys had webbing between their toes – I recognised it in an instant this afternoon, as the degree to which they had the condition was so unusual. But Caleb…'

I looked across at Cheryl involuntarily, her face completely impassive.

'…he had something else that made him so easily distinguishable in the early days, until his hair grew.'

Luigi leant forward in his seat.

'And that was?' he asked in a sibilant whisper.

'A birthmark. It was on the back of his head, just behind his right ear. About the size of an English fifty-pence piece and bright red, shaped like a badly drawn map of Australia.'

'And it would still be there?' said Luigi, his eyes burning into mine.

'Oh, yes,' I confirmed, looking steadily back. 'A birthmark is a birthmark. It never fades away, wherever it may be…'

I have never known such stillness. Across the lawn to the swimming pool all was suddenly quiet, even the birds curtailing their evening chorus. In our palatial sitting room, everybody was holding their breath – so much so that at least one of us was possibly going to pass out unconscious any second, and I didn't want it to be me.

Luigi squared his shoulders, swallowed a couple of times, and then came to a decision.

'We are in need of some hair clippers,' he said finally.

'So how did you feel when they were shaving Luca's head?' asked Cheryl. 'How did you know what they would find?'

'It didn't matter,' I said. 'Luca… Caleb… whichever of them was alive, we both wanted them to inherit, didn't we? But Caleb had what is called in medical language a capillary haemangioma on the back of his head. They shrink and then fade away mostly within a year of their birth. Neither of them would have had a mark on their head now. I couldn't have known after all this time which of the twins I'd just met.'

We sat in silence for the rest of the journey, until Cheryl pulled up in front of my hotel and I opened the door of the car.

'Why did you come, Mike,' she asked, 'when you hadn't a clue what you were coming to?'

I shrugged, mainly because I didn't have the answer she was looking for. Or maybe because I did.

'Because,' I began, thinking carefully, 'life isn't always quite what you expect it to be... I guess we all like a bit of unpredictability every now and then.'

'Different worlds, Dr Sparrow,' she said softly. 'We all start from someplace and finish somewhere else, whether that's up, or down, or just scrabbling eternally sideways. We meet people that matter, and others that don't. And sometimes we lose the ones that are the most important. I've often wondered...'

'I often wonder too, Cheryl,' I admitted with a grin, 'but mostly I don't come up with any answers. As for the boys... I wish you and Luca well. Whoever he is.'

'But you do know, Mike, don't you?' she persisted. 'You've known right from the start...'

I stood on the pavement, watching the car drive away into the distance. A family dynasty, a multimillion-pound inheritance, a question of honour...

Night was falling, music from a lone saxophone drifting down the empty streets, melancholy and uplifting.

I never saw or heard from Cheryl again.

# 12

# You Can Get Anything in a Volvo

I have an old school friend, Ern, who is a vet, though I try hard not to hold that against him. Shortly after I began my first job in the Air Force, at RAF Chivenor in North Devon, Ern drove down for a weekend visit.

He was at the time working in Grantham – deemed the most boring town in England, I understand, but no doubt by a panel who had never been to Wellingborough, our home town.

It was in the middle of a blisteringly hot summer spell, and we naturally repaired to the pub for a spot of timely rehydration. The following lunchtime, having finally arisen from the ashes of the previous night's refuelling, we seemed to be in need of further – and this time rather more urgent – rehydration. We went out to his car to go for some supplies.

But when Ern opened the car door, an appallingly sweet, sickly odour crept out and swirled around our feet. His face grew even more ashen than it already was from the night before.

'Oh, my God,' he breathed. 'It's the beagle.'

His last call, before leaving for Devon, had been to an elderly lady whose much-loved companion – yes, you've guessed it, the beagle – had just died.

'I held her hand,' he said faintly, 'and promised I would take her beloved Jasper to the dog cemetery and arrange for his burial. And she thanked me so profusely, tears running down her cheeks, for being so kind and understanding and thoughtful.

'So, let me get this right,' I said. 'She thinks her beloved beagle, Jasper, has been buried in a dog cemetery in Grantham…'

'Yes,' he agreed.

'...whereas in actual fact he is rotting to bits in the boot of your car in an out-of-the-way bit of North Devon.'

'Yes,' he mouthed, starting to look rather pathetic.

'Well,' I said encouragingly, looking for that elusive silver lining, 'Devon is nicer than Grantham...'

'Anywhere's nicer than Grantham,' contributed Martin, the pilot who was my next-door neighbour, and who just happened to be passing by. 'My God, what on earth have you got in that car? Smells worse than a dead dog,' and he wandered off, holding his nose.

'Now, Ern,' I said, 'this beagle isn't going to make it back to Grantham in anything less than liquid form, so I suggest we do some serious digging. Sort of soon.'

A few minutes later we were driving round the airfield trying to find a suitable spot, and trying even harder not to be sick before we found it. Not only was the weather unbearably hot, the ground was incredibly hard, and it took some considerable time to locate an area our spades could even begin to make an impression upon.

We finally dug our hole, all the while sweating profusely, and dragged Jasper the beagle in his black plastic bag along the ground from the car, leaving a foul-smelling liquid trail in his wake.

'I didn't realise beagles could be so heavy,' I panted.

'Only dead ones,' grunted my partner in crime. 'Live ones jump about a lot.'

As we prepared to lower Jasper into his final resting place, I stood, looking around for a moment. It could be worse, I thought. Here, on this glorious summer afternoon, Jasper would be laid to rest by the side of the runway with a view over the valley and the estuary. How calm and peaceful it all was...

And that was precisely when two Range Rovers full of heavily armed Military Police rolled up to find out what we were doing.

Of course, only a vet could ever leave a dead patient in the boot of their car. No doctor could ever do that. Could they?

The ambulance service in this part of the world is wonderful, the men and women who staff it without exception supremely efficient and professional, and they wear some really nice tunics as well.

Bur even the best of ambulance personnel can only be in one place at one time, and in Devon and Cornwall that one place is usually miles away from where you would really like them to be. Down here – especially at night – there are vast tracts of uncharted country lanes without an ambulance to be seen. You are more likely to run into a badger or a fox.

There quite simply aren't enough ambulance personnel to go round. It doesn't matter whether you blame the goverment, or the Health Authority, or the juxtaposition of Mars and Venus and the pull of the neap tide, it just won't help if you need an ambulance and the nearest available vehicle is over two hours away. So you have to learn to think on your feet, and improvise.

There are, in essence, only three forms of improvisation available to you:

(1) Decide the patient is nowhere near as ill as you first evaluated and does not need to go into hospital after all. This normally works a treat as long as they do not actually die before the following morning, and can be circumnavigated even then if you manage to persuade the surviving relatives that at least you saved the undertaker a fifty-mile round trip to retrieve the body, and some £150 off their resulting bill.

(2) Utilise any available local transport. Am I the only GP in the country who has sent a patient in the final stages of labour to the local Maternity Unit in a combine harvester with only one gear working (and that was reverse)? Of course not. And anyway, everything was going splendidly until the driver passed a field of unharvested wheat and developed a sudden conflict of interest.

(3) Buy a Volvo. You can get anything in the back of a Volvo. Remember that advert in the late seventies which showed a horse reclining comfortably in the boot of the latest Volvo estate? And it's true, you can get a horse in there, although getting them out again is a different matter altogether. And it requires an awful lot of valeting before you can get another one in. A colleague once suggested a wheelbarrow would be more economical, and my practice nurse proposed the acquisition of a supermarket trolley, which would avoid the initial financial outlay of buying the Volvo.

But I am a GP, and I have standards. I waited until I had my 2.4 children and then purchased the biggest Volvo money could buy, resolving to test its storage capacity at the earliest available opportunity.

It was two o'clock in the morning, and Mr Newport was in terminal heart failure.

I was young, inexperienced. I'd left my medical bag in the surgery, my stethoscope at the scene of my last visit, and I needed help. Mr Newport was going to die unless I did something now, and the nearest ambulance was over an hour away.

At this early stage in my career I was still driving a 4x4 Fiat Panda – yes, they did exist and they were the ultimate off-road vehicle of their day. They could go anywhere, and mine frequently did. Just very slowly, and with an absence of style.

I picked Mr Newport up – he was so light, and so frail, and he had such a tenuous hold on life – and carried him to my car. The local GP-run hospital was only ten minutes' drive away, and I just prayed we could both get there before he died.

If you will forgive me a temporary lapse into vocational outpouring, this is what general practice is all about. Total care, if you can provide it, is as satisfying and rewarding as it comes. It almost pained me the following day to send his wife the bill for the taxi service I provided to the hospital.

Mr Newport, I should add, survived and lived another five years. I still feel the warm, encompassing glow from my selfless humanitarian gesture, and from the sheer wrath and contempt of his wife, who failed to inherit his considerable estate as early as she had hoped, and then had to nurse him at home throughout his final months.


It was an ordinary morning, during an ordinary February day, in the course of an ordinary year. I arrived at my surgery full of the joyous anticipation that each new day in public service inevitably brings.

Sally, my receptionist, was on the telephone as I entered, probably running through her usual list of fake alibis:


'He's in a meeting, Mr Johnstone, and can't be disturbed.'

'He's just dashed out on an emergency visit to a young farmer who thinks his wife might be pregnant.'

'We have an outbreak of bubonic plague, and he's got himself stuck in his protective clothing...'

All our potential employees were obliged to learn these very realistic excuses – and so very many more – prior to signing their preliminary contract.

'Excuse number six!' I might bellow during a meeting at the practice.

'Um, your mother-in-law has been gored by a bull?' they would reply nervously.

Which was wrong, of course, as that was excuse number five – and the complete answer, in any case, was 'His mother-in-law has been gored by a bull and he's gone to give the vet a hand trying to catch it. I think he wants to congratulate it on a job well done.'

On this particular occasion, however, Sally was saying, '...and you're pretty sure he's dead, Mrs Jenkins? You've notified the undertaker already? That's good, very good. There'll be no need for him to hurry, then...'

I grasped the phone in uncharacteristically compassionate vein, and mouthed to Sally, 'Who's dead? Dog, goldfish, long-lost brother from Indonesia?'

'Husband,' she mouthed back, but she didn't say exactly whose.

And this is the woman who, on her first day in the practice, ran screaming from the building when a middle-aged lady came in and said, 'I think I've got an infection in my ingrown toenail. It's oozing pus and stuff.'

We desensitise them so well.

'I'm so sorry...' I began, looking at Sally inquiringly.

'Ruby,' she mouthed helpfully.

'...Ruby,' I said (using their first names makes our patients think we actually remember who they are). 'I'll be round as soon as I can. Would a week on Friday be all right?'

I do feel that, at difficult times like these, a little humour can lighten the load.

In the event, I drove out that same afternoon and pronounced poor Mr Jenkins duly deceased – not a difficult task, as it transpired, because the undertaker, the immaculately coiffured Leon, was already crouched over the body with his tape measure in hand.

'Hallo, Mike,' he said gaily, 'long time no see. Been curing the odd one for a change, have we?'

I have never in fact encountered a miserable undertaker. I suppose we only ever meet each other when my loss of income is their gain, but why do they have to be so infernally chirpy about it all?

Having declared Mr Jenkins well and truly no longer among the living, and having agreed that he was six foot one inch tall, forty inches in circumference and a good 250 lbs in weight, I prepared to leave. Time, as ever, was in short supply – and, more importantly, I had spotted his newly created widow coming down the corridor from the kitchen. It was imperative I should make my escape before she pressed upon me the worst cup of tea north of the equator along with one of her indigestible rock cakes.

Leon laid a hand gently on my arm.

'Um – you couldn't help me out here, could you, Mike?' he asked. 'You see, there's only me available at the moment… combination of a busy day and Peter's leaving party at the Arundell. Mr Jenkins is too big for me to throw over my shoulder, and I can't just drag him along the carpet and bump him down the outside steps, now, can I?'

I looked down at my watch and grimaced.

'Well,' I said, 'I have got commitments…' (the semi-finals of *Countdown* were due to start in less than half an hour), '…but how much does an undertaker's assistant generally charge per body, per hour?'

'Sometimes, Dr Sparrow,' he said, peering over the top of his half-moon glasses, 'you can be a very funny man. But this isn't one of those times. Do you want to take the head or the feet?'

We transferred the unfortunate Mr Jenkins down to the hearse in two separate journeys – carrying Mr Jenkins in the first, his wig, false teeth and wooden leg in the second, and stood back admiring our handiwork.

'If there's anything else I can do, Leon?' I offered kindly.

'I'll ask for an estimate,' he countered, and climbed into the driver's seat.

Of course, I should have been there long before Leon arrived in the first place. Of course, I should have refused point blank to help him move the body. And, of course, I should have driven away before he tried to start the hearse.

'Um… Mike…?' he said, five frustrating minutes later as the engine failed to engage. 'You know how you keep telling me you can get anything in a Volvo?'

It was beginning to get dark.

We transferred Mr Jenkins' corpse to my car in a body bag – you can get anything in a Volvo, except a coffin – and covered his inert figure with the groundsheet I keep there for special occasions.

'See you back at your office,' I called over my shoulder, 'if you ever manage to get there.'

So there I was, driving back to town, the late Mr Jenkins resting uneasily (my perception, he was probably as comfortable as he had been for several years) in the boot of my car, when my bleep went off.

I was poised to write that, although I do have a bleep, I don't have a mobile phone, but actually I do. I've had one for some years now, I just don't know the number or how to plug it in, or what the security code is or how to use it.

Every other doctor I know, though, has a mobile phone, and I feel it is now my duty to share with you, the public at large, a little-known fact. There is a company, existing purely for the benefit of the medical profession, which contracts to ring us at specially predetermined times – on the way to the altar for an unwanted matrimonial ceremony, for example. Their remit is to provide us with fictitious medical emergencies that enable us to sound compassionate, dynamic and wholly indispensable. I have a lifelong subscription – money wasted, of course, what with me being incapable of remembering where it is or how to turn it on.

The point of all this is that should my bleep ever go off, I cannot pull into the nearest lay-by and check the details on my mobile because my mobile is still in the box it first came in and I'm not quite sure where I left that. So, when my bleep relayed the message 'Gemma Wilkinson is having an asthma attack – please visit ASAP', I just drove straight there, oblivious to everything save my obligations to the living.

Gemma had frequent 'severe' attacks, inveterately requiring 'urgent medical attention', so much so that we had emblazoned the side of one of the local emergency vehicles with 'The Gemma Wilkinson needs to go to casualty *now* ambulance'.

There was, in fact, nothing much wrong with her, save for an admittedly impressive ability to exaggerate her complete lack of symptoms to a degree designed to disturb and distress the family and friends who gathered around her. The whole affair had to my mind become something of a ritual, which sooner or later had to be addressed.

The appropriate opportunity had never arisen, but now an idea was beginning to form in the inner recesses of my mind. I arrived at the house and found Gemma, a sallow-faced girl of about nineteen, in her usual state of 'semi-collapse'. Her parents stood close by, looking threateningly at me, as if to dare me not to admit her to hospital that very instant.

'No time to waste,' I said briskly, after a quick examination. Gemma's parents' faces lit up with surprise. 'Must get her in as soon as we can. May I borrow your phone?'

I rang ambulance control and said, 'Hi, it's Dr Sparrow from Lifton here. I'm out in St Giles and I have a patient that needs admitting urgently. Can you tell me where your nearest ambulance is?'

'About five minutes away from you,' came the reply. 'Your luck is in, it's just on the way back to Launceston.'

'Oh, that's no good at all,' I replied, allowing a note of concern to creep into my voice. 'Don't worry, I'll just have to deal with it myself.'

Smiling inwardly as I heard a startled 'You what?' at the other end of the line, I replaced the receiver and looked across at the gathered assembly.

'No ambulance for miles around,' I lied unflinchingly. 'Will my car do? I could take you there myself.'

'It's an emergency, doctor,' said Gemma's mother angrily. 'Wot's the bleedin' use of an ambulance service if they can't bleedin' 'elp you out in an emergency. S'wot we pay our taxes for, innit?'

I tried not to look guilty – a task made less difficult by the fact that none of the Wilkinson family had worked or paid a single day's tax for several generations.

'Look at 'er, dying she is,' carried on Gemma's mum, 'one breath at a time.'

'How lyrical,' I thought. 'There's only one problem, though,' I continued. 'There's somebody else in my car already. Is that all right, Gemma? Mrs Wilkinson?'

Gemma nodded weakly and took another full breath closer to her apparently imminent demise. Her mother clasped my hand in her podgy damp ones. 'It's so good of you, doctor. Do you think they'll mind?'

'I rather doubt it,' I said. 'Now, let's get Gemma out of here and on the way to safety, shall we?'

Gemma, it transpired, was feeling too faint to walk, and Gemma's gathered family, friends and general passers-by were too weak to carry her the short distance down the drive. I duly obliged, slinging her over my shoulder and making my way out to the car with the whole entourage following in a neat little crocodile down the path behind me, like a well-rehearsed play.

I put Gemma down briefly, on the bonnet, while I opened the door. None of the assembled audience seemed to think it necessary to help, perhaps reckoning I would just tip her in through the open window. Gemma herself stared unblinkingly through the windscreen.

The fresh air must have given her a second wind. 'I thought you said there was someone else in 'ere?' she said.

'Under the tarpaulin,' I said. 'He's there all right, if you want to look just a little closer.'

She looked a little closer. 'Is 'e asleep?' she asked.

'In a manner of speaking,' I replied. 'Asleep on a permanent basis, you might say. In fact, he's dead. I was just on the way to the mortuary with him when I got your call.'

Gemma's face went completely white, then grey, and then an interesting shade of vermillion. Not that vermillion would be a colour she would ever have encountered. She drew a deep breath and screamed at the top of her voice, 'Mum, there's a dead man in 'is car and I ain't goin' to 'ospital with no dead body an' I think I'm feeling alright now.'

And with that she hopped nimbly off the bonnet of my car and sprinted back into the house, brushing aside the startled crowd around her. They all turned back slowly to look at me with expressions of varying astonishment on their faces.

'Looks like we've effected a bit of a cure,' I remarked mildly. 'I wonder if it might just turn out to be permanent?'

And with that I climbed casually into the driver's seat and drove off.

I was becoming quite used to having Mr Jenkins in the back of my car by now.

He was the perfect travelling companion – no trouble, didn't interrupt my train of thought, and seemed completely at peace with the world. So it was with a strange sense of impending loss that I eventually arrived at the undertakers late that evening, only to encounter another minor logistical difficulty. The place was shut, and in complete darkness. Of Leon, there was not a sight to be seen.

There was, however, a note addressed to me on the door, which I read with an increasing air of resignation.

'Mike, the car's been fixed but I've been called away to Barnstaple on a coroner's case. Sorry – can you let yourself in? The trolley's in the usual place, and Mr Jenkins can go on the third shelf in the big fridge on the left. Hope that's okay – help yourself to coffee if you want it, you know where the kettle is. Thanks for everything – owe you at least one drink for this. Leon.'

As he well knew, I had my own key to the back entrance of the mortuary and I could easily have transferred the late Mr Jenkins to the trolley, and thence to the big fridge on the left, but for one small fact. I had not the least idea what I had done with the key.

I looked helplessly at the door, which remained stubbornly closed, and then back at the car. Mr Jenkins seemed entirely unconcerned by this latest twist of fate. It was by now pitch black, and it was becoming chillingly cold. 'As cold as a morgue,' I thought, shivering a little. What on earth to do? And then the idea came to me.

It was so simple, really. Mr Jenkins could stay overnight in my car, in the security of my garage, and I would deliver him bright and early the next morning to his next resting place. No one would know, no harm would have been done.

I drove back to my surgery. There was still work to be done.

It was nearly midnight by the time I arrived home.

I had rung and left a message for my wife on the answerphone, telling her I would be late and not to worry about waiting up. The house was in complete darkness. As I crawled wearily into bed, next to her soundly slumbering body, I breathed a final sigh of deep relief.

A long and difficult day successfully negotiated, I decided. At least nothing else could go wrong now.

It is well known amongst my friends, relatives and compatriots that I am not all that good at remembering the daily minutiae of life.

Like taxing my car on time, or close relatives' birthdays, or even when my wife is going abroad on business. That sort of thing.

A bell was ringing in my head. It kept ringing, and ringing, and as I finally stumbled through various layers of consciousness, I realised it was the telephone. I picked it up and mumbled a sleep-ridden 'Yes?' into the mouthpiece.

'I'm at the airport,' said my wife. 'You were sleeping so peacefully when I left. I knew you'd had a late night, so I didn't want to wake you. I'll be back on Thursday.'

'Mmmm,' I responded. 'Have a nice time, then.'

'You hadn't forgotten, had you?' she asked perceptively.

'No, no, of course not,' I lied, maybe a little unconvincingly.

'Thought so. Now, try not to do anything too ridiculously stupid while I'm away, won't you. It's only three days and surely even you can keep out of trouble for that long. Oh, and by the way, your car was blocking me in, so I've taken it and left the keys to mine on the kitchen table. Funny smell in the back of yours, though – better get it checked out when I come back… Oh, they're calling my plane, must rush. Bye now, and just make sure you behave.'

The phone went dead just as the full enormity of those last few sentences struck home.

I sat bolt upright in bed, suddenly wide awake, and to the steady burr of the dialling tone I yelled out forlornly:

'Airport? Which bloody airport…?'

# 13
# Cynthia (and the Ogre and the Vicar)

Cynthia was a regular.

She had the thickest set of notes in the entire practice, and although Emily Watson and her clan were making a determined bid for the top slot, they still had a precipitous climb to negotiate. And Cynthia was relentless.

She came to see us at least twice a week, sometimes more, which might have been almost acceptable apart from one minor detail.

There was absolutely nothing wrong with her.

She also had the irritating habit of ringing the surgery just after arriving home from a consultation, ostensibly to check she had got all her medications right.

'Did you say rub it in three times a day or four?' she might say, or 'Can I take it with a glass of orange?'

'You can try,' I replied on this latter occasion. 'But do remember they are suppositories, won't you?'

I once encountered her in town, outside the Post Office, holding court to a small coterie of her cronies. She tried to avoid my eye. What we both knew is she had rung earlier that day asking for a visit, saying she was too weak to come in.

'Feeling better now then, Cynthia, are we?' I asked pointedly. 'Better than you were, say, first thing this morning?'

'Perked up no end, thank you, Dr Sparrow,' she responded shamelessly, without a hint of embarrassment.

Now she sat before me once again, for the fourth time that week. My partner, Dr Harper, had just returned from holiday and it had fallen to me over the past two weeks to do a double Cynthia shift. She was halfway through some diatribe about how the cat seemed to have the same water trouble as herself when a grey mist descended before my eyes. I think it was prompted by fear because I was at the time envisaging a future populated entirely by Cynthias, stretching on to eternity.

I was drowning in them, unable to breathe. Cynthias everywhere, spreading beyond the horizon as far as the eye could see, thousands upon thousands of them pouring over the hills and down into the valleys. Flooding the plains.

Serious and immediate action was called for.

'Cynthia,' I said suddenly, interrupting her just before she got to the fascinating section where she began to grade her urine output in terms of colour, volume and ease of passage, giving it marks out of ten for clarity and degree of froth. 'Take a look at your notes, will you?'

I held the first volume up, my arms quivering under the weight.

'They are the thickest in the county, if not the entire galaxy,' I continued. 'The Guinness Book of Records have been begging me to count the pages, or at the very least measure their circumference. They wanted me to leave out the cardboard folders, but I said no, the twenty-two of them are an integral part of the collection.'

She sat there, for once dumbstruck, completely taken aback. I decided to push home my advantage.

'All over Brazil they are preparing plantations as we speak, dedicated to you. In twenty years' time these plantations should provide enough paper to see us through volumes 50 to 200, should we both live that long. The British Library wants to preserve your records for posterity, and is already preparing another two wings for their storage.'

Cynthia remained very still, marshalling her defences.

'I've not been so well, doctor,' she began at last, but I was ready for that. It was how she had started every conversation we had ever had, and there had been enough of those for several of my lifetimes. I'd heard it a thousand times before.

'I've heard that a thousand times before, Cynthia,' I said. 'You start every consultation and phone call I've ever had with you that way, and then continue to punctuate your conversation with it at every available opportunity.'

I put on my best 'This is getting really serious' face and persevered. 'But now I want you to face something. You have been to see either Dr Harper or myself twenty-six times in the past eight weeks, ninety-two times in the last six months. I've counted. And that's not to mention the emergency service – fifteen times – or casualty – nine times – and goodness knows how many phone calls to the surgery in between. The local ambulance crew know their way to your house blindfold – they've started running time trials between there and the station, and there's a sweepstake on for the fastest trip every month.

'And yet throughout all these consultations, not once have we ever said anything different to you, or treated you in any different way. So why do you keep coming to see us, for goodness' sake?'

'Because I'm just not well, Dr Sparrow,' she said doggedly. 'You don't understand.'

She had spirit; I'll give her that.

'But you are well, Cynthia,' I said. 'I say so, Dr Harper says so, the cardiologist says so, as do the gastroenterologist, the urologist, the neurologist, the chest physician, the dermatologist and the entire surgical department. The collective opinion, Cynthia, the overwhelming weight of evidence, is that you are all right. You are okay. You are not ill. There is nothing medically wrong with you. You are devoid of physical ailments. You just ain't sick.'

I later offered the transcript of this conversation to the Monty Python team. But they said they had already done it.

'But…'

She managed to squeeze the 'But' in just as I was pausing for breath, but I wasn't about to let her off the hook, not now I was warmed to the task in hand.

'But what, Cynthia? Look, I've recorded the gist of our last fifty phone calls with you, and our resultant advice, and they all boil down to just two things – we either say that it's okay to take another Valium or we tell you shouldn't be taking the cat's water pill just because you can't find your own.'

'But…' she tried again, more weakly this time as she began to wilt under the pressure.

'But nothing, Cynthia,' I persevered. You even rang me last week to ask if I thought All Bran or Bran Buds would be better for your digestive system.'

'And which one did you say again?' asked Cynthia, spotting an opening. 'I forget things so easily these days. My memory...'

'All Bran,' I said, exasperated.'

For a moment, Cynthia just sat and stroked her chin. She had quite a lot of chin, and it took a fair bit of stroking, but this was a sure sign that she was thinking.

It was the quietest I had ever seen her.

My phone rang, and as Cynthia was still lost in some world of her own, no doubt wondering how she might ultimately turn all this to her subsequent advantage, I answered it surreptitiously.

'How are you doing?' whispered Dr Harper. 'Are you winning?'

'In the balance,' I muttered, raising a quick eye to look at Cynthia, who remained oblivious to the conversation. 'What are the odds I can get a month without her making an appointment to see either of us?'

'My Ferrari for a fortnight,' he said without hesitation, 'and no mileage limit.'

'Make it a month,' I replied.

'Against?'

'You being on call for the rest of the year, or £1,000 in the currency of your choice.'

'Done,' he said instantly, 'I'll have it in used fivers, please.' He put the phone down, still chuckling.

I turned back to Cynthia, with renewed resolve. This was now more than just a crusade – this was business.

She stopped stroking her chin, opened her mouth and set off in earnest. 'Then what you're saying, doctor, is that I shouldn't come and see you anymore?' Her top lip started to quiver as she made a show of fumbling in her handbag for the tissue I knew full well she kept up her sleeve.

Cynthia was about to cry. My role was to crumble quietly and beg her to forgive me for having been so impossibly hard-hearted. Just like last week, in fact.

Now this actually raises a serious point – what should a doctor do when a patient begins to cry in front of them?

Without wishing to sound in the least bit chauvinistic, crying is mostly done by female patients in front of male GPs, and sometimes that happens before we have managed to say anything at all, so it can't always be our fault.

I think sometimes they cry because something has been building to a crescendo while they waited to see us, and they just can't keep it in any longer. And sometimes I think they cry because they are in the privacy of a room where it doesn't matter who sees them, as long as it is someone who is on their side.

I once went on a course where, hidden amongst the usual lectures about bowel cancer, Parkinson's disease and do-it-yourself cardiothoracic surgery, was an hour's slot innocuously titled 'Patients, doctors and their relationship'.

I ambled towards the lecture hall, groaning inwardly as I considered the subject of the talk to come.

'Pubs are open,' I whispered to the pleasant-looking chap walking next to me.

'Yes, they are,' he agreed amiably. 'Can't go myself, though.'

'Why not?' I asked. 'Go on, live dangerously. It's bound to be more exciting than this next talk. God, who wants to listen to an hour of "Patients, doctors and their relationships"?'

'I can't,' he repeated. 'I'd like to, but I can't.'

'Why not?' I asked.

'This lecture,' he said. 'I'm giving it.'

I generally detest this sort of lecture.

They tend to start with the speakers establishing their own credentials for fifty-five minutes, itemising the research they've carried out, the letters they've accrued after their name, the invitations they've received to garden parties at Buckingham Palace (or 'Buck House', as they cosily refer to it), and what they've had published in the *British Medical Journal*. They then spend the last five minutes answering any questions you have.

But this chap was different.

He sat quietly behind the desk, waiting until we settled, as if totally undeterred by our presence. Only when the lecture theatre was completely still did he begin.

'We are about ninety per cent men in here today, and I would like to ask you all – what do you do when a female patient suddenly starts to cry in front of you?'

Having never really thought about it to any great extent before, I was fascinated, and genuinely surprised by the collective response. What should one do? How had I approached it up until now?

Around eighty per cent of the male GPs said that they would walk over to the patient and put an arm around them, as if crying was some unwritten invitation to a hug. But I had never done that, and I began to wonder if it was me that wasn't getting it right.

On reflection, I virtually always reacted in precisely the same manner.

'I'm out of tissues,' I would say sympathetically. 'Hope a bit of kitchen towel will do,' and as I walked slowly past them to my examination room, I would rest my hand briefly on their shoulder if I thought it was the right thing to do.

By the time I came back, they had either composed themselves or were weeping inconsolably. And for me, although I am no expert, companionable silence was the answer, until they were ready to tell me what they needed to unload.

So there was I, and there was Cynthia.

She sat looking down at her interlocked fingers in her lap, poised to launch into her frequently rehearsed 'Poor little me, I'm so ill and misunderstood' speech, which she did so remarkably well it had never yet failed to get the desired response.

Not until then, at least.

'Cynthia,' I said firmly, 'go and be well for a change. It's a bit of a challenge, I know, but see what you can do. At least just try it for a month.'

I don't know who was more shocked, Cynthia or myself.

In a fit of petulance, she gathered up her belongings, thrust out her chin and stumbled out into the waiting room with her best 'He doesn't understand me at all' expression on her face.

After a moment, I strode out into the waiting room, where I felt a 12-ton weight lifting from my shoulders as I watched Cynthia trudge slowly back to her car. Dr Harper's Ferrari was as good as mine.

Later, my last patient of the morning disposed of, I leant back in my chair, put my feet up on the desk and settled down, eyes closed, for a few minutes of blissful repose. Peace at last. A whole month of Cynthia-less consultations to come.

And then the intercom buzzed, and somehow I knew. I just knew who it was going to be. I picked up the receiver with a heavy heart, and my receptionist spoke the words I was dreading.

'It's Cynthia on the phone,' she said. 'She wants to know, when you said a month, did you mean a calendar month, or just twenty-eight days?'

There is a completely true, if slightly unexpected, footnote to this tale.

Cynthia had a husband, Hubert. Whereas she was large and always completely in your face, he was rarely seen, a small man with a seemingly non-existent personality, probably subsumed by her presence.

They owned a silver Smart car, which Hubert invariably drove, with Cynthia somehow shoehorning herself into the passenger seat. Viewed from behind, Hubert's head barely showed above the driver's backrest, and all too often it appeared surreally that Cynthia was alone, in the passenger seat of the vehicle, as it weaved itself along our winding country lanes.

Hubert hardly registered a blip on our radar, and even after twelve years I barely knew the man. He was either remarkably thick-skinned, or totally under his wife's control, or much more of a man than we gave him credit for. I used to joke that the reason she was so large, and he so small, was that she ate all his food before he sat down to dinner.

I met them, once, in the local supermarket, and I realised for the first time that Hubert had a surprisingly dry sense of humour.

'Hello, Dr Sparrow,' he said, 'nice to see you. I would introduce you to my wife, Cynthia – over there by the fish counter – but I understand you know her rather well already.'

The phone call came in from the out-of-hours service just before seven o'clock in the morning.

'Sorry to bother you, Dr Sparrow, but Cynthia Hall rung in a few moments ago. And, yes, I know you will go "Not again" but she says she needs to speak to you urgently.'

'She always wants to speak to me urgently,' I sighed wearily. 'No matter what time of day. Bank holidays, Christmas morning…'

There was a short delay at the other end of the phone, and then…

'Sounded like it was important, though. Her number is…'

'I know her number off by heart,' I said.

I had a quick shower and a cup of coffee before succumbing to the inevitable with an inward sigh, dialling pretty much with my eyes closed. Cynthia answered on the first ring.

'Oh, Dr Sparrow, it's so terrible,' she gasped. 'I don't know what to do.'

'Same as always, Cynthia,' I said. 'Take another Valium and ring in for an appointment when the surgery is open.'

'No, no… you don't understand.'

'I do understand, Cynthia. We have been here so many times before, haven't we, and we always manage to find a way round it.'

There was an eerie silence at the other end of the phone for a few moments, and I thought I could hear her sobbing.

'No, you really don't understand,' she managed at last. 'It's Hubert –I've just come downstairs and found him dead in his chair. Could you come? Could you come now, please?'

I sat and looked at the phone for several minutes after I had put it down, then picked up my car keys and walked out of the door.


'I've been out with Mary, the new student, on that visit you asked us to do,' said Sally, the district nurse, shuddering visibly. 'You didn't tell me, did you?'

'Tell you what?' I asked.

It had apparently taken them a while to find the house, tucked away down a long drive on the outer reaches of the practice.

'Oh, we found it in the end,' she said, 'despite your meticulously detailed directions. But when we got there…'

'After fully five minutes of knocking,' she continued, 'the door was finally opened by what at first sight appeared to be a human version of Shrek, and at second sight seemed to be something darker, more sinister and scary. He didn't even have any of Shrek's humorously redeeming features, and at least computer-generated images are devoid of overpowering body odours and are unlikely to drip green slime over your uniform. It was terrifying.'

The ogre had then apparently spoken.

'Have you come to see Jorrrrge?' he drawled in a low, guttural monotone.

'Er, no,' stuttered Sally, completely taken aback. 'We've come to change Mrs Arnolds' dressing,' her voice rising to a squeak, 'if we're in the right place, that is.'

'But what about Jorrrrge?' he persisted, glowering down at her.

'I'm afraid I don't really know who Jorrrrge is,' stuttered Sally, trying unsuccessfully to recover her composure. 'According to the notes of my predecessor – that would be Emily, she's been here a lot – there's never been a Jorrrrge here before.'

'Well, there is now,' bellowed the giant, rocking from one club foot to the other. 'There is a Jorrrrge here now, madam, and I think you should be seeing him.'

'Are you Jorrrrge?' asked Sally suddenly, a flash of inspiration striking her.

'No!' came the answer as he stamped his foot on the slate floor and half the living room ceiling fell down behind him, 'I'm Fernley, but this...' he said, dropping his voluminous trousers surprisingly adeptly, 'this is Jorrrrge. Shouldn't you be taking a look...?'

'I've never seen anything like it,' said Sally, beginning to shake uncontrollably.

I was trying unsuccessfully at this point to keep a straight face.

'It was like something out of one of those futuristic Arnie films,' she continued, 'or anything with Sigourney Weaver in it. This... this huge fungating mass was growing out of his leg like some sort of self-sustaining life form. I half expected it to detach itself and crawl across the floor before wrapping itself round my neck and draining the life from me with blood-curdling wolverine howls.'

'Oh, you have to be exaggerating,' I said dismissively, in that middle-aged GP put-down voice I have worked so hard to perfect. 'Or maybe not,' I reflected quickly, catching the look of horror on her face.

There were, I knew, some branches in the car park, but none of them bore olives. I improvised quickly.

'So what did you do?' I asked.

'I suggested he brought Jorrrrge in sometime to see Katrina,' she said, recovering her composure for a second and grinning wickedly. 'I thought it would be good for the both of them...'

Katrina was our then 'retainee' in the practice, working four sessions a week to keep her hand in while bringing up her young family. She hailed from the dizzy proletarian heights of Kensington, and had moved with her husband down to the West Country only a matter of months before. Tall, blond and willowy, she had yet to fully acclimatise to the earthy realities of rural life.

'She burns all them oils in 'er room,' one of my patients informed me mysteriously. 'Them homophallic ones you see on the telly. Don't 'alf smell nice, bu' you never quite knows what's in 'em, do you?'

'Homeopathic,' I corrected, 'or at least, I would imagine so…'

Sometime later, we were all waiting expectantly as Katrina came out from the resultant consultation, looking positively green and apparently in need of somewhere to vomit.

'I asked if I could see it,' she said in wonderment, 'but if only I'd known…'

We don't keep smelling salts and brandy in the practice for nothing. I poured myself one of the latter.

'…so I explained to him that the best approach would be for me to take a biopsy, to investigate further.' She gulped.

'And?' I asked, trying hard not to seem too unsympathetic.

'Oh, you don't need to be worrying about thart,' he replied. 'I'll just break a bit off for you…'

Our vicar has a particularly droll sense of humour, and I always looked forward to his infrequent visits to our home.

We soon set aside his blood pressure, weight and recently alarming cholesterol levels and got down to the real business of the day.

We both believe God will prevail, but in largely divergent ways. Graham, like most of his creed, does the important stuff – births, marriages and deaths – in his own inimical style. And he does it brilliantly. He's married me twice, christened or blessed all of my five children (from six different mothers) and one of us will ultimately attend the other's funeral.

Our conversation soon turned to recent occasions he had officiated at, and, marriage being a singularly unhumorous event, we inevitably started contemplating the latest batch of funerals to have come his way.

'You would have enjoyed my last Saturday afternoon,' he said, smiling in that uniquely benevolent way of his. 'A couple of interesting funerals I had. First chap, he was a farmer I knew, died of a heart attack at the age of forty-five.'

I pursed my lips. 'Worryingly close,' I admitted, adding 'Forty-two and counting' to address his gently enquiring expression.

'Oh, he'd had some sort of problem for years,' continued Graham, 'medical, you know – your department, not mine – needed an operation or something, but kept saying he was far too busy working to bother with little things like that. And so he died as he lived, just as he would have chosen, toiling away at home on the farm.'

I could see him beginning to bite his lip. I was already chewing my own, dinner being late again that evening.

'The service was quite interesting, though. Full of reminiscences from his friends.'

I could see this was going somewhere. I just didn't know where.

'He was quite a character, was Alan. He wasn't married, you see, and he put an advert in the paper one day for a wife.'

'Really?' I said, intrigued. 'Did he get many replies?'

'I'm not all that sure,' Graham grinned, 'but he certainly deserved something for his efforts. He wrote "Fit, active farmer in early forties, sense of humour, likes outdoor activities, seeks like-minded woman with tractor with view to long-term relationship, possibly marriage." And then he finished with "Please send photo of tractor".'

I was giggling helplessly by this stage.

'The next funeral,' Graham expanded, 'was of a chap a bit older. A sad story, really. He was a road digger, quite healthy as far as anyone knew, but as he and his wife were preparing for bed one night he just keeled over with a heart attack too, quite unexpectedly.'

'Two in the one day,' I mused. 'You were a busy chap.'

'Ah, but that's not all,' Graham went on. 'His wife, who was of course in the bedroom with him, panicked and decided to run round to the neighbours for help.'

'No telephone?' I asked, wondering what was coming next.

'Didn't stop to think,' said Graham. 'Down the stairs, across the hall, out through the front door and down the path she ran – she wasn't a small lady, you understand, and in the heat of the moment she had neglected to notice that she had undressed for the evening but had not as yet actually got round to putting her nightdress on.'

The picture was forming vividly in my mind.

'And what did the neighbours say?' I asked.'

'Well, she didn't get quite that far,' explained Graham, now totally deadpan. 'Her husband – being a road digger, as I believe I had mentioned, had been doing a little late work that night, and unknown to her had dug a hole in the road outside their house to check on a leaky water pipe.' Pantomime pause. 'But he hadn't quite had the time to fill it back in again.'

'And she…' I began.

'Filled it in for him,' nodded Graham, 'breaking her leg and getting wedged in the bottom of the hole in the process, calling out in the darkness for someone to come and help her.'

'And what happened then?' I asked, scarcely breathing.

'It was a cold night,' he said, 'and unfortunately nobody heard her, or came by even.' He drew a deep breath and added, straight-faced, 'I did her funeral just after her husband's.'

You could never quite be sure, with Graham, just how much to believe.

# 14
# Matters of Life and Death

Jack lived in Bratton Clovelly, a small rather cut-off village some ten miles north-west of the surgery, past Roadford Reservoir and up hill and down dale thereafter.

He was a widower of some ten years, having nursed his wife through the end stages of breast cancer with great dedication and tenderness. Physically, he could have auditioned for any production of *Snow White* as Happy, a smile always on his face and a sunny demeanour that rarely altered. I am sure he wouldn't have minded me referring to him as rotund, and as for his hair...

'When I lost what I had on the top of my head, I thought I'd better make up for it on the bottom,' he would declare cheerfully, stroking his white/yellow beard that the old man in the Edward Lear limerick would have been proud to possess. His only daughter, Vicky, lived just over an hour away and would drop in whenever she could, and Jack seemed as content as one could be, given his circumstances. In those days I used to undertake a weekly branch surgery in the Bratton Clovelly village hall and would generally call in for a coffee and a chat with Jack on my way home. He always seemed glad of the company.

Mostly I would find him seated at his dining table, surrounded by the accoutrements of his new-found love, painting.

'Never drew a thing in my life before,' he told me one day, 'until after Cynthia was gone. But I needed something to do, and I potter away. Helps pass the time in the quiet moments. Not that I'm any good, mind.'

But he was good, more than good, producing intricate depictions of local village cottages and other scenes. One used to hang on my wall at the surgery, but now adorns my office at home. The painstaking detail and reproduction are uncanny, and I continue to marvel at his talent, especially as he was self-taught in his latter years.

Jack disappeared off the radar for a while, as patients often do, and re-emerged with a terminal diagnosis of widespread prostatic cancer, with a prognosis of just a few months.

'I'm so sorry, Jack, I didn't know,' I apologised when next passing by, shortly after he had been discharged from hospital, looking grey and unwell.

'It's not your fault, Mike,' he shrugged ruefully. 'I didn't know either. I went into hospital over a weekend in retention, and then it all went from there. It's like they suck you up at the beginning of your diagnosis, and then spit you out at the end when you are either cured or beyond any further help. They did all these tests, and I wanted to ask you what they meant, but I knew you were so busy...'

I have now just torn up my CV for Doc and am rewriting it for Grumpy. The oncology (cancer care) department at Derriford employed good people with generally poor communication skills. And I felt I had somehow let Jack down. I should have known what was going on in his life and been there to help.

All that was left for me now was to pick up the pieces as best I could, and see him through to the end.

Jack died quietly at home three months later, as uncomplaining as ever. I rarely drive past his house these days, but when I do I stop by his front gate and gaze across the valley behind his makeshift studio, admiring the shifting colours he encapsulated so beautifully in his sketches.

I had so many lonely patients without a purpose, but Jack showed there is a way to move on, if you can just summon up the energy and accept that life may not always be how you would choose it to be.

'I thought you were going to Jack's funeral,' said Jo, my practice nurse, a week or so later.

'I am,' I answered. 'It's not until one o'clock, and it's only just gone twelve. Plenty of time. I was just writing up the notes for my last patient and then I'll be on my way.'

'Funeral's at twelve thirty,' Jo sighed. 'Sometimes I wonder how you ever get anything right.'

It is, I think, just under thirty miles from the surgery car park to Bodmin Crematorium, and I can now report to you that the journey can be done in nineteen and a half minutes. Not should be done, but can be.

As I screeched to a halt and threw myself out of the car, I saw with relief that the hearse was just pulling away from the front of the building and that the last couple of mourners were still filing in. My running days were pretty much over by then, but, ignoring the pain in my knees, I sprinted across the divide, slid in through the automatic doors and sank gratefully on to a wooden bench at the back of the chapel of rest.

Job done. Except...

After a couple of minutes drawing breath, I started to look around. The vicar was quietly eulogising down at the front, the congregation were listening with solemn intensity and all was as calm, peaceful and serene as any such proceedings should be. There was only one problem.

I didn't recognise anybody there.

I craned my neck over the couple in front of me, hoping to see Vicky, Jack's daughter, in the premium seats, in fact hoping to see anyone I knew. When something of magnitude happens in Bratton Clovelly, the whole village celebrates, or mourns. It was beginning to dawn on me that the whole village wasn't there.

I motioned to the gangly usher on my left, who glided Jeeves-like across to my side and bent down obsequiously to my level.

'Um,' I said tentatively, 'whose funeral, exactly, is this?'

'Clearly not, I think, sir,' he intoned nasally, 'the one you were anticipating.'

Have you ever tried surreptitiously leaving a funeral you didn't intend to be at?

I met Vicky in the car park half an hour later, at the right time, in the right place, for the right service, and told her my story.

'He would have liked that,' she said, her eyes brimming with tears. 'And he wouldn't have been surprised. Because much as he respected you... Thank you for getting it so wrong, because when I remember today in years to come...'

She fell silent for a moment.

'...it will be with a smile on my face. It's what Dad would have wanted.'

I loved Friday summer evenings at work – the sun sinking towards the distant Dartmoor hills, the birds singing joyously, the surgery waiting room finally empty as barbeques were lit and cold cans of beer and bottles of wine were opened, and laughter was all around.

But that's enough about my staff before they went home.

It was one such Friday summer evening, and the waiting room was empty. I sat, as usual, on the back step, a beer in my hand, and watched as the Canada geese squawked their way across the sky in a jagged V shape, same as usual, regular as clockwork. There was a knock on the door, and Sally, the last receptionist standing for the week, poked her head through.

'We've had an urgent call from Mrs Brice,' said Sally, pausing for a moment before she spotted me out at the back. 'It's her mother – they think she might have had a heart attack, and they are on the way to Launceston Hospital. They're wondering if you could meet them there.'

'I could,' I agreed, 'but somehow I don't think I'll be needing to...' I said as an ageing and wheezily asthmatic Ford Cortina pulled up with a screech of what was left of its brakes. 'I hope they haven't left any rubber marks on the tarmac.'

'You're all heart,' replied Sally, peering closely at her reflection in the computer monitor and adjusting her lipstick. 'You got a mirror?'

'What,' I wondered out loud, 'do I pay you for? Because it's not your compassion and empathic tendencies.'

She looked at me disparagingly.

'Cute. You do the healing and macho posturing,' she decreed. 'I do reception and staff manicures. We get paid accordingly. Go treat.'

Mrs Brice and her impossibly tall husband had uncoiled themselves from their vehicle and were standing uncertainly in the car park beside it, waiting for me to come down and join them.

'I think,' said Mrs Brice faintly as I descended the back steps. 'I think she's dead...'

I moved round to the passenger side of the car and stood looking inside for a moment or two. And then I nodded.

'I'm very much afraid that she is,' I agreed.

'So what happens now?' Mrs Brice asked quietly.

'Well...' I hesitated.

Just over eighteen months ago, Mrs Brice's father, a man with advanced Parkinson's disease, had fallen down a flight of stairs and been admitted to our local major hospital in a coma. Rather than allowing nature to take its course they had pulled out all the stops to save him, much against the family's wishes.

'We felt like we were not in control,' I remember their daughter telling me at the time. 'It was like they were always pursuing their own agenda, not ours, and kept quoting protocols at us. But grandad was never a protocol, he was family, our flesh and blood. None of them had ever seen him as a real man, who dangled me on his knee and told ridiculous stories to my brother and sisters about a life before we were born. A man who survived two world wars, and so much else. A man we all cared about passionately, and wanted to die with dignity, and in peace.'

He never regained consciousness, dying more than six long months later. And if that wasn't hard enough for them all to bear, there was then an inquest into his death, which meant his body could not be released until that was all over – another four months of torment.

I knew what was in her mind.

'We can't go through all that again, Dr Sparrow,' she said, looking to her husband for confirmation. 'We just can't.'

He took her hand, and they stood and looked at me in anguish, obviously praying I could come up with an answer for them.

'What should happen now is that I call the coroner,' I said gently, 'as this is a sudden death and I haven't seen your mother for several weeks. They will send out the duty policeman to take down all the details, and then your mother...'

Tears were forming in her eyes.

'Your mother will have to go to Barnstaple for a post-mortem to be done. It shouldn't be more than a couple of days. Hopefully no inquest this time.'

Mrs Brice had now folded herself in her husband's arms. He looked at me over her head.

'Is there another way, Dr Sparrow?' he said, a note of desperation in his voice. 'Is there anything else you can do?'

Ethel and Maybelline Hutchings lived in one of the neighbouring towns in the far reaches of the practice. They were spinsters, both in their mid eighties, and Maybelline was wheelchair-bound following a series of minor strokes.

Ethel cared for her sister as diligently as anyone could wish, and would invariably bring her into the surgery when she needed to be seen. So many times I had said to her: 'Ethel, if you need one of us to visit, I promise you we will always come. You should never have to struggle in to see us. Dr Harper and I both understand how difficult it is for you to make your way in here, and you must know by now that Dr Harper only lives a mile down the road from you.'

But so independent were they that they would not dream of paying any attention to our protestations. Whenever Maybelline needed a consultation, her sister would somehow get her to us, no matter what the cost or difficulties of the journey.

'It's so far for you to come,' they would both say. 'The last thing we ever want to be is a nuisance to you, and we've been patients here for so long. We don't want to change to somebody nearer, not at our time of life. Not till we have to.'

'You are never a burden, Ethel,' I would reassure her. 'I just wish I had more patients like the pair of you.'

Maybelline had been diabetic for many years, and was now on insulin after a long – but eventually unsuccessful – spell of oral therapy. Despite Ethel's meticulous care she had now developed several painful leg and foot ulcers which had proved resistant to all our routine therapies.

'I don't know what else to do, Mike,' said Lexi, our district nurse. 'I've tried just about everything I can think of, but nothing seems to be doing the trick. Have you got any bright ideas?'

'Just about everything?' I replied, picking up on her choice of words. 'What does "just about everything" mean? Have you tried acupuncture, voodoo… a pressure wash at the local garage?'

She screwed up her nose in quiet contemplation.

'You really have no right to be a GP, do you?' she observed good-naturedly. 'I can't understand how you've deluded the local population for so long into thinking you have the vaguest idea what you're doing here. But yes, in answer to your question, there is something we haven't tried yet. As far as I know it's only been used in hospitals up to now, and that has been on a trial basis. I'd need to go and do some research.'

'Oh, research,' I mused. 'That's what proper doctors and nurses do, isn't it? It's not for us backwater folk with our cloth caps and handcarts.'

'And,' I continued, 'I'm guessing "new" and "hospital-based only" equals "expensive"?'

'Isn't Maybelline worth it?' shot back Lexi. 'Aren't any of our patients worth it? Would you deny someone a possibly life-saving treatment purely because of the cost? Are you that cold and calculating?'

'Ouch,' I said, raising my arms in submission. 'I guess I deserved that. Go research, then, and come back when you have something to show me.'

A gentle smile of victory spread across her mouth.

'You pretend you're so tough, Michael,' she purred, 'but you're as soft as putty, right there in the middle, where you don't want anyone to see.'

'Get out of here,' I growled.

Research, indeed. Nothing wrong with a good old-fashioned poultice, that's what I say.


I didn't see Lexi for a couple of weeks. She had been on holiday and came bounding back into the surgery a fortnight later looking tanned and buoyant.

'Maggots,' she announced brightly as she entered the back office.

'Whatever you choose to eat when you're away from us is entirely your own affair,' I replied. 'But despite that, I have to say you look pretty good on it.'

'Do you eat them while they're still wriggling?' asked Sally, aghast. 'Like those celebrity jungle people? Or do you wait until they're stunned from being put on the hook?'

Lexi and I exchanged glances.

'Trouble is, she means it,' I said. 'But she's good with the patients. I think that's why we employ her.'

'Maggots,' repeated Lexi, 'I think they might just be the answer.'

'Well, eventually,' I agreed, after a moment's thought. 'Dust to dust, ashes to ashes, flesh to maggots...'

'Oh, shut up, Mike. Look, I've been reading up about it. It's never been tried in general practice, as far as I can tell, but I don't see why we couldn't give it a go. Here,' she said, reaching into her briefcase, 'I've brought you some literature. It's okay, it's not in joined up writing or anything. Take a look at it and tell me what you think.'

Later that night I read through what she had given me, trying my utmost not to get excited but growing ever more intrigued by the prospect. It might possibly work. It just might…

I glanced at the clock. Not too late. I picked up the phone.

'Lexi,' I said, 'I think you might just have something here.'

'That's what I've been telling you,' she said. 'I'll order some first thing in the morning.'

The great day finally arrived – as did the maggots, by special delivery. The courier handed them over with a look of distaste, as if we were indulging in eighteenth-century witchcraft.

'Sign here,' he said. 'Anybody. I just want to be out of here.'

'Good God, would you look at the price of them,' I spluttered. 'I could have just left a couple of pheasants rotting in the garage for a fraction of that.'

'Ah, but it's not just the maggots,' Lexi explained. 'It's the dressings, and the home visits as well. And anyway, these guys have been specially bred to eat only rotting flesh. They leave the healthy tissue alone.'

And they were in truth rather cute, these maggots. Little white wriggly things, like newborn lambs gambolling in the early spring meadows… maybe a simile too far.

'Sweet, aren't they?' I observed. 'And so tiny.'

'Yes, but they're only babies,' Lexi advised. 'Give them a couple of weeks and they'll be the size of marrows, if we let them.'

'Bit of a strain on the dressings, then,' I ruminated.

'Well, it would be,' Lexi said, 'but that's why we change them every three days. After that they get a bit frisky, and go wandering up the nearest available limb looking for something more exciting to eat.'

I peered into the flask again, reassessing. They now had a certain… how can I put it… voraciously hungry look about them. These maggots were ready to get to work.

Lexi and I drove out for the inaugural application. Maybelline was really quite intrigued.

'Will it hurt?' she asked curiously.

'No,' Lexi assured her, 'they only feed on the dead flesh. It may itch a little, but otherwise you shouldn't feel a thing.'

We all watched intently as Lexi applied the maggots, dressings and relevant phone numbers to one of Maybelline's feet.

'In case of emergencies,' she explained. 'Not that we are expecting any.'

'And very tasty you must look to them, too,' I suggested. 'A little salt and basil, perhaps, maybe some melted butter... yum.'

Maybelline and Ethel took it all in good spirit.

'You will have your little joke, Dr Sparrow,' they said in unison. 'Not all that funny, of course. But we are so grateful to you for allowing us to give it a try.'

'Save your thanks for Lexi,' I said, registering internally that if anything at all should go wrong it would be entirely her fault. But if it went right... I could be a trend-setter. I'm still young enough to appreciate an official recognition from Her Majesty for all that I've done. Or maybe a road in the village named after me when they next start building.

It was a Friday night again, but winter now, and it was cold, and dark, and miserable outside. In my office the heating still warmed my aching limbs, a last cup of coffee sat on my desk. I almost didn't want to venture out into the inclement evening.

I had just turned the computer off and was shutting down for the evening. The weekend beckoned, full of hedonistic pleasures such as... well, maybe some gardening and a visit to the local council tip. Live life to the full, that's my motto.

The security light in the car park flicked on suddenly, bathing the back of the surgery in a brilliant white light. A car I didn't at first recognise pulled in, probably a last-minute prescription collection, I assumed. I carried on checking I had everything I needed and wondering whether that bottle of gin from a new local distillery a patient had brought me in earlier that day merited a quality control tasting session before braving the elements.

I was inclined to think it did, when the phone rang.

'I have Mrs Davey here at the front desk,' said Mandy, the only other member of staff left in the building. There was a sense of déjà vu building here. 'She was bringing her father, Graham, back from a hospital appointment, but she doesn't think he is very well and wonders if you would mind taking a look at him.'

I sighed inwardly, mouthed 'Sorry, not just yet' at the bottle of gin, and said 'Okay. Ask him to come through.'

'He's not actually in,' said Mandy. 'More sort of… out. Still in the passenger seat, in fact. Could you take a look at him outside?'

I let myself out through the back door, descended the half-dozen steps to the car park and crossed to where Mrs Davey had pulled up at an angle to the building. Inside, I could just make out the worryingly static figure of a plump man in his late sixties, naked from the waist up, head sagging on his chest. I crossed to the passenger side, opened the door and took stock of the situation.

I had been here before, but in such different circumstances.

'How do you think he is, Dr Sparrow?' came a voice from behind me, making me jump. 'He took his shirt off because he said he was so hot. How is he?'

Mrs Davey's father was cold and not breathing. Mrs Davey's father was dead.


I leant into the car, reclined the seat, and pushed Graham's head back as far as it would go, opening his airway as best as I could. I had no equipment, no back-up, no plan B. I wasn't at all sure if what I was about to do constituted a plan A. But it was all I had. Even if I could have dragged him out of the car and lain him on the tarmac, his chances of successful resuscitation, I calculated in a nanosecond, were zero.

The car park light, time-controlled, had switched off again, and it was so dark Graham's daughter could not see what I was about to do. I thumped him so hard on the chest I was convinced I had fractured a couple of my wrist bones. Less importantly, maybe several of his ribs as well. Graham jerked forward, coughed and took a one-off laboured breath.

'Get in the car,' I said tersely to his daughter, 'and drive as quickly as you've ever done in your life to Launceston Hospital. Just do it, do it now, and don't stop for anything or anyone.'

'But…' she stuttered.

I pushed her roughly into the driver's seat, switched on the ignition, and stood back.

'Go now,' I shouted at her. 'Go now if you want a chance for your father to live...'

I had sent a dead man on a seven-minute journey into another county. If he lived, I would be a hero. If he died...

I had been in the minor injuries department at Launceston earlier that day. Peter, the head nurse and the most competent man in his job that I knew, was on the late shift. As Graham's daughter revved up her car and sped off up the drive, I was already on the phone to Peter.

'There is a dead man heading for your car park,' I said bluntly. 'Get all the staff you can mobilise out there, resuscitation equipment to hand, and have an ambulance all sirened up and ready to go. His life and my future depend upon it.'

'I'm on it,' said Pete.

I do hope so, I prayed silently.

He was as good as his word. By the time Graham's daughter arrived, Launceston Hospital outpatients department was like *ER* with bells on. On reflection, I didn't save his life. I just made the decision that allowed better qualified people to do it for me.

Graham arrested three times in the ambulance journey from Launceston to Plymouth, so it was touch and go, but the paramedics, the ever fantastic paramedics, resuscitated him each time and kept him alive until they reached A & E at Derriford Hospital in Plymouth, when the emergency staff took over. Against all the odds, he survived to live another twelve years into his eighties.

I don't think he or his family have any idea what I did. I sleep better, knowing that.

There is always another way, if you think long and hard enough about it. Mr Brice was waiting expectantly for my decision.

'Well,' I said, 'suppose when you drove into our car park your wife's mother was still alive, and died just after you had arrived here. Then I could have issued a death certificate without any problem. Suppose...'

'What are you saying, Dr Sparrow?'

'Suppose we realised she was still alive for a moment, after all?'

There was silence for a moment.

'I can't believe we are having this conversation,' Mrs Brice said, 'on this beautiful evening, with my mother dead in our car. Things like this are not meant to happen to people like us. We're just ordinary folk, trying to live ordinary lives.'

'There are four of us here with a say in this – the three of us out here and your mother in there.' I looked them both in the eye. 'Is there any one of us who would choose a different way?'

'No,' they agreed together, without a moment's hesitation.

'Okay,' I said, 'Let me reconsider this. I think your mother is still moving.' I reached into the car and took her hand. 'And there is a pulse – weak and thready, but definitely there.'

We all held our breath for a minute. I let go of her wrist.

'I'm afraid she's gone,' I announced sadly. 'May she rest in peace.'

'No one must ever know,' I added, 'a sort of career-defining moment, you see.'

'No one ever will,' Mrs Brice said, clasping my hand in her own. 'Thank you, Dr Sparrow. Thank you so much for what you have done.'

And then they got back into the car and drove her mother home again.

The first time I ran into Mrs Brice after that day was outside the crematorium, when I was part of the procession of mourners shaking her hand after the service.

'My husband and I, we've been so worried about you,' she said. 'We know what a risk you took for us, and we can never thank you enough for it. Are you comfortable with what you did?'

'I am,' I confirmed, without a second's thought. 'How about you?'

'So are we,' she said. 'So are we.'

The maggots worked a treat.

We returned as planned three days later, and Maybelline's foot was looking wonderful. Lexi changed the dressings expertly, rescuing a couple of itinerant wanderers from Maybelline's knee, and one particularly adventurous specimen close to her groin, without comment. Until later.

'That one was probably on heat,' she said as we drove away.

The experiment had been a wonderful success, so far, and I decided to leave the follow-up in Lexi's capable hands. If all was to go well from now on, I would happily try leeching again in the future.

That visit to treat Maybelline happened on a Friday afternoon, and I went off in good spirits for the weekend. Sadly, however, Maybelline died the following day from a massive but unrelated stroke. It happens. It was my weekend off, so I did not learn of it until Monday lunchtime.

And, as is so often the way in general practice, I reflected quietly for a moment and then moved on, until later events brought it back to the forefront of my mind.

One of the routine tasks of a GP is to sign death certificates (and, if relevant, a cremation form, which is always good news, because we get paid for that). Maybelline was due to be buried and had already been certified deceased by another doctor over the weekend, so I did not need to travel to the undertakers to see her body.

One of the undertakers we visit most frequently is just down the road from my children's school, and it was not uncommon for me to call in there after collecting them in the afternoon on the nights they were staying with me.

'Where are you going, daddy?' asked Cressie, then aged six, as I pulled into the car park on the first such occasion.

'To see a dead body, darling,' I said honestly.

'Oooh, can we come in too?' they chorused.

'No, of course not,' I answered immediately, appalled. 'What would your mother say, for goodness' sake?'

'She'd be very, very cross with you,' grinned Cressie perceptively.

'No change there, then, daddy,' put in Charlie brightly, and we all started giggling.

'Pleeeease, daddy,' begged Cressie. 'Pretty, pretty, pretty please.'

'Don't pout,' I said, turning off the ignition and opening the door. I had my own key to the funeral directors' building and as I fumbled in my pocket for them two little figures sidled up to me with 'we'll be very good' smiles on their faces.

'Well, okay then,' I relented, making a sudden decision. After all, maybe this was the right time to introduce them to some of the harsher realities of life. 'If you really want to...'

'We do, we do,' they squealed excitedly.

In truth, Charlie, aged eight, was the more timid of the two, hanging back a little as we entered the chapel of rest. Cressie strode boldly ahead.

'So where are all the bodies?' she demanded. 'I thought they would be on slabs like on the telly, covered in vinegar running down a drain and with their chests cut open.'

'That's what's called a post-mortem,' I explained patiently, 'where they try and decide what people died of. And it's formalin, not vinegar. This is where the bodies come afterwards. It's a place of peace and quiet contemplation. Where their relatives come to grieve, if they want to, before the funeral. To say their last goodbyes.'

'So where are the bodies?' she persisted. 'I can't see any of them.'

My daughter was then six, going on seventeen, and totally fearless. I'm not sure if at that stage I worried for her future, or for the man who might one day share it.

'They keep them in a really big fridge,' Charlie piped up unexpectedly. 'Is that it over there, daddy?'

It was. To the right was a whiteboard with the names of the occupants written in red crayon. I opened the door. The lady I had come to see was the second one down in a column of five, covered in a white shroud. The top shelf was empty.

I thought for a moment about what I was doing, but Cressie was getting impatient.

'Can I see that one first?' she asked, pointing.

I slid the trolley half out and lifted the sheet.

An elderly lady, beautifully laid out, was lying serenely within. Cressie took a long, hard look.

'Just like she's sleeping, daddy,' she observed.

Charlie finally plucked up courage, tiptoed across the tiled floor and peeked hesitantly under my shoulder before scampering back to the safety of the doorway.

'Yuk,' he announced expressively.

'That one,' said Cressie, tapping the bottom shelf emphatically. 'Now I want to see that one.'

'That one,' I checked. 'You're sure?'

'Yes, daddy. And then that one and that one,' she continued, jumping up and down excitedly. 'I want to see them all.'

I wondered, during the next twenty-four hours, if I had done the right thing by letting them in. What with early mornings and late nights, it was a couple of days before I saw them again, collecting them once more from school.

But I need not have worried. They were both waiting there at the gate for me, with a little knot of their friends, chattering away excitedly together.

'Daddy, daddy,' they called out as soon as they saw me. 'They all want to know if they can come and see a dead body too...'

The day of Maybelline's funeral dawned. Ethel had decided in the end that it would be a cremation.

'I'm an old lady, Dr Sparrow,' she had said, 'and we were two spinsters. No children, no close relatives. We were all each other had, really, all our lives, so there would be nobody to tend her grave after I have gone. Or mine, I suppose, and we would neither of us have wanted that. So we will go out the same way together. Ashes to ashes.'

The service was scheduled for two o'clock in the afternoon. I didn't routinely attend my patients' funerals, unlike my predecessor, Dr Margaret, who went to each and every one. Time generally just didn't allow, and besides, I only had the one suit. It didn't do to be seen out in it too often in the same year.

Lexi came in late and we discussed her morning visits. She was just leaving when she turned back suddenly, saying, 'By the way, Mike, did you remove Maybelline's maggots and dressings when you went to see her body?'

I sat back, open-mouthed.

'I didn't need to go,' I said, my mind racing. 'She'd already been certified by somebody else, and she wasn't for cremation then. Besides, I thought you would have done that.'

'But I never went back,' she stuttered. 'I was away for a few days, and we nurses don't, generally, anyway. There isn't much point.'

We turned as one and glanced at the clock. An hour before the service.

'Quick,' I said decisively. 'There's probably still time. I'll drive...'

We intercepted the hearse on the way to the church, flagging it down in a side street.

'I'm not quite sure how we are going to explain this,' I murmured, but Lexi, resourceful as ever, had a quiet word with the undertaker who had pulled up by the kerb with a bemused expression on his face.

He walked back to the following entourage and waved them on to the church, following which Lexi and I climbed into the rear of the vehicle to reclaim our lost charges. And then we thought again, as a low humming and buzzing noise assailed our ears.

'What happens if we open the coffin now?' I said suddenly. 'What do maggots become if you leave them too long?'

'They become flies,' Lexi said soberly. 'Hundreds upon hundreds of them...'

We looked at each other, and we both sighed.

'Let's get out of here,' I suggested, and Lexi nodded in agreement.

They cremated Maybelline that afternoon as planned, just a little later than originally intended. Or at least, they cremated what was left of her...

'They only eat dead flesh,' Lexi had said presciently.

# 15
# Bill and Ben, and Some Unusual Bequests

If you come from my generation, you grew up with black and white television and the 'Watch with Mother' programmes. You remember Bill and Ben the Flower Pot Men, and their friend Little ('Flobbolobodob') Weed. I am no longer ashamed to admit I fervently believed they were real, and secretly searched for them at the end of our garden when my parents thought I was grubbing for worms or checking on the welfare of the frogs in the next-door neighbour's garden.

Well, we had our very own Bill and Ben. William and Benjamin Gladstone, to be precise, who came to register at the practice in my early years. One tall and stooping, the other upright and virtuous. From that moment, they disappeared off our radar, neither of them in need of our services. No illnesses, no past medical history, no medication in need of surveillance. Cheap patients to run. I wished I had more of them.

I would see one or other of them on the odd occasion in the village shop when I collected my morning paper, Bill polite and communicative, Ben withdrawn and taciturn in his ubiquitous windcheater, turned-down cap and ever-present dark glasses.

'Morning, Ben,' were generally two words wasted for the day.

He tripped over on the pavement one morning as I drew up outside the shop, wincing as his elbow struck the path. I leapt out of the car and helped him to his feet, dusting down his jacket and picking up his shades, holding them out to him until he had regained his composure.

'You okay, Ben?' I asked. 'I could run you back home if you want.'

He met my eyes briefly.

'Thanks, but no thanks,' he answered gruffly. 'I can take care of myself.'

I watched him walk unsteadily down the road, unsettled but not knowing quite why. Perhaps I should call him in for a health check soon, I thought, run some blood tests and maybe get to know the private man a little better. Or maybe I should just mind my own business, I argued with myself, and let him live the life of his choosing. It wasn't like we were related or anything.

'You have to understand, Dr Sparrow,' Bill confided in me when I bumped into him later that week, 'we come from such a different upbringing. Our parents were so well off when we were young, and we, especially me as the older son, had all the privileges – private school, our own ponies, servants in pinafores, the real *Upstairs, Downstairs* dream. But my father was a gambler, and one day he lost it, lost it all. Our mother left and we never saw her again. Ben, he didn't mean to be rude to you, but…'

'You never married?' I asked. 'Either of you?'

Empathy my middle name. Curiosity my first.

'My wife and children were killed in a car accident over twenty years ago,' he said sadly. 'Killed by a young girl who had her first and only epileptic fit at the wheel, they said, not to blame. She still sends me a Christmas card from time to time. She's now married with two young children, and I know she continues to carry the guilt, and will take it to her grave. And I want to forgive her, but yet…'

He turned away, though I knew his eyes were watering. I pretended not to notice.

'We all have sadness in our lives,' he said finally, 'and our crosses to bear. Ben is an ex-serviceman, four tours during the Northern Ireland troubles. When he left, he joined the fire brigade. First responder to any accident on his patch – motorbikes in the days when riders weren't obliged to wear helmets, buses that went under bridges without a low height warning sign, blazes that ate up all the oxygen in the surrounding area and devastated lives. Corpses that were unrecognisable, blackened and decaying. You name it, he saw it. It scars a man, and he has never recovered.'

'I'm sorry,' I admitted with a sigh. 'I didn't know.'

Bill shrugged and held out his hands in a gesture of resignation.

'How could you? We don't talk about ourselves much, we Gladstones. It's all I can do to get him out of the house once a month to collect his pension. Everyone has to live with their memories, Dr Sparrow, and I guess,' he added shrewdly, 'you will have some of your own. You rarely see us, but we know what you do, what the village thinks of you.'

Three weeks after that conversation, Bill was admitted to hospital by the out-of-hours team with a heart attack, teetering on the brink in intensive care for a couple of days before pulling through. I called at the house two or three times in his absence when I was passing, but Ben was either out or more likely refusing to answer the door, locked in his self-imposed hermitage.

'He's not been in for his pension this week,' observed Tony behind the counter of the village shop as I stopped by for my health-giving lunch ingredients – a pork pie and two packets of Smarties. 'No one's seen him since his brother was taken ill, Dr Sparrow. Do you think we should be doing something?'

'I'll try and call again,' I promised. 'I guess it's just his way of dealing with things outside his comfort zone.'

We all hide away from reality when the Grim Reaper parks his car at the end of our lane, sitting casually on his scarlet red bonnet, watching and waiting for our next move.

People surprise you, though.

'Morning, Dr Sparrow,' said Bill breezily, emerging from the local farm shop as I skidded to a halt in the gravelled car park. 'Sudden attack of hunger?'

'Elderly lady collapsed in the restaurant,' I sighed. 'No paramedics within thirty miles. But I thought you…'

'A brief brush with my maker,' he said wryly. 'But a couple of stents, a bucketful of drugs and they tell me I'm as good as new. Well,' he shrugged, grinning broadly, 'second-hand at least. You take nothing for granted at my time of life.'

'And Ben?' I asked. 'I tried to look in on him while you were in hospital, but…'

'You know Ben,' he said. 'Well, mustn't keep you from your little emergency. See you around, Dr Sparrow.'

191

My patient, Mrs Soby, was slumped in a chair by the window, looking grey, her daughter Heather hovering uncertainly beside her.

'We tried to put her head between her knees,' she said, 'but it wouldn't reach.'

I glanced quickly around.

'On the floor, now,' I ordered briskly. 'No, your mother, Heather, not you. A cushion for her head, a chair for her feet.'

'I'm not wearing a petticoat,' Kathleen Soby muttered feebly.

'Nor am I,' I said. 'Just do as I say, and everything will be okay.'

Five minutes later, Kathleen was looking pink and respectable again, sitting up in confusion.

'Dr Sparrow,' she said indignantly, looking down at her décolletage. 'What were you doing holding on to my feet?'

'Saving your life,' I explained. 'Nice lunch?' I added, casting an eye over the remnants on the table. 'You know, pasties and sherry don't normally mix all that well when you reach a certain age. Have a nice rest of the day.'

She had the grace to blush, and I had the decency to look away as if something else had caught my eye. I smuggled an aubergine and a sweet potato into my pockets on the way out.


'Derek on the phone for you,' said Lynne, my receptionist, putting him through before I had a chance to ask 'Derek who?'

Derek the policeman would have been the answer, despite the fact that for the first few years I knew him I always referred to him as Geoff, for no particular reason either of us could understand. Just like I always called Wendy the cleaner's husband 'Norman' when his name is actually Tony. Derek was a comforting presence whenever one was needed.

'Mike, I'm outside at the Gladstone's bungalow,' he said, 'and I think I'm going to need your help. Three days of milk on the doorstep, and a cat crying to get in. Have you seen either of them lately?'

'No, not for a while. Give me five minutes, Derek, and I'll be with you.'


He was sitting outside in the sunshine, relaxed and at ease and talking on his radio as I drew up.

'Tough life for a copper,' I greeted him. 'How are we going to get in?'

'Never met a policeman who didn't know how to kick a door down,' he answered. Thirty seconds later, we were in.

The front door opened into the living room, which was neat, orderly and empty of all human life. As was the kitchen, the small dining room and the first bedroom. We found Bill lying on the floor next to his bed in the second, right arm tucked awkwardly beneath him, a small wound on his forehead presumably from when he fell.

'Death confirmed at?' I asked, holding up my bare wrist and raising an eyebrow.

'14.05,' Derek replied. 'But don't you want to hold a mirror to his mouth, or feel his carotid pulse or something?'

I gave him a withering look.

'Thought not,' he said.

And then we looked at each other, and said simultaneously...

'Where's Ben?'

They never found him, nor did they locate a single living relative.

But the mystery was finally resolved when a young couple moved into the empty property several years later, and on clearing the living room found a concealed safe beneath an old dresser.

'Thought you might like to take a look at this,' Derek said casually as he tossed a letter on my kitchen table.

'Off duty or on?' I asked.

'End of shift and on my way home.'

'Bottle of beer and a cigarette?'

'Thought you'd never ask.'

We sat outside in the evening sun as I read Bill's spidery scrawl.

To whom it may concern

If you should ever find this, then I know I will be long dead and buried, but questions will still hang over us. There comes a time when I have to address them.

My brother Ben died a few days after we moved here, ironically in the passenger seat of the car as we drove back from registering at the local doctors' surgery. I was devastated, but I had to think quickly. I took him out to a place where I knew he would be at rest, somewhere you will never find him. The bungalow was mine, but our income was almost exclusively Ben's – his soldier and fireman pensions, his disability allowances would die with him. So I became both of us, with trepidation at first but then with more confidence as no one noticed. History will of course judge me, but was it so wrong? And in the end, a greater power than any of us will decide on our destinies.

No one ever guessed, because no one ever asked. We always regarded ourselves as outsiders, welcomed into the village on the back of our histories, but never worthy of a grave or monument in the place of our choosing.

I am sorry for anyone who feels let down by my actions, but ask yourself – what would you have done in my situation? A man has to live, after all.

William Gladstone

'What would you have done if you had known?' I asked.

'I have no idea,' admitted Derek, 'but that's all immaterial now. We none of us knew, did we, and you can't second guess anything all this time later. Thanks for the beer, Mike. Catch up with you in due course.'

It was an unusual bequest. My predecessor, Dr Margaret, was once offered the pick of a treasure trove of antiques, but my best offer to date had come from Mr Sandyman, an elderly and rather lonely widower up on one of the small village estates.

'I shall be gone soon,' he said sadly, 'and you've been so good to me I want to leave you something. Take a look around you – is there anything you would like?'

'Not really,' I admitted honestly. 'But,' I added as a thought struck me, 'are you aiming for a burial or a burny-up job.'

'Oh, I don't want to be buried,' he shuddered, 'and besides, Betty and I couldn't have children. There would be nobody to tend my grave,' he finished wistfully.

'That's okay, then,' I reassured him. 'I'll get myself something nice from the cremation fee.'

His next-door neighbour, a spritely, mischievous spinster, had planned her own deathbed surprise in the event of her unexpected demise.

'I've left the house…' (in fact a very upmarket four-bedroom bungalow with magnificent views over the valley) '…to my estranged sister in New Zealand,' she confided in me one day.

'A sort of final gesture of reconciliation,' I mused. 'That's rather touching.'

'Not really,' she twinkled. 'You don't know my sister – she gives bitter and twisted a bad name. I've made her the sole executor of my will so she'll have to come over here and deal with it herself. It will take her months and cost her a small fortune, but what she won't know is that five years ago I remortgaged it to the hilt and spent it all on an eighteen-month round-the-world trip. It'll probably kill the old trout when she finds out, but I rather hope not – I'd like to think she could suffer a bit longer at my expense.'

'Anthea Thomas!' I said in mock indignation, 'I didn't think you had it in you.'

'Yes, you did,' she said with a wink. 'And I shall have a last request for you, too, Dr Sparrow.'

'Anything,' I agreed readily.

'I'd like you to meet her for me when she comes over, keep her alive for as long as you can and check that she is as miserable as she can be.'

I never knew what Anthea's sister had done to deserve such displeasure, but it didn't matter.

'It's a deal,' I grinned.


I have often said, and even more frequently thought, that a well-trained chimpanzee could do much of my job as well as I could.

Sore throat and fever for three or more days? Give them some penicillin. Marital problems? Hand over the Relate leaflet. Brittle, unattractive nails? Wear gloves more often, or stay home. Easy, isn't it?

But there are just those one or two times when you do make a difference, which sort of makes up for all those other times when you don't.


I had just visited Hazel, a recently widowed lady in her mid seventies who was badly crippled with arthritis. Reg, her much-loved husdband, had recently died suddenly from a ruptured aortic aneurysm and she was struggling to cope.

'It's too much for me,' she said. 'I can't even manage the stairs, let alone the garden – he loved his garden, did Reg, especially his greenhouse. I have so many memories here but I think I'll have to move. Maybe I'll find a warden-controlled flat somewhere – I shall hate it but it's all I can think of doing.'

'Oh, something will turn up, Hazel,' I reassured her. 'Something always does.'

'I wish I could believe that, Dr Sparrow,' she sighed, 'Oh, how I wish I could believe that.'

As I walked down the short drive from Hazel's house, deep in thought, a man in his mid sixties hailed me apologetically. It was Mr Parish, a semi-retired local journalist, obituaries his speciality. A trail of blood dripped in his wake.

'Sorry to touble you, Dr Sparrow,' he said, 'but as you can see I have a bit of a problem.'

He held up his heavily bandaged hand.

'Years of rigorous training and a keenly developed sense of observation,' I said thoughtfully, 'make me suspect you have in some way damaged your left hand.'

'That's why we all think so highly of you,' he concurred. 'Your uncanny perception and unrivalled clinical acumen. Witches were burned at the stake for less.'

'What have you done to it?' I asked.

'Rearranged the contours of my index finger with a chisel,' he grimaced. 'Would you like to see?'

He unwrapped his temporary bandage, a large rather oily rag, and displayed his finger to me. There was a bit missing. From the second joint up he had sliced down the thumb side of the finger, neatly bisecting the nail in half.

'Nice work,' I congratulated him. 'Where's the rest of it?'

He rebandaged his hand, reached into his trouser pocket and carefully withdrew a piece of kitchen paper.

'Ah, there it is,' I exclaimed as I unwrapped it. 'All in one piece then.'

'I wondered whether I should put it in my mouth to preserve its tissue viability,' he said, adding, as I raised an eyebrow, 'read all about it in the *Reader's Digest* once. What do you think?'

'Well it's certainly not going in mine,' I said firmly.

Joking apart, I was uncertain what to do next. The nearest hospital capable of dealing with this was more than an hour's drive away, and that was before you had to negotiate the minefield that is the casualty department. I was no expert in half-severed fingers, but I was sure that the detached segment would not survive the delay until surgery could be arranged.

'Well,' I said thoughtfully, scratching my head, 'it's an unusual situation, I must say, and not one, to be honest, I've encountered before.'

I explained to him my concerns about what might happen if I merely transferred him to the local hospital.

'How about you stitching it back on?' he asked.

'The problem with that,' I admitted truthfully, 'is that I'm not at all sure I'm capable of doing it. It's a bit out of my league.'

'I'll sign any disclaimer you like,' he promised, 'and a large cheque to any charity of your choice if it's successful. Anyway, to be honest, do we have a viable alternative?'

'No,' I said slowly. 'I don't believe we do.'

I drove him back to the surgery and for an hour and a half painstakingly and diligently sewed back the severed part of his finger with tiny, delicate stitches. Eventually I stood back, surveying my handiwork.

'Looks pretty good to me,' said Mr Parish.

'Looks absolutely bloody wonderful,' I confirmed, 'considering I think I might have sewn it on upside down. Only joking,' I added as he raised his eyebrows, 'No promises, Trevor. I've done the best I can.'

Three days later he was back for a dressing change, and we both held our breath.

'My God,' I said faintly, as Jo, my Rolls-Royce of a practice nurse, gently removed the last piece of bandage. 'Oh, my God.'

Far from being the necrotic mass I was anticipating, it looked wonderful – pink, healthy and healing far beyond my wildest expectations.

'About that cheque,' I reminded him, 'I don't think I'll be needing it. This is the best reward I could ever have wished for.'

Over the next four weeks his finger progressed steadily, and after two months it was as good as new. You could still see the scar, but even that faded over the following months, and was fully functional to a degree I would never have thought possible. His fingernail, about which I had had the gravest doubts, was impeccable, having regrown without so much as a blemish.

Trevor Parish was now entrenched as one of my greatest fans, an ever faithful advocate of my surgical skills, and he would brandish his finger to one and all with a ready explanation of my prowess. And for once I would suspend my natural reticence and self-deprecatory demeanour and admit that I was proud, in fact very proud, of what I had managed to achieve.

I dislike receiving solicitors' letters. At best they bring with them an additional workload, and at worst every doctor's dread of an intended legal suit. But this one was different. I sat and read it twice at the end of morning surgery, smiled to myself and set out on a visit.

'Hallo, Dr Sparrow. It's nice to see you, as always, but I didn't ask for a call. I'm quite well, really, or as well as I ever shall be.'

'Are you going to ask me in, Hazel, or shall I just stand here and freeze to death on the doorstep.'

'No, please, what was I thinking of?' she apologised. 'Do come through.'

'Well, it's like this, Hazel,' I explained as we sat down in her lounge. 'You remember Mr Sandyman, from up on the Churchlands estate?'

'Yes,' she said, puzzled. 'Poor man, so lonely after his wife died, and for so many years.'

'I had completely forgotten,' I continued, 'but because he had no surviving relatives – he left the bulk of his money to a range of charities – he asked me several years ago if I would be one of his executors.'

'He always spoke highly of you,' she nodded.

'One of my tasks is to help in the disposal of his assets,' I said, 'which includes his bungalow up on the hill. Lovely view over the valley, a small easily maintained garden, kind and helpful neighbours and I was wondering... would you know anybody who might be interested?'

'You mean...?' she gasped.

'I've checked with the solicitors and estate agent and they have assured me there would be no problem in offering it to you without putting it on the open market. What do you think, Hazel? No warden-controlled flat among strangers somewhere, but a home you can easily manage close to all your friends.'

She sat quietly for a few moments, blinking heavily.

'If a woman of my age could throw her arms round her doctor, I would do it right now,' she said finally. 'Thank you so much, Dr Sparrow. I don't know what to say.'

'You just said it,' I smiled. 'Don't forget to invite me to the house-warming party.'

Amidst the seemingly never-ending drudgery of daily life as a GP, it is rare indeed for me to feel proud of myself twice within the same month. Moments like these are what makes it all worthwhile.

And then there are other moments that are just... well, you'll see.

'Mike,' said Alisson determinedly, 'I'm having my baby this weekend, at home, and I want you there, but I don't really want to see you.'

I wanted to say 'How do you know?' but Alisson of the immaculate blonde bob already had three other children, and sat on lots of important committees. I wasn't about to argue.

'I realise you'll technically be off duty,' she continued, 'but having known you for the past twenty years I know you won't let me down. The midwife will do all the important stuff, as they always do, but I want you there as my security blanket. We'll provide the daily papers and a wet dog to stroke, and you can go away when it's all over. Oh, and we're not at home at the moment – we're renting while the house is being done up. Turn right past the Portgate pub, up and down a couple of hills and we are round the corner from where Stan and Martha used to live. You remember them, I expect?'

A force of nature, Alisson, and not one to be denied. I gave her my home number – again – and promised I would do what I could. Which I knew would be doing just what she was asking.

How did she know, though? My home phone rang at 10 a.m. on Sunday, a time when even my dogs are usually still asleep.

'Hope I didn't wake you,' she said, knowing me of old. 'Midwife is on the way, my husband Pete is out with the dogs and the kids have been banished to friends. We'll be expecting you by eleven, if that's okay with you. Time for you to grab a coffee before you come, if you want.'

I was about to speak but the line went dead, and I sat there looking at the phone in my hand. Same old Alisson, but we had been friends for years and I didn't mind one little bit.

I found their temporary home easily enough – the first of two rows of semi-detached cottages at right angles to the road. Although I had forgotten to check out the number of the house, I recognised the midwife's car parked outside the nearest front door.

I let myself in and took a quick look around. Wet dog in the corner, tick – although it was a lugubrious-looking basset hound who peered at me over the rim of his bed and clearly decided I wasn't interesting enough to leave the warmth and comfort of his cushion to come and investigate. Strange, though, I'd always had Alisson and her family down as golden retriever/black Labrador people, but then you never know.

Spread out on a table inside the door was the *Sunday Independent* and yesterday's *Daily Mail*, but there was no need to panic – I'd stopped off in Lifton on my way there and collected my treasured *Sunday Telegraph*. I spread it out, sank into a beautifully aged brown leather armchair, and started to read.

A man and his Sunday crossword can easily get lost in each other's company, and so we did. The final clue, one that had been troubling me from the start, came to me with one of those 'Doh!' moments. As I wrote it in with a beam of satisfaction, I heard footsteps on the stairs and glanced up.

A well-preserved man in, I guess, his mid fifties stood there with two stunning-looking girls of no more than thirty, all staring at me with amazement. They were none of them wearing a stitch of clothing. We regarded each other in silence for a moment.

'And you are?' said the man at last.

'Dr… um… Sparrow,' I admitted, too slow off the mark to adopt a classy alias.

'The midwife made the same mistake,' he acknowledged, pointing over his shoulder with his thumb. 'Left her car outside. But she arrived earlier, before we… anyway, you should be next door, immediately behind us.'

I slunk out, shaking my head, and trudged round the corner.

Right house, wet Labrador nudging my leg, *Sunday Telegraph* open on the table, bacon sandwich awaiting and coffee on the hob. Newborn baby uttering its first cry, and proud mum tucked up in bed cradling her first son delightedly.

'Good to see you, Mike,' said Alisson. 'Been here long?'

'Long enough,' I sighed.

Like I said, we don't get it right all of the time. But we usually get there in the end.

And then there is the out-of-hours car shift – that last bastion of unpredictability in the comfort zone of general practice. There you are at the coalface, the lives of thousands in your hands, poised to strike at the twin evils of injury and disease wherever they should arise. It is the cutting edge of the emergency services, where critical and challenging decisions must be made in the blink of an eye when faced with the unexpected… well, sometimes at least.

Saturday afternoons often brought international rugby matches live on televisions we couldn't sit down in front of. On one occasion, Mike, the driver, and I had already encountered the critical case of a woman in a warden-controlled flat who had rung in saying she was unable to get out of bed. When I finally managed to gain entry – the warden apparently being out at the cinema – I moved her Zimmer from across the room by the door to next to her bed without comment.

Next up was Olive, who had had a 'funny turn' the day before – from which, I should point out, she was fully recovered – and was surrounded by interfering neighbours.

'She's on her own, you see,' one of them gushed, 'and we were so worried.'

'So, Olive,' I asked, suddenly curious. 'How long have you been on your own, exactly?'

'Nigh on forty years,' she replied promptly.

It was time for a very deep breath…

'Give me strength, Mike,' I said, as I climbed back into the car. 'That or a double brandy.'

'Another good call then, was it?' he said, grinning. 'Well, never mind, maybe the next one will make you happy.'

George and Mary Colwill lived in a tiny end-terrace house with a dramatic view overlooking the castle. Fortunately, they were both pretty tiny themselves. If you stood one on top of the other – well, they would probably both fall over to be honest, but, if by some miracle they managed to balance – they would have made barely ten feet between the two of them.

'It's me 'usband,' said Mary by way of introduction. 'Fell over the back o' the settee this morning, 'e did, and 'ad to get those nice paraplegics in to pick 'im up – I'm too little, you see. On 'is way to the toilet, 'e was, an' they took 'im for me. Ever so kind, they was.'

'Yes, ever so kind,' agreed George suddenly, obviously feeling a bit left out of the conversation.

'...an' then they brought 'im back in 'ere again after. Well, we 'ad a bit of breakfast, didn't we George, 'im on the settee there, 'e don't move around too much these days, an' then 'e needed to go to the toilet again an' you can't keep calling them paraplegics, can you...'

'Paramedics,' I interjected.

'...cos they've got their own Olympic Games and stuff, and what with washing the ambliance... but luckily our friend Arthur came round, an' 'e took George to the toilet – 'e's good like that, Arthur, isn't 'e George – an' brought 'im back as well. But Arthur's gone now an' George needs to go to the toilet again an' we don't know how we're goin' to manage. So, could you 'elp us, doctor, in our hour of need?'

You couldn't be cross, could you? Well, I couldn't. They were so endearing with their contradictory dependability on others on the one hand but fiercely determined intent to remain in their own home on the other. But there was a bit of a dilemma looming.

I am of the old school and will, in general, turn my hand to most things not directly involving vomiting children. But I do not do toilet runs, not ever. Not even for George.

'Okay,' I mused. 'Do you have any family that might be able to help?'

'Well, there's Alfred,' said Mary, brightening. ''e'd always do anything for anyone.'

'Good,' I enthused. 'Let's go for Alfred, shall we? Can I give him a ring for you?'

'No, dear, I'm afraid not. Alfred's not on the phone, you see.'

'Could we send someone round, then?'

'You could try, dear, but it wouldn't be very much 'elp. Poor ol' Alfred's passed away some time now, dear love 'im.'

'Landmine,' said George suddenly.

'I'm sorry,' I said. 'How awful for you.'

'I know, dear,' said Mary wistfully. 'Loadin' it on the lorry, 'e was, when 'e put 'is back out and couldn't get out of the way of the tank comin' up be'ind 'im.'

You couldn't make this up, could you?

'But there's Gertie, my niece, she's always ever so good too, an' she lives just down the road from 'ere, doesn't she, George?'

I liked the sound of Gertie.

'And she's alive, is she?' I asked guardedly.

'Oy yes, dear, we 'ad a card from 'er yesterday, didn't we, George? Always kind and thoughtful like that, is Gertie... it's on the mantelpiece, dear, if you care to look. Looks rather nice there, doesn't it?'

'Yes,' I agreed, looking over my shoulder. 'I've heard Australia can be very pleasant at this time of year.'

There were no more Arthurs or Gerties or Alfreds, and I was just beginning to wonder what Mike's price might be when inspiration struck. There's always an answer, isn't there, if you know just where to look.

'So, who looks after you?' I asked. 'On a day-to-day basis? Helping around the house, shopping, that sort of thing?'

'Well, there's Elizabeth, our 'ome 'elp. She's our lifeline, isn't she George, always so cheerful an' does everything she can for us.'

'And she's not dead, or on holiday, or visiting her mother in Cleethorpes?'

'Oh no, dear, nothin, like that,' said Mary, a look of sheer delight enlivening her face. 'In fact, she'll be 'ere in about twenty minutes. She can take George to the toilet, can't she? Oh, thank you, doctor, thank you so much for your 'elp.'

Eat your heart out, *ER, Casualty, Holby City*. This is where you find the real cutting edge.


Ten years later.

I had just returned from holiday, facing the usual runaway juggernaut of unopened mail. Two-thirds of the way down the pile, there it was, by recorded delivery and stamped with the name of the most litigious firm of solicitors in the county, if not the entire world. I groaned inwardly.

'At the request of our late client we have been instructed,' I read, expecting what followed to involve hanging, flogging or surgical removal of my life's savings, 'to inform you of a legacy.'

A holiday villa would be nice, I thought. A season ticket to West Ham, maybe, or just rather a lot of gin.

I read further.

'This will be delivered to you at the above address within the next few days.'

There goes the holiday villa, I thought, given how difficult it would be to post through the letter box. But the reality, when it arrived, was more bizarre than I could ever have imagined.

A well-wrapped parcel arrived the following day, marked for my personal attention. As I pulled back the layers, intrigued, a small mahogany box finally lay before me, a gold inlaid inscription on the top. There was an accompanying note.

'It has been many years,' it said, 'but I have never forgotten. I wanted you to have this as a mark of respect and appreciation for your help far beyond the call of duty. It is of course of absolutely no financial worth, but I hope by now you will not be in need of such things. I am glad that the one other service I might have done for you I will not be around to attend to, and wish you a long and healthy life.'

I opened the box. Encased, Damian Hirst-like, in plastic, was the like of which I had never seen. I re-read the inscription.

'Mr Parish's Finger,' it said.

# 16
# Mrs Axleby's Knickers and the Tractor Episode

My life as a GP ranged from the sad and mundane to the bizarre and unaccountable. And I although I mostly wouldn't have had it any other way, just occasionally I think I might have.

'Sorry,' said Sally, cradling the phone to her ear as I wandered towards the back office looking for something soft and uncomplaining to kick. Maybe the surgery cat. 'It's one of the local paramedics,' she continues, 'can't think of his name but I recognise his voice. He says he needs to talk to you.'

I took the call in my room.

'Hi, Mike... it's Marcus,' came a familiar voice over the phone.

'Hi, Marcus. You well?'

Small talk my speciality.

'Uh – yes, thanks. Look, Mike, I'm at Ken Pitcher's house...'

'What a great place,' I enthused. 'That view from the upper balcony, and those gardens – just incredible. What's he up to, then? Haven't seen him for a while.'

There was a pause at the end of the phone.

'Mike... we've been called out on a 999 call. He's.... um... he's not up to anything, I'm afraid. He's dead, Mike. I'm so sorry.'

'Oh, you're joking,' I said faintly, sagging back into my chair. 'Tell me you're joking...'

But I knew that he wasn't.

Ken's grandson had played rugby at every schoolboy level with my eldest lad. We had stood on cold, wet, windy touchlines together, driven back triumphantly from unexpected tournament wins, and sat proudly in the empty stands at Twickenham as our boys strutted their stuff on the hallowed earth, sublimely unaware of the magnificence of their surroundings, before a Barbarians–New Zealand match.

I had been to Ken's place a couple of times before, but it still took my breath away as I drove down into the vast bowl of their valley. The house oozed class and wealth and was as opulent as the wood-and-leather-upholstered Bentley he had dropped me home in the previous Sunday.

His wife, Christine, was out on the front lawn, looking small, lost and alone in the beautifully landscaped gardens. An elderly man with receding grey hair hovered uncertainly beside her, unsure what to do or say.

'This is Tom,' she said distractedly. 'He sort of does everything here. He's a treasure – I don't know how I would manage without him. I don't know…'

Her voice tailed off. I stood quietly as her shoulders heaved and silent tears coursed down her cheeks.

'I can't believe he's dead, Mike,' she said abstractedly. 'Look at me – I've been handing out chocolate biscuits and decaff coffee… the postman's just been and I've been opening letters from people I've never heard of as if nothing had happened. I was out here gardening…'

Her voice faltered, and she shook her head in disbelief.

'…I thought he was asleep, having a lie-in. He was out with friends last night, and I knew he was tired. What sort of wife does that make me?'

I didn't know what to say. Marcus was beckoning in the periphery of my vision.

'I sort of need you to go and confirm death, Mike,' he whispered in an aside, 'because we are no longer allowed to on our own, and we have another shout. It's just that…'

He ground to an apologetic halt, but I knew what he needed to say.

Ken was dead, but his next call might be alive and desperately waiting for an emergency ambulance. It was a question of priorities, and they needed to go. We mostly only ever meet when sad circumstances dictate.

'See you again, Marcus,' I acknowledged, standing to one side as they climbed into their vehicle and drove off. I gave Christine a hug, took a deep breath and walked slowly towards the house.

Ken was lying undisturbed in his bed, livid bruises on his downturned cheek. An open book lay unfinished in his hand. I picked it up and choked back a sigh.

'Oh, Ken,' I thought, or maybe said out loud without realising. 'What a way to go.'

West Devon has an abundance of country lanes; some I knew, and a few I didn't.

A decade ago the verges were cut by the council at least six times a year. Now it is an annual ritual – if you are lucky. Which means you never quite know what you might find in the hedgerows, or where the road ends and the verge begins.

As I drove back from Ken's house, taking an almost-forgotten detour I had not driven down since a previous fateful day, old memories returned to haunt me.

It was spring, two or three years earlier. An outlying visit on a busy day. Just an elderly lady who probably needed some company more than my medical expertise. A cup of tea that I pretended to drink, a scone that I smuggled into my pocket. A promise to return whenever I could.

I had taken a wrong turn on the journey home, straying into uncharted territory. Two miles down an unfamiliar lane I rounded a stray sheep and stopped abruptly by a corpse protruding from a grassy bank, clad in his Sunday-best tweed suit.

My phone had no signal.

Blackwater village was a few minutes ahead. I came across Mrs Axleby just around the next corner, sweating profusely as she clung on to her walking stick, a frantic look on her face. It would have been so easy to drive on past and continue looking for a phone box from which I could report what I had just found.

But there was something about the way she looked. I stopped and wound my window down, with an ominous feeling that I knew what she was going to say.

'I'm looking for my husband,' she gasped, between heavy breaths. 'He's not been himself recently, but he went out for his morning walk today, just as usual. Except he dressed up in his Sunday best today, which is unlike him, and he's been gone over an hour longer than usual. Have you seen him, Dr Sparrow? Have you seen him anywhere?'

Coincidences do happen.

As I had left the surgery that morning to go and confirm Ken's death, my staff had rearranged most of the rest of my clinic. Some had simply rebooked, Dr Harper had taken on a couple, and Jo, the practice nurse, had hoovered up the rest.

There was only one left waiting to see me.

'Doesn't she look well!' Debs was exclaiming as I walked heavy-hearted through the back door. 'All new wardrobe, and hasn't she lost so much weight?'

'I've been internet dating,' said Mrs Axleby, grinning smugly. 'You just never know what you can find out there, do you? This young chap, he says he's only thirty-five, and he's asking me what colour knickers I wear. Red,' she roared explosively, 'I told him they were red, and he believed me.'

She glanced over her shoulder and looked back at me conspiratorially.

'But now I've been out shopping,' she confided darkly.

'There are some things about you I don't believe I need to know, Mrs Axleby,' I responded solemnly.

'I ought to feel guilty, shouldn't I?' she continued. 'But when my Fred went out for his final walk, he said suddenly, out of the blue, "I don't think I can go through another winter, Maureen. And if I can't, I want you to move on, and make another life for yourself."'

She leant across the desk and grasped my hand earnestly.

'You see, I know it was his sign to me that he was ready. It's okay, Dr Sparrow, isn't it? Because I've come to say goodbye and thank you. I'm moving up country with my new man this afternoon. Furniture van is all packed, and I've had the neighbours round and everything. Wish me luck, Dr Sparrow. Wish me luck.'

A vision of Ken floated back into my mind.

That book by his side? It was the first of the two that I had written, which I had signed for him. I still have no idea what to make of that.

I just hope he died laughing, and not bored to death.

From the sad demise of a friend to Mrs Axleby knickers. All in the one day.

Only in Lifton. Surely that was enough for the day. I needed a drink, and maybe a little light relief. Driving home, lost in contemplation, I rounded yet another corner. And there it was, waiting for me. Daring me to engage. It was not an entirely unusual sight in our practice.

A tractor was blocking the road.

If it's not a tractor, it's a herd of sheep. If it's not a herd of sheep, it's a cow, a goat or a mystery outing of the Women's Golden Circle, who've taken a wrong turn at the abattoir and are busy spending an hour and a half consulting the map so they can find their way back to the village hall.

If it's not the Women's Golden Circle, it's the council, who have managed to dig up the road – again – but need a couple of weeks to read the yet-to-be-published directive which explains how to fill it in again.

But the culprit that day was indeed a tractor, a dirty, decrepit-looking beast which had obviously pulled one bale of hay too many and just expired on the spot. Try as I might, I could not squeeze past it, even in my then racing-green 4x4 Fiat Panda – which could mostly go anywhere, just not very quickly.

Generally speaking, there is at the very least a farmer or farmhand within the offing of whatever blockage they may have left in their wake. Be it a dead cow, an eviscerated sheep, a decapitated European Commissioner or a tanker innocently transporting a three-week collection of slurry to an unidentified destination, they undoubtedly enjoy the discomfiture of the poor traveller trapped behind the obstruction in question. Most farmers I know have an enlarged rear-view mirror in order to count the number of stacked-up vehicles behind them, and would never dream of pulling over until the enraged queue reaches well into treble figures. And even then, should the verges remain unmown due to local council cutbacks, they plough on, slowing down even further with a smug smile on their face. Each month I endorsed a plethora of shotgun renewal certificates from the non-farming community, living – as we all did – in the greatest of hope.

I looked around carefully, but on this occasion it seemed that this was a tractor undeniably alone, a tractor wholly abandoned to its fate, marooned, cast into an uncaring world... but it was also in my way. I gave a blast on my horn, followed quickly by a second. There was no response.

Cursing, I got out of my car and clambered into the cab, hoping to find out who owned the obstructive vehicle. This would not only give me an identifiable target for my wrath, it might also allow me to plot a suitable revenge – like sharpening my fingernails when they were next due a rectal examination. But instead of a clue to the vehicle's ownership, I found something infinitely better – the keys, and in the ignition, at that.

Now, with the benefit of hindsight, I should have anticipated a potential catastrophe just around the corner. But then, with the same benefit of hindsight, I would have ceased to support West Ham long before I was six; decreed no interest in biology at eleven; and said yes to the girl next door when I was fourteen. But I did none of those things, and over the years I came to regret them all.

And I think it is only fair to say that I was not an expert tractor driver. To be brutally honest, I have to admit I had never actually driven one at all. But there I was, upset, angry, late for my next appointment and feeling desperately sorry about the loss of my friend.

If you have never driven a tractor before, but should unexpectedly encounter one on a downhill slope and find you have the perfect opportunity to move it, please take my advice. Don't.

The tractor and I ultimately went in the direction the tractor wanted to go. It just seemed easiest that way. I did at one point attempt to turn the wheel and travel for a few moments in a direction I thought we could both be happy with, but the tractor had other ideas, free at last to give rein to the formerly repressed inner feelings it was not about to be denied.

Two ploughed fields later – we were on a very steep downhill slope – a milking shed turned up out of the blue, but only for as long as it took me to destroy the entire edifice in the blink of an eye.

As silence fell, I considered my options… and ran for it.

I shot back across the two ploughed fields, up the bank and into my car. I was just about to beat a hasty retreat when, lo and behold, a farmer loomed rapidly into view.

But this was not just any old farmer. By the law of Sod, it was Jed Williams, the farmer who until very recently had owned a fully functioning tractor parked in a quiet country lane and a fully functioning milking parlour.

I clambered out of my car with that sinking feeling you get when you are about eight and the doorbell rings shortly after you were spotted scrumping again in the mad old lady's orchard at the end of your street. I stood as innocently as I could by the roadside as the farmer drew to a halt and surveyed the damage, his face bright red and sweating.

'Hello, Doc,' he wheezed, looking worryingly blue around the gills.

Please God, I prayed, don't let him have a coronary right now. Not when I'm feeling so guilty already and have forgotten to replenish my portable oxygen cylinder.

'Good to see you,' he continued. 'Just been after a loose cow, I have, bugger of a job to get him back in his field again.'

He surveyed the scene of devastation before him and shook his head wearily.

'What the bloody hell's happened here? Have you been here long – did you see anything?'

I tried to be good, I really did.

'Not a thing,' I lied, a shade too convincingly for my own liking. 'I've only just got here myself, Jed, and I thought I'd better stop and see what on earth had been going on.'

'Bloody kids, again, I suppose,' he sighed, turning to spit into the ditch. 'Better go and see what damage the little buggers have done. Want to come and take a look with me, be a witness, like?'

That would be a no, then.

'Sorry, Jed, but I'm a busy man,' I said. 'You know how it is, much to do, things on my mind…' (like a recently demolished tractor and a prized milking shed). And off I drove.

I know what you're thinking, and I agree. It was sheer, unadulterated cowardice. I still blush at the thought.

A couple of weeks later I ran into Jed in the local pub.

To my surprise he was looking the picture of health, and he was obviously more than a few pints into what promised to be an extremely lengthy drinking session. I tried unsuccessfully to blend into the background, but he spotted me within minutes and waved me across to where he sat with his entourage of fellow imbibers.

'Ah, here's the boy,' he bellowed joyously. 'Have a drink, Doc. A double, please, Peter,' he added, waving imperiously at the barman.

Such was my state of trepidation I didn't even ask 'A double what?' I would at that stage have drunk a double anything that came my way. Okay, maybe not Campari.

'I was just telling my friends here,' Jed continued, 'about that tractor of mine, and my milking shed, and how you just happened to be passing at the time. Didn't see a blessed thing, did you, Doc?'

I swallowed nervously. 'Not a thing,' I agreed hastily. 'I just wish I had, Jed, but I was too late arriving.'

'Ah, pity, more's the pity, that.' Jed laughed uproariously, slapping his grotesquely deformed left knee in great delight. 'Like to find out who did it, I would. Best day's work they ever did for a man, if you ask me.'

He took a huge draught of his pint. I thought he was going to swallow the glass.

'That old tractor of mine,' he reminisced, and I swear there was a tear in his eye, 'was fit only for the knackers yard, and as for my old milking shed – well, that had seen better days before the war...' He turned and winked at his engrossed audience, 'and I don't mean World War One or Two, neither.'

I think I gulped at this point, but he was smiling delightedly at all around.

'I've got a shiny new tractor, I have, and a brand-new milking shed coming, all courtesy of me insurance. Ah, I bless the day them kids did me a favour, I do. What a shame I can't give a bit of a reward to them as done it.'

And he slapped his thigh again, but even more heartily, bursting into further gales of uncontrollable laughter.

'Best day's work I've ever 'ad done for me, it was,' he gasped. 'Best day ever...'

So, it is time to come clean.

Farmer Jed Williams, of Netherwood Farm, somewhere in West Devon – if you should happen to be reading this, then my conscience can hold out no longer. It was me, all the time it was me. And I've been wondering...

Is it too late for that reward you were talking about?

# 17
# Lost for Words – Part IV

I didn't get out so much in these days, so when an invitation that actually had my name on it arrived at the surgery, I took it home and waved it triumphantly.

'We've been invited out,' I said. 'An evening drinks do.'

'We've been invited out?' said Laura, my other half, with an air of disbelief. 'By someone who knows you?'

'Yes. Well, knows me professionally,' I admitted. 'Sort of.'

'Do they know what you're like?'

'I was a friend of his father.'

'And that will be who, exactly? And where?'

'The High Sheriff of Cornwall,' I read from the invitation, 'and Mrs Cynthia Watkins will be at home on Monday 10 September.'

'It's at Werrington Park, on the other side of Launceston,' I added.

'And they really want us to go?'

I paused for a moment, reflecting upon my current standing in civilised society. 'Almost certainly not,' I admitted.

'Then we will,' she said firmly, 'and you can show them how well behaved you can be, for a change.'

Well, it started out like that…

'Mike, how nice to see you,' said the High Sheriff, shuddering visibly as I shook him by the hand.

'Yes, lovely,' agreed Cynthia faintly as her husband prodded her in the ribs. 'You will be gone by eight, won't you, because we have to put the children to bed.'

'And how old are the children?' Laura asked me as we made our way into the magnificent reception room.

'Forty-six, forty-one and thirty-eight,' I replied. 'But we still have an hour and three-quarters. Let's go mingle.'

We mingled amongst the great and the good for a while, drinking fine quality champagne and consuming delicate vol-au-vents. I was just deliberating the diplomatic time to leave when I spotted an old colleague across the room, leaning against the fireplace. We moved across, weaving through the crowd and picking up another glass each from the waiter as he glided past.

A slim bespectacled man, prematurely receding, early forties, turned to greet us with a smile, an attractive blonde by his side. He held out his hand.

'Mike. It's been a long time.'

'Hello, Neil, nice to see you again. This is Laura.' I turned towards his blonde companion. 'And your wife is…?'

'At home looking after the kids,' he replied. 'Allow me to introduce you to Anna.'

He observed my air of disconcertion with an amused smile for a second or two.

'I'm joking, of course. She's not at home looking after the children at all.'

He paused for a second, ever the comedian.

'She's actually in South Wales, visiting her mother.'

I looked across to Laura, who was clearly struggling with what to make of it all.

'It's okay,' I explained. 'Neil's a psychiatrist.'

An hour later, we were still firmly entrenched by the fireplace, reminiscing. Anna and Laura had spotted mutual friends and had drifted away for a while.

Neil, in reflective mood – more than one doctor gathered together equals shared nostalgia – had turned the conversation towards patients we were both well acquainted with.

'What did you do with Simon Tompkins?' I asked, when it was my turn, 'after we'd extracted him from the delicatessen freezer?'

'By the time we'd thawed him out a bit he was almost rational,' he said, 'and he was nothing like as much trouble as Emily What's-her-face. Where in God's name did you find her? I've seen more evolutionary advanced specimens embedded in plastic in the Natural History Museum.'

The fire was dying down, and the waiter came across to toss on another couple of logs.

'My name is George,' he said, as he stood up, brushing his hands. 'I like tips, and I despise most of the people here. Anything you want, just give me a wave.'

'Thank you, George,' I acknowledged. 'When you see our glasses empty on the mantelpiece, just pop back.'

'I will,' he promised. 'We have lamb chops on the way.'

I had lost the thread of our conversation for a moment, and then the mist cleared.

'And Michael Johnson, Neil?' I hesitated to ask. 'I've been away for a while. Whatever happened with him?'

'Oh, Michael Johnson,' he sighed. 'You mean you didn't hear? I'm going to need another drink, a large one. I'll bring you one back too. And I need directions to the nearest loo, if you know them.'

'Through the door over there, up the stairs and it's on your left.'

Michael Johnson had been a patient of mine for ten years.

A local farmer, he had exhibited increasingly bizarre behaviour over the past six months since his wife had left him, taking their two sons with her. I had become increasingly worried about him living in the comparative isolation of what used to be a bustling family farm, keeping only cattle and heavy machinery as his companions. He now filled every available waking hour with work, and he had contracted himself out for a while deep in the Cornish hinterlands.

A fortnight or so after he began there, I received a phone call from a Dr Chandler, one of the local GPs.

'I know he's out of your area for the time being,' he began, 'and not really your problem, but boy is this guy strange. I've been called to see him three times in the past week, and although I don't feel he's actually sectionable (able to be forcibly detained for the safety of himself or others), right now it would be a real help if you gave me some background information and told me what you think.'

'To be honest,' I said, 'I've been expecting something like this to happen. Look, do you know Neil Roberts? I'll give him a ring. He's always pretty good in a situation like this. I can probably get him to visit. After all, what else do psychiatrists have to do with their days apart from collating their off-shore deposit accounts?'

'The loo is actually on the right,' said Neil good-humouredly on his return. 'I won't tell you what I found through the door on the left, but I may be traumatised forever.'

'Sorry,' I said. 'Been a while since I've been here.'

He handed me a brandy, and I nodded my thanks.

'So, Michael Johnson,' I said, reverting to our previous conversation. 'What did you do?'

'Oh, I went all right,' Neil said. 'It's all part of the job, and besides, it gets me out of the hospital for a while.'

He fell silent, remembering.

'You've been there, Mike. Anything that does that on a bad day is a blessing. I found the field he was working in without any difficulty – nice spot, just down the road from Craggy Head, the field slopes down to the cliffs…'

'Yes, I know it,' I said. 'One of my patients tried to commit suicide there a couple of years ago by launching himself off the top.'

'Tried to?'

'Yeah… failed. Hit a grassy slope a hundred feet down, rolled over and stood up completely unharmed, wondering how on earth Hell could look so much like southern Cornwall.'

'Really,' said Neil, intrigued. 'What did he do then – climb back up again a bit further down the coast and have another go?'

'No, he's a changed man,' I said. 'Revolutionised his life, he's never looked back since. He's a glass engraver in Streatham now. The bit I really liked, though, is when I asked him what he was thinking about while he was standing at the top of the cliff.'

George arrived with a tray of desserts. The girls were now back, and Laura took three.

'She's eating for two,' explained Anna. 'Has she not told you?'

'You're as bad as your husband,' Laura giggled, but I noticed her fingers were crossed behind her back. I shrugged all thoughts aside that would not keep until later and resumed my tale.

'Well, Michael,' he said, 'I was at peace, totally relaxed and confident that what I was about to do was the right thing for me, and the right thing for my family and my friends. Funny thing was, though, the second I stepped out into thin air I remember thinking, "Oh, shit. I really wish I hadn't done this." Sorry, Neil, I interrupted. Do carry on.'

'Er... yes, where was I? At the field, that's it. There's a track runs down the side of it towards the clifftop...'

'Yes, I know it,' I put in, 'I've been there before with...'

'Stop interrupting, Mike,' said Laura.

'Yes, stop interrupting, Mike,' repeated Neil, 'it's my story, thank you... I couldn't see anyone at first, the field slopes down away from the road...'

'I know,' I agreed, 'away down to...'

'Shut UP, Mike,' chorused Laura, Anna and Neil.

'...so I drove along the track,' continued Neil, glaring at me with mock ferocity, 'right to the far end until I spotted his tractor weaving its way across the stubble. He'd obviously seen me, so I parked my car, got out and waited for him to draw up alongside. Which he did, sort of, but that's when it got all out of hand.'

'Why's that, then?' I asked.

'Because he didn't stop,' said Neil. 'He just kept going, right past me, and right into my car.'

'What?' I exclaimed.

'I only just had time to get out of the way. He was shouting something at me I couldn't hear, and then there was this almighty crash as he smashed headlong into my car and just carried on, shunting it closer and closer to the edge.'

'What did you do?' asked Laura, enthralled.

'Ran like buggery,' said Neil, 'as fast as I could, and just kept on going. I only looked round once, just in time to see my car tumbling over the edge of the cliff.'

'Jesus,' I whistled.

'Could have been worse though, I suppose,' he shrugged. 'I might have been still in it. It's funny, though,' he added ruefully, 'it's not been a lucky spot for me, down there.'

'Why is that?' I asked, little realising what might be about to come.

'A year ago,' he said, 'almost to the day. I was down at the bottom of the same cliff, my car parked at the edge of the beach, when there was a huge commotion and this bloody great bale of hay came tumbling out of the sky and thundered on to the roof of my car, flattening it to a complete pulp… I was just a few feet away. I could have been killed.'

I gulped, and it wasn't just another vol-au-vent.

'What's the matter, Mike?' asked Anna, concerned. 'Are you all right? You've suddenly gone awfully pale…'

I was, in fact, lost for words.

# Also Available

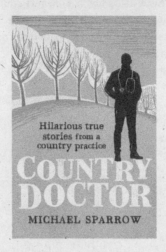

Hilarious true
stories from a
country practice

## COUNTRY DOCTOR

MICHAEL SPARROW

Have you ever had to decide what to do with an unidentified corpse by a Devonian cowshed when the herd is due in for milking? And how would you react if one of your patients was abducted by aliens?

If you are a GP it seems these are routine matters. From coping with the suicide of a colleague to the unusual whereabouts of a jar of Coleman's mustard, this is the story of one rural doctor's often misguided attempts to make sense of the career in which he has unwittingly found himself.

Dr Sparrow's adventures would be utterly unbelievable were they not 100% true stories. His bedside manner may sometimes leave a little to be desired but, if you're in dire straits, this doctor will have you in stitches.

OUT NOW

# Also Available

Dr Sparrow is back, coping with more bizarre, macabre and hilarious situations. Following his successful debut with Country Doctor, he once more guides us through the daily rounds of the weird and wonderful in his practice on the Devon/Cornwall border.

What would you do if faced with the unsuccessful resuscitation of the wrong patient, being held at gunpoint as a suspected terrorist or confronting a blind man who refuses to stop driving? And what about the little old lady who presents you with a supermarket bag stuffed with £20 notes? Add to this, jets crashing on the runway, fleeting glimpses of the Royal Genitalia and the haunting tale of the suicidal stranger and an abducted child – and you will start to have some idea of the unpredictable life of Dr Sparrow.

OUT NOW